D1266133

THE BALLAD

OF HUP & BARFINNIOUS

Published by

ARCHAIA™

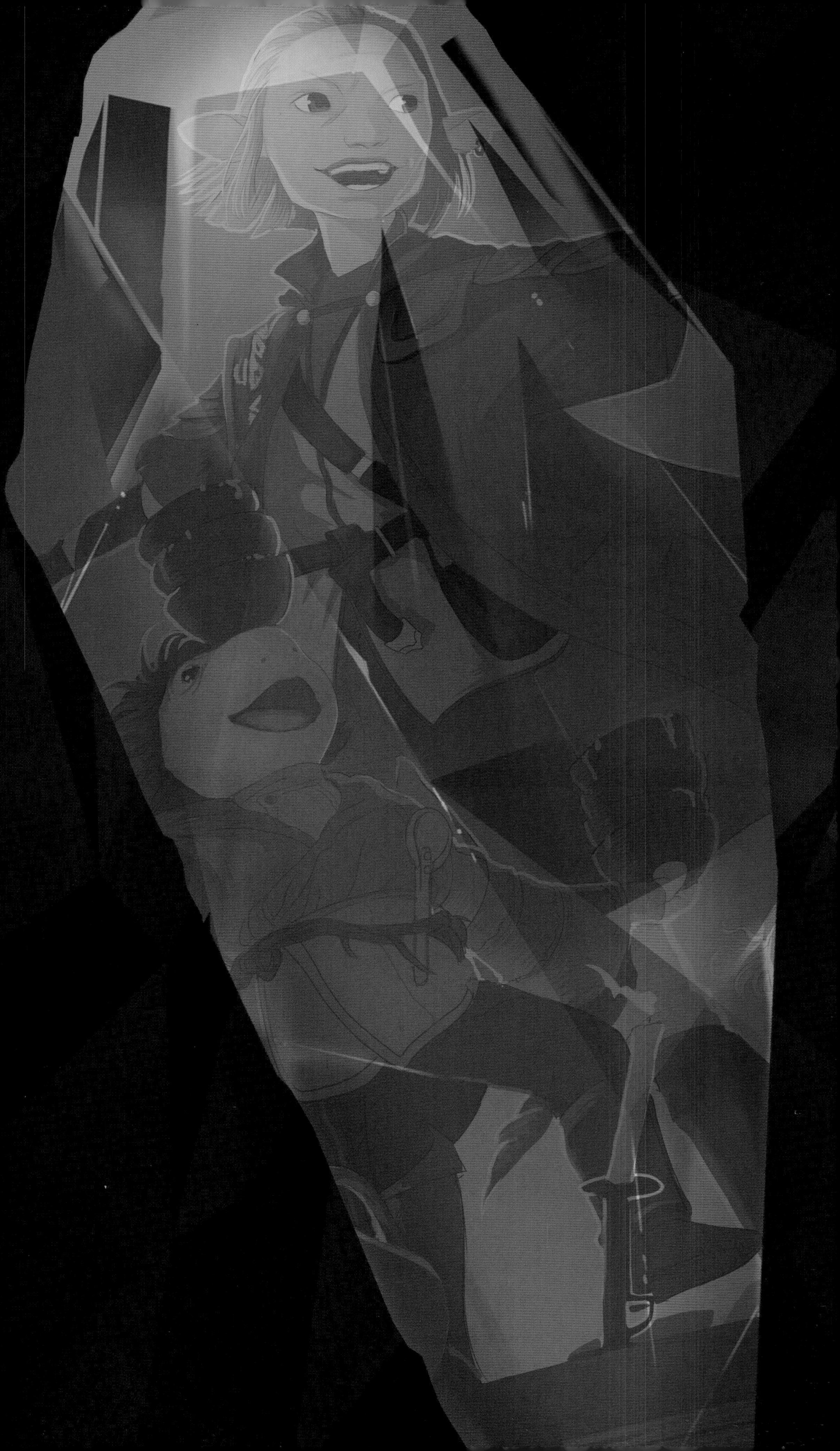

Jim Henson's™

The Dark Crystal: Age of Resistance

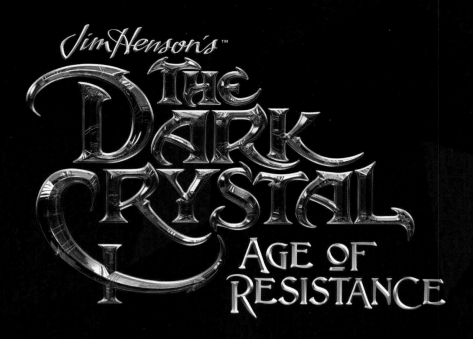

THE BALLAD
OF HUP & BARFINNIOUS

Story by **Jeffrey Addiss** & **Will Matthews**

Written by **Adam Cesare**

Illustrated by **French Carlomagno**

Lettered by **Jim Campbell**

Cover by **Conor Nolan**

ARCHAIA™
Los Angeles, California

Series Designer **Michelle Ankley**
Collection Designer **Chelsea Roberts**
Assistant Editor **Allyson Gronowitz**
Editor **Matthew Levine**

Chapter Breaks Illustrated by **Mona Finden**

Special Thanks to **Brian Henson, Lisa Henson, Jim Formanek, Nicole Goldman, Carla DellaVedova, Karen Falk, Blanca Lista, Jessica Mansour, the entire Jim Henson Company team, Wendy Froud, Brian Froud, Francesco Segala, and Sierra Hahn.**

JIM HENSON'S THE DARK CRYSTAL: AGE OF RESISTANCE: THE BALLAD OF HUP & BARFINNIOUS, October 2020. Published by Archaia, a division of Boom Entertainment, Inc. ™ & © 2020 The Jim Henson Company. JIM HENSON's mark & logo, THE DARK CRYSTAL: AGE OF RESISTANCE, mark & logo, and all related characters and elements are trademarks of The Jim Henson Company. Originally published in single magazine form as THE DARK CRYSTAL: AGE OF RESISTANCE No. 5-8. ™ & © 2020 The Jim Henson Company. All rights reserved. Archaia™ and the Archaia logo are trademarks of Boom Entertainment, Inc., registered in various countries and categories. All characters, events, and institutions depicted herein are fictional. Any similarity between any of the names, characters, persons, events, and/or institutions in this publication to actual names, characters, and persons, whether living or dead, events, and/or institutions is unintended and purely coincidental.

BOOM! Studios, 5670 Wilshire Boulevard, Suite 400, Los Angeles, CA 90036-5679. Printed in China. First Printing.

ISBN: 978-1-68415-629-0, eISBN: 978-1-64668-041-2

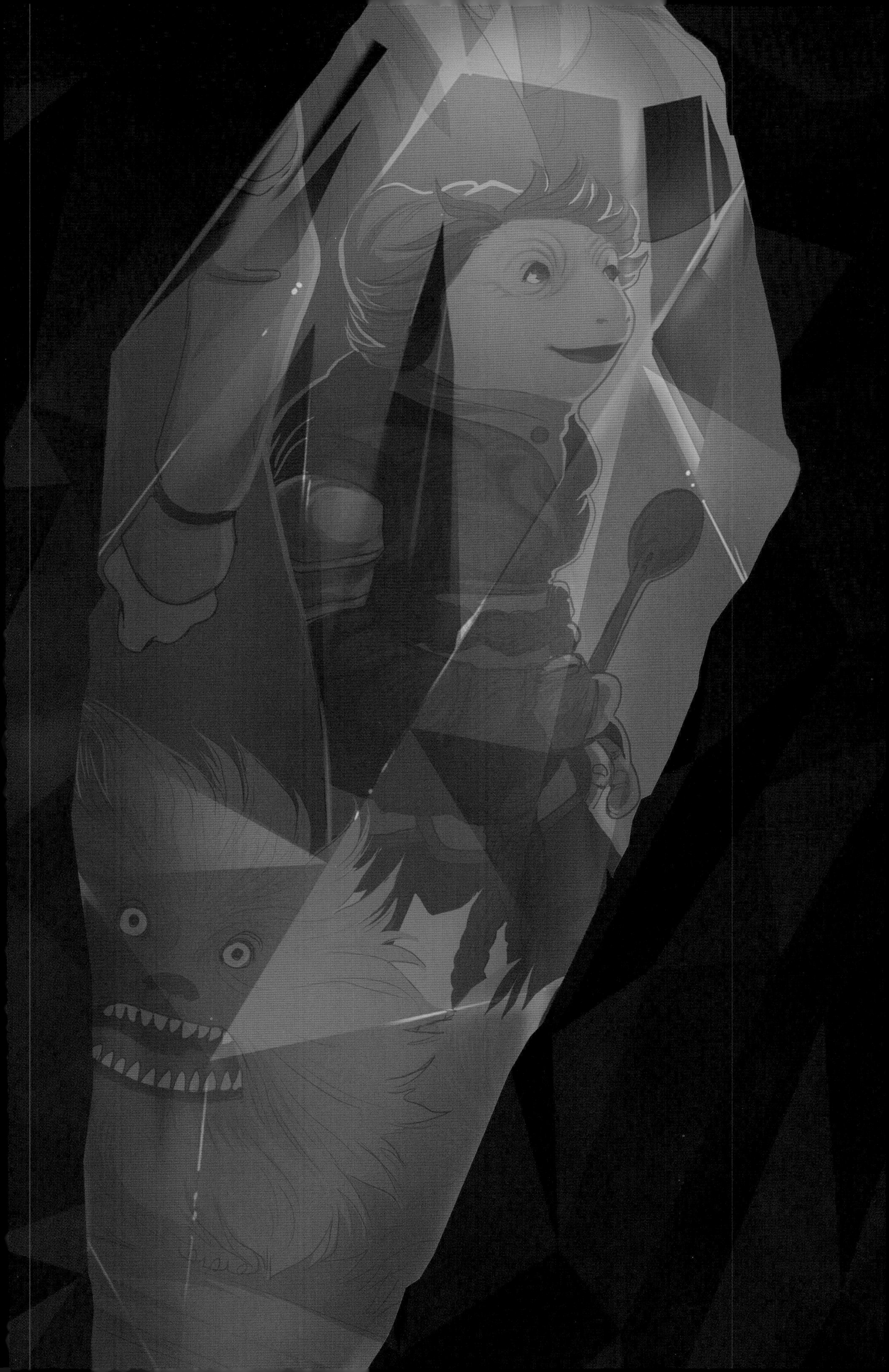

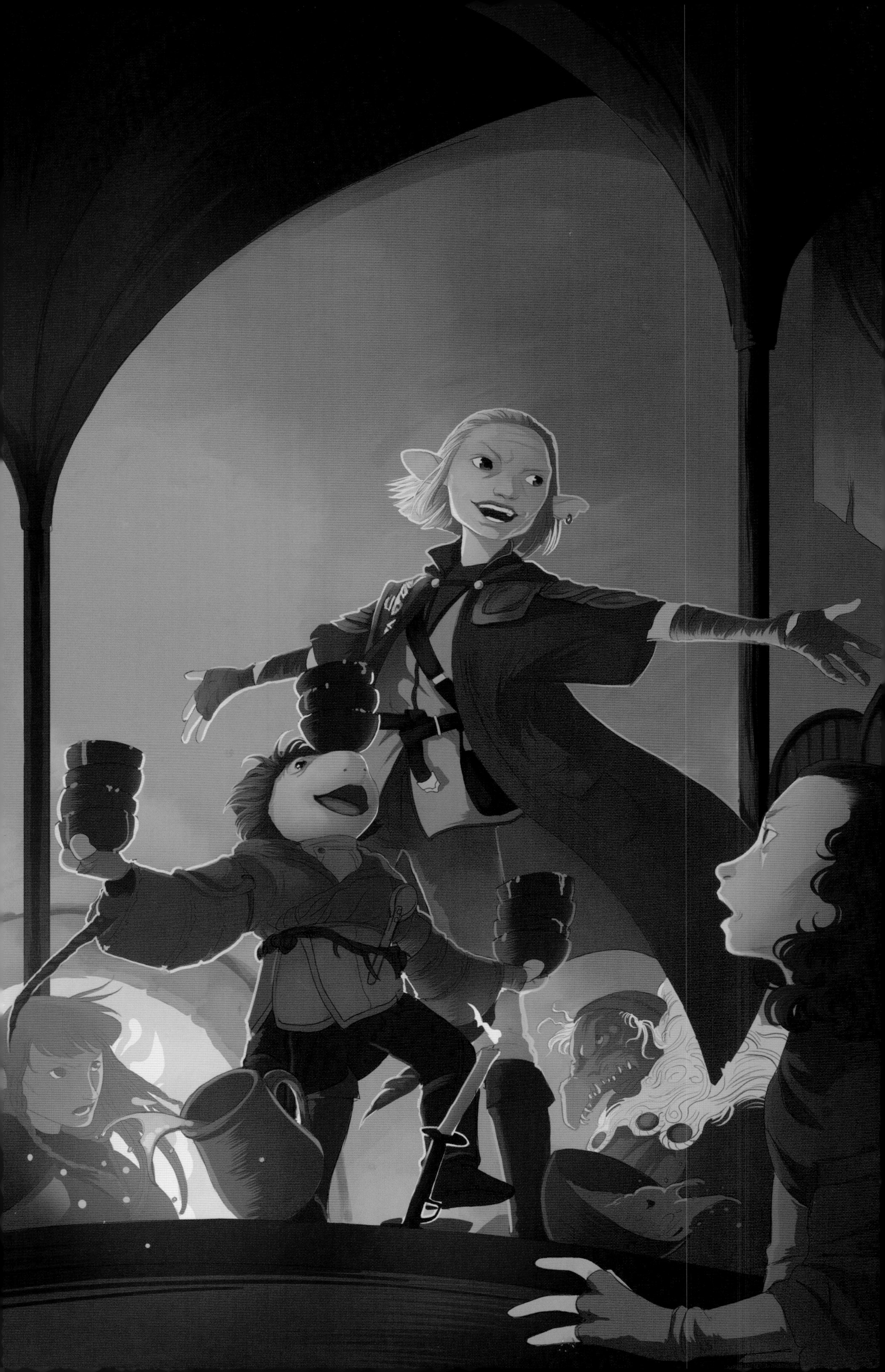

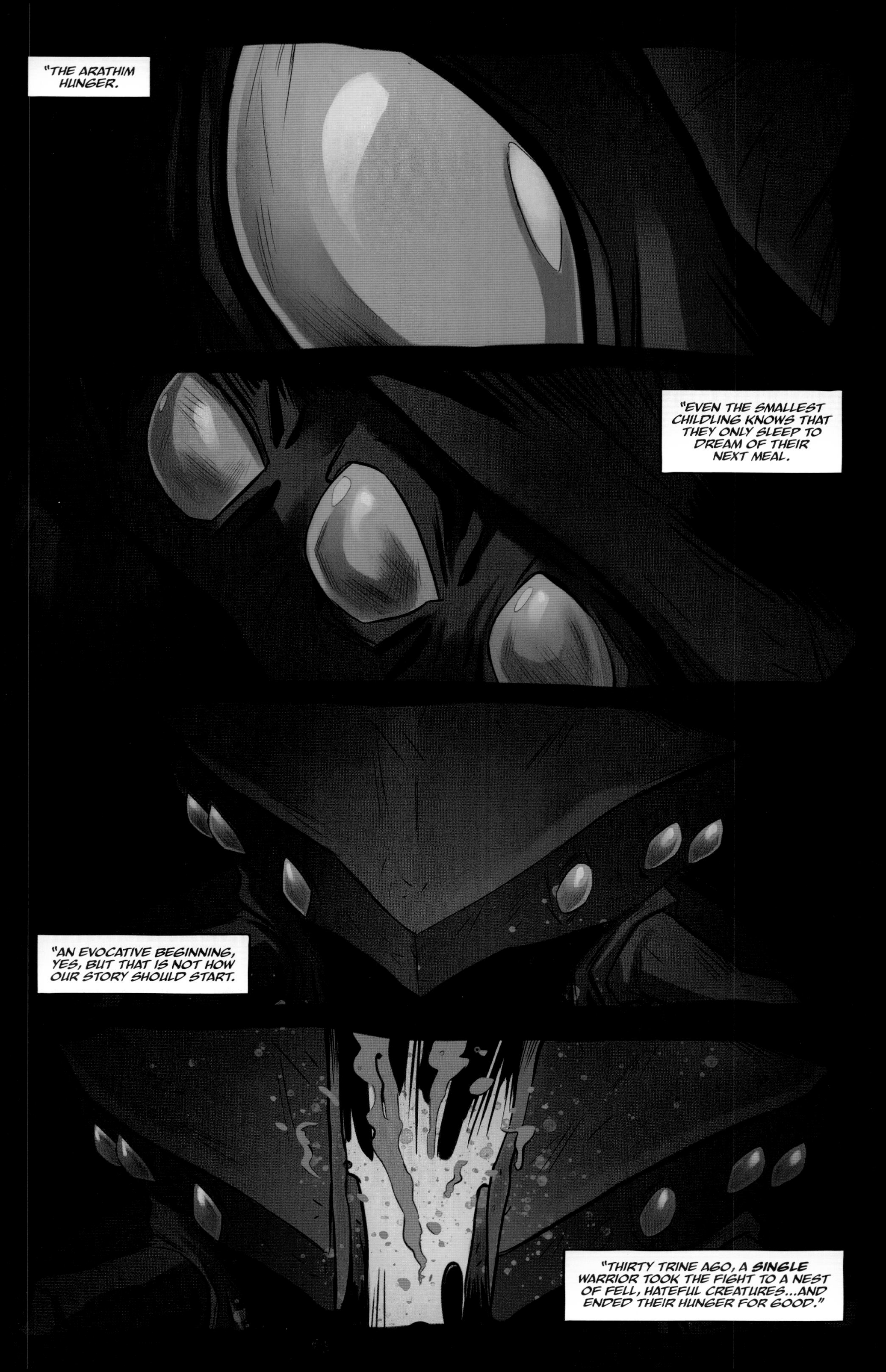
"THE ARATHIM HUNGER.
"EVEN THE SMALLEST CHILDLING KNOWS THAT THEY ONLY SLEEP TO DREAM OF THEIR NEXT MEAL.
"AN EVOCATIVE BEGINNING, YES, BUT THAT IS NOT HOW OUR STORY SHOULD START.
"THIRTY TRINE AGO, A SINGLE WARRIOR TOOK THE FIGHT TO A NEST OF FELL, HATEFUL CREATURES...AND ENDED THEIR HUNGER FOR GOOD."

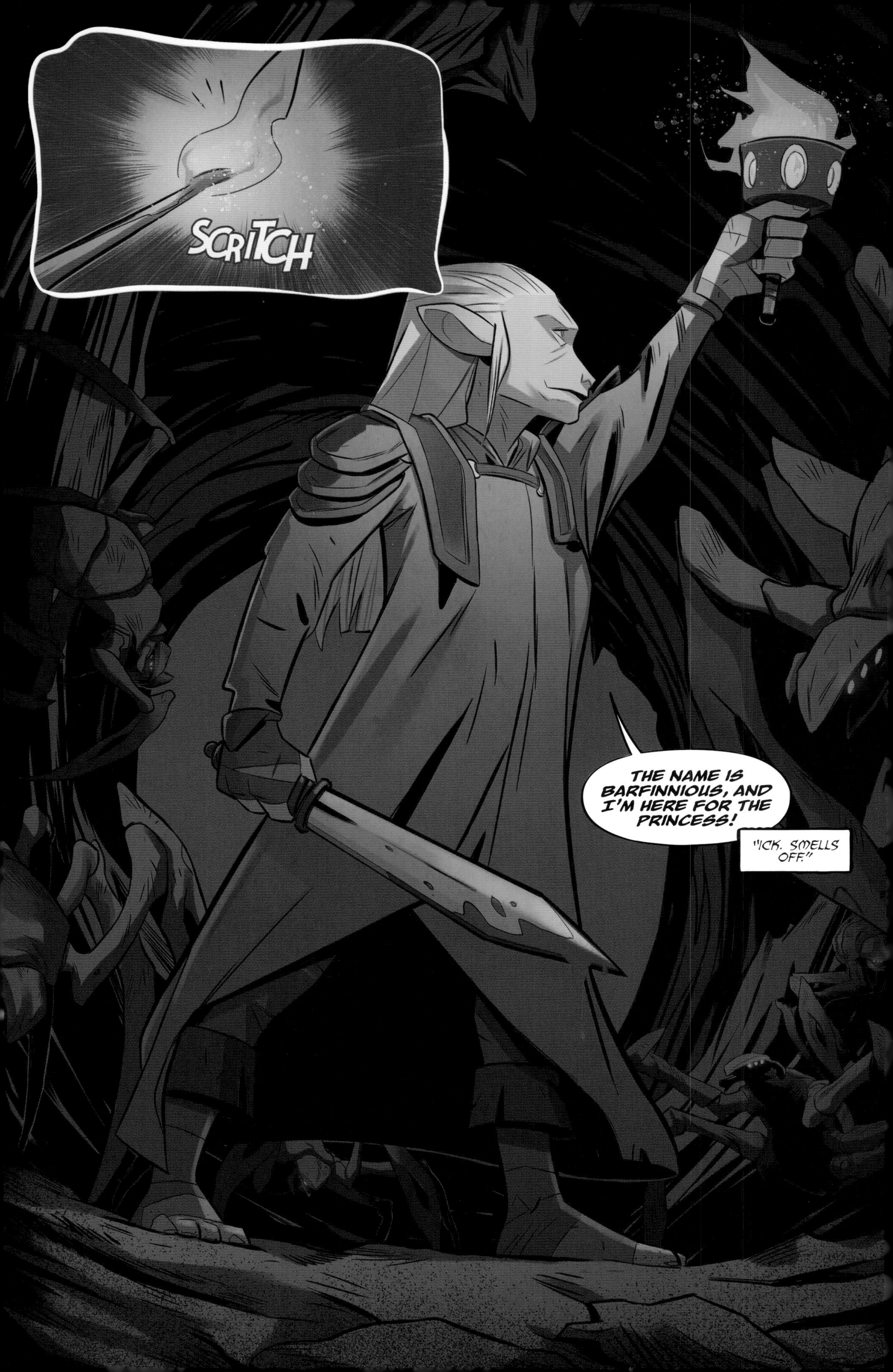
SCRITCH
THE NAME IS BARFINNIOUS, AND I'M HERE FOR THE PRINCESS!
"ICK. SMELLS OFF."

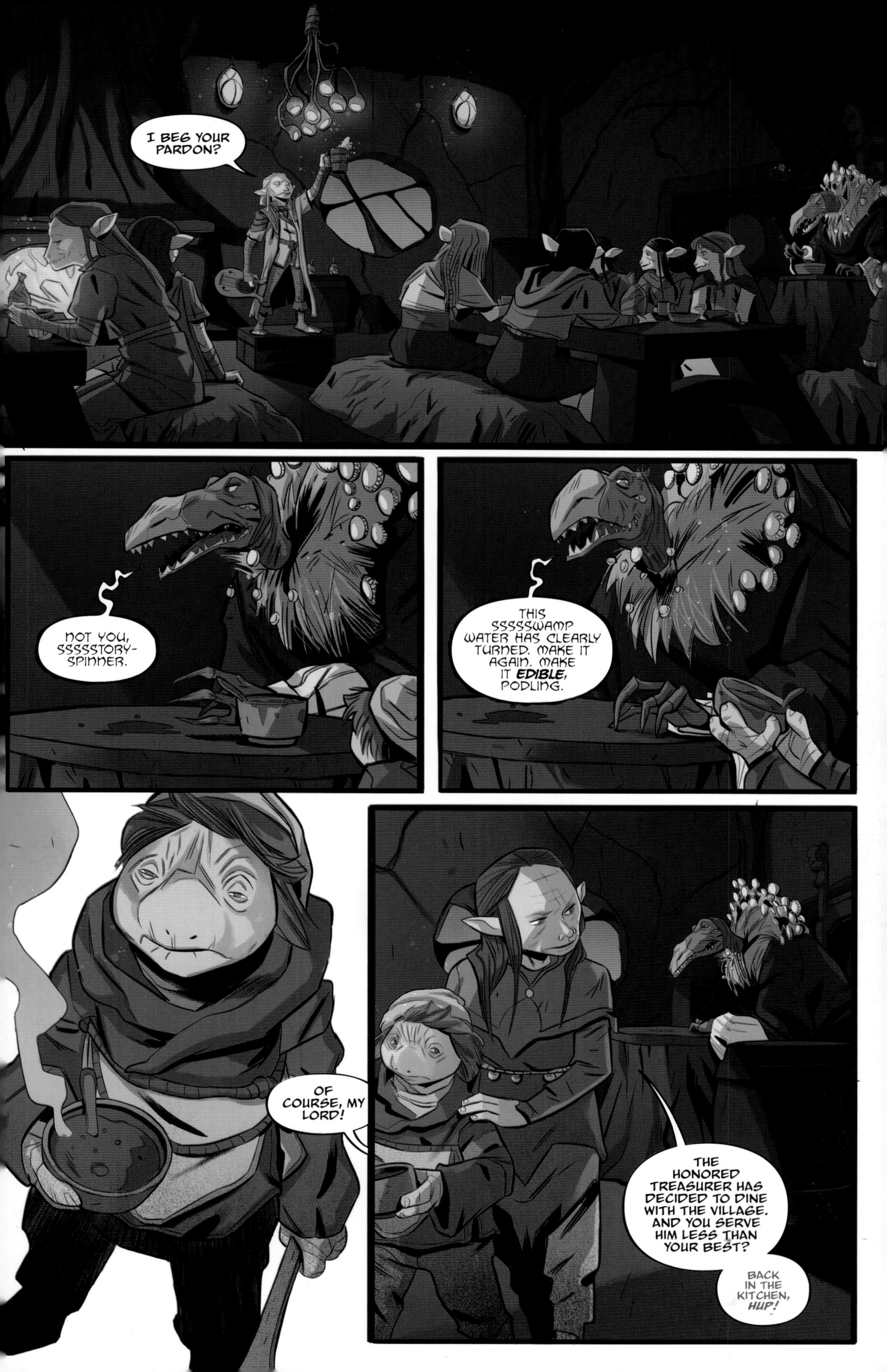
I BEG YOUR PARDON?
NOT YOU, SSSSSTORY-SPINNER.
THIS SSSSSWAMP WATER HAS CLEARLY TURNED. MAKE IT AGAIN. MAKE IT **EDIBLE**, PODLING.
OF COURSE, MY LORD!
THE HONORED TREASURER HAS DECIDED TO DINE WITH THE VILLAGE. AND YOU SERVE HIM LESS THAN YOUR BEST?
BACK IN THE KITCHEN, *HUP!*

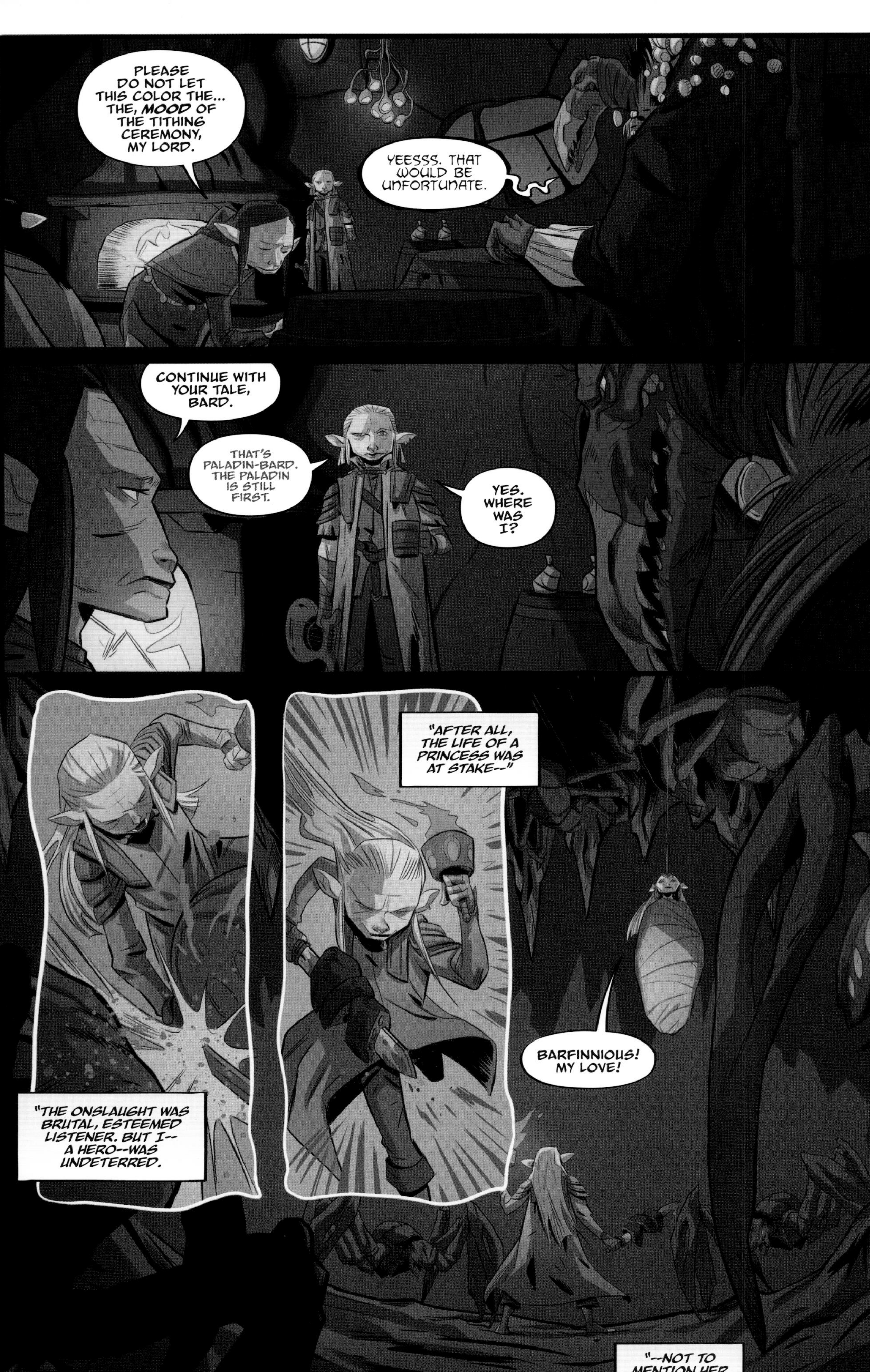
PLEASE DO NOT LET THIS COLOR THE... THE, MOOD OF THE TITHING CEREMONY, MY LORD.
YEESSS. THAT WOULD BE UNFORTUNATE.
CONTINUE WITH YOUR TALE, BARD.
THAT'S PALADIN-BARD. THE PALADIN IS STILL FIRST.
YES. WHERE WAS I?
"THE ONSLAUGHT WAS BRUTAL, ESTEEMED LISTENER. BUT I-- A HERO--WAS UNDETERRED.
"AFTER ALL, THE LIFE OF A PRINCESS WAS AT STAKE--"
BARFINNIOUS! MY LOVE!
"--NOT TO MENTION HER HEART."

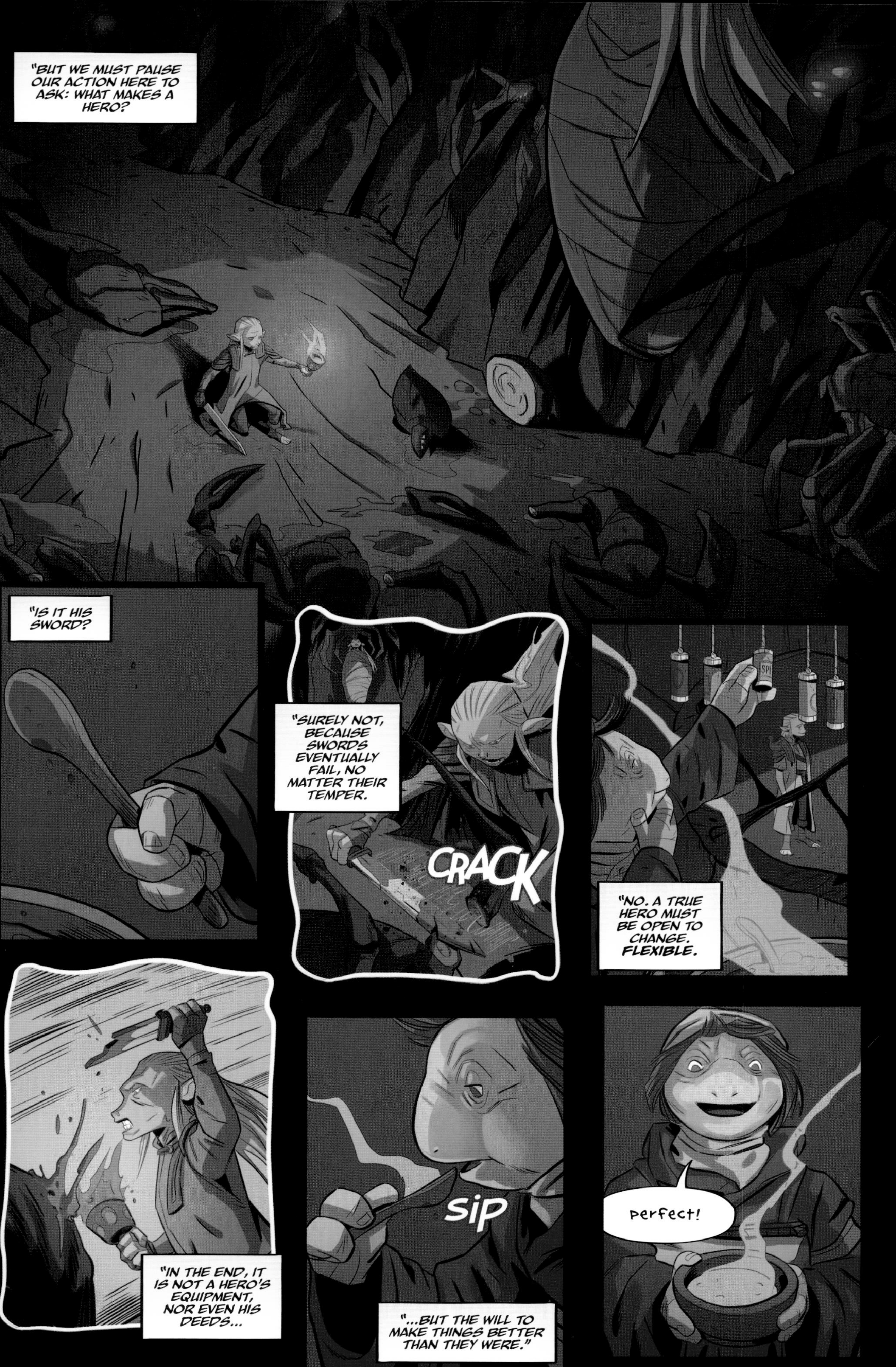
"BUT WE MUST PAUSE OUR ACTION HERE TO ASK: WHAT MAKES A HERO?
"IS IT HIS SWORD?
"SURELY NOT, BECAUSE SWORDS EVENTUALLY FAIL, NO MATTER THEIR TEMPER.
CRACK
"NO. A TRUE HERO MUST BE OPEN TO CHANGE. FLEXIBLE.
"IN THE END, IT IS NOT A HERO'S EQUIPMENT, NOR EVEN HIS DEEDS...
sip
"...BUT THE WILL TO MAKE THINGS BETTER THAN THEY WERE."
Perfect!

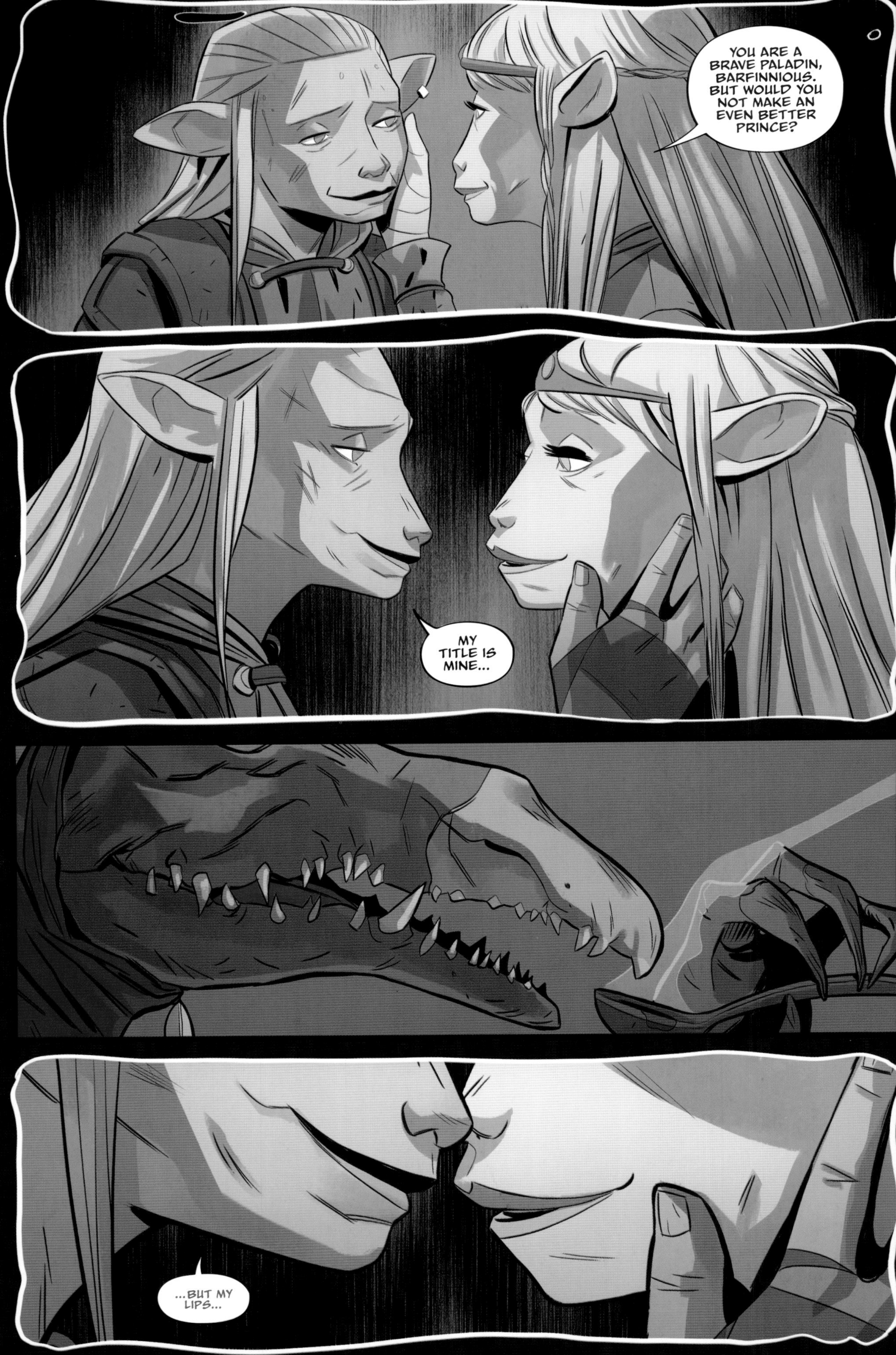

YOU ARE A BRAVE PALADIN, BARFINNIOUS. BUT WOULD YOU NOT MAKE AN EVEN BETTER PRINCE?
MY TITLE IS MINE...
...BUT MY LIPS...

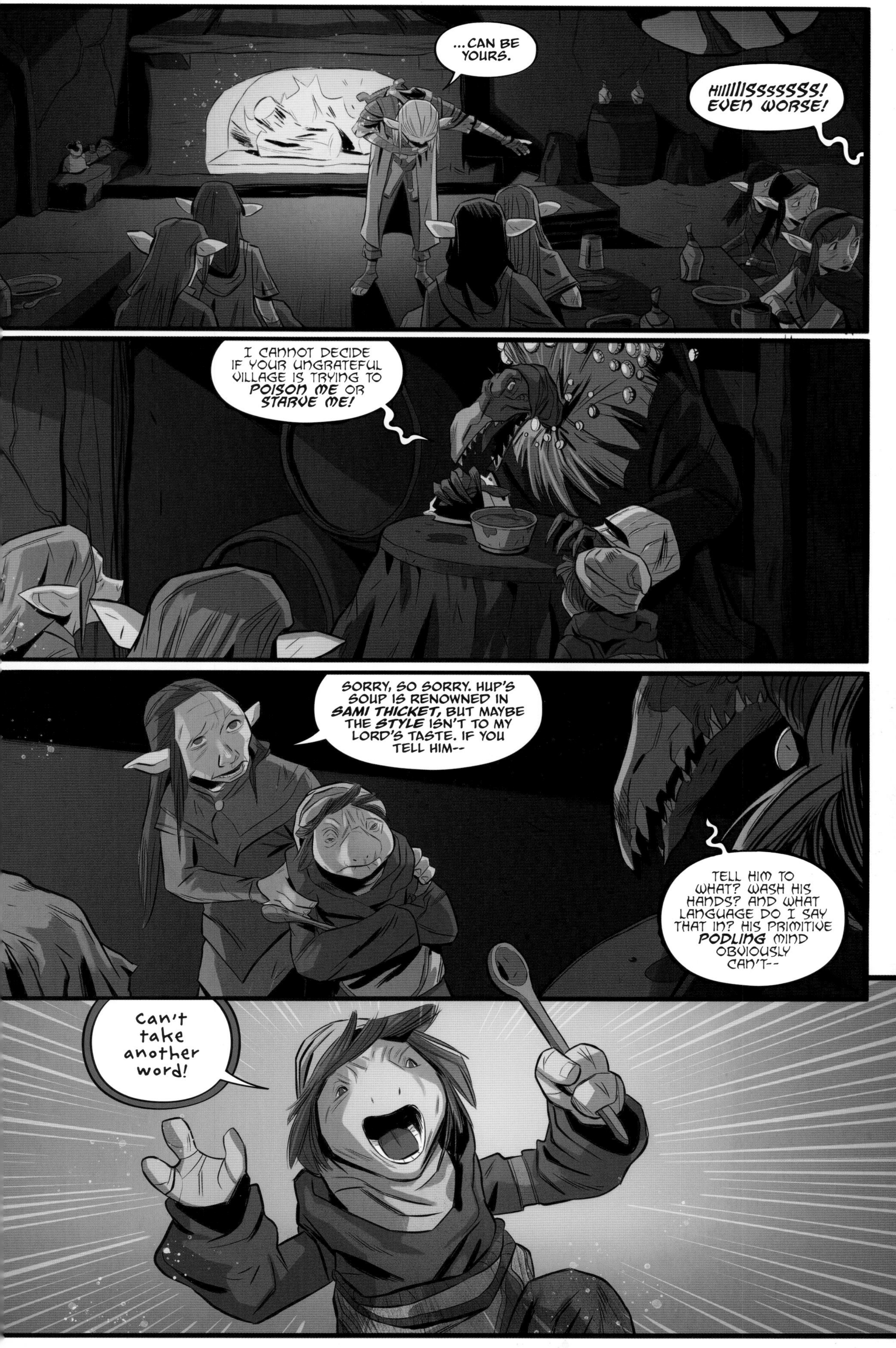
...CAN BE YOURS.
HIIIIIISSSSSSS! EVEN WORSE!
I CANNOT DECIDE IF YOUR UNGRATEFUL VILLAGE IS TRYING TO POISON ME OR STARVE ME!
SORRY, SO SORRY. HUP'S SOUP IS RENOWNED IN SAMI THICKET, BUT MAYBE THE STYLE ISN'T TO MY LORD'S TASTE. IF YOU TELL HIM--
TELL HIM TO WHAT? WASH HIS HANDS? AND WHAT LANGUAGE DO I SAY THAT IN? HIS PRIMITIVE PODLING MIND OBVIOUSLY CAN'T--
Can't take another word!

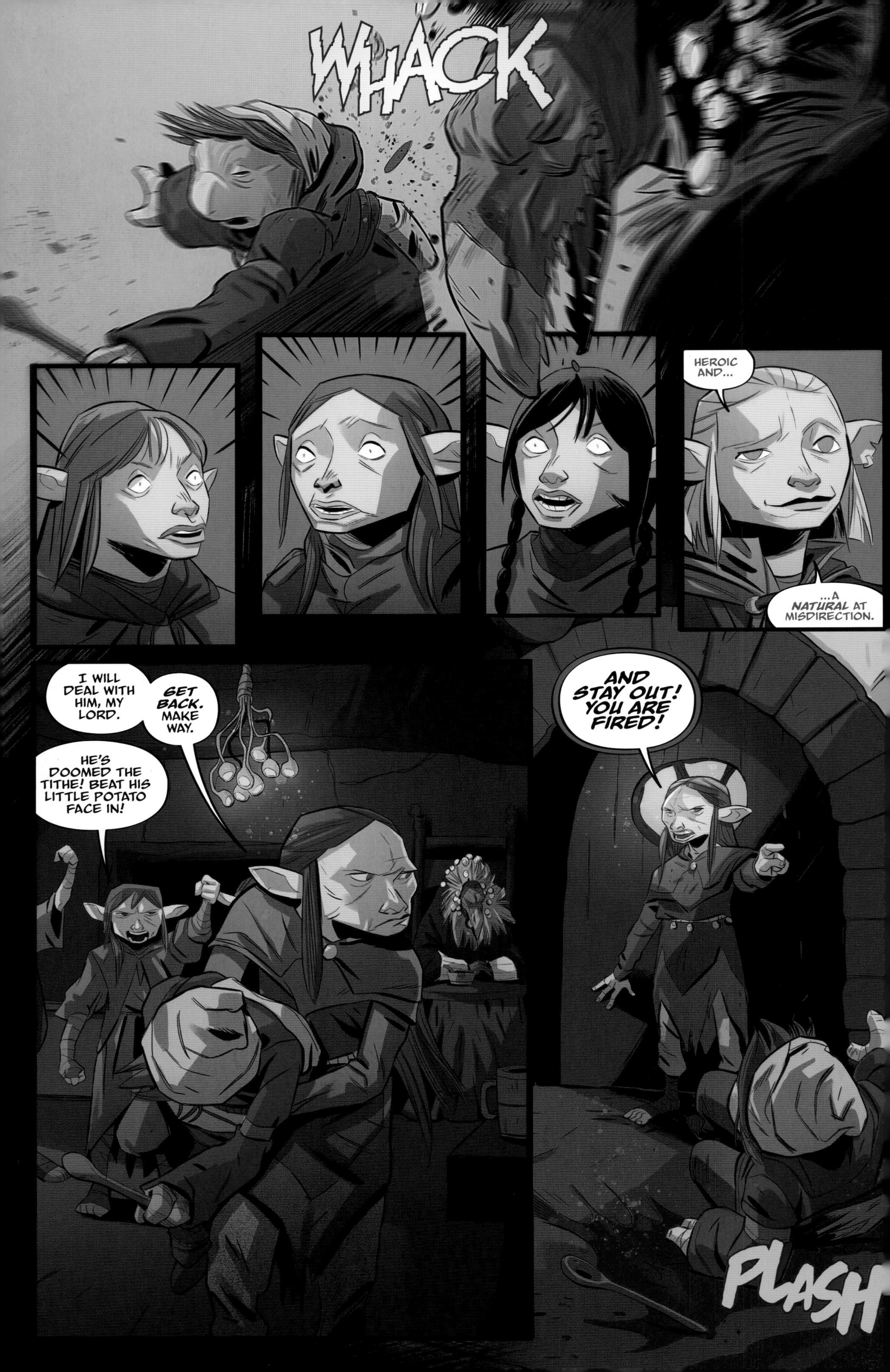
WHACK
HEROIC AND...
...A NATURAL AT MISDIRECTION.
I WILL DEAL WITH HIM, MY LORD.
GET BACK. MAKE WAY.
HE'S DOOMED THE TITHE! BEAT HIS LITTLE POTATO FACE IN!
AND STAY OUT! YOU ARE FIRED!
PLASH

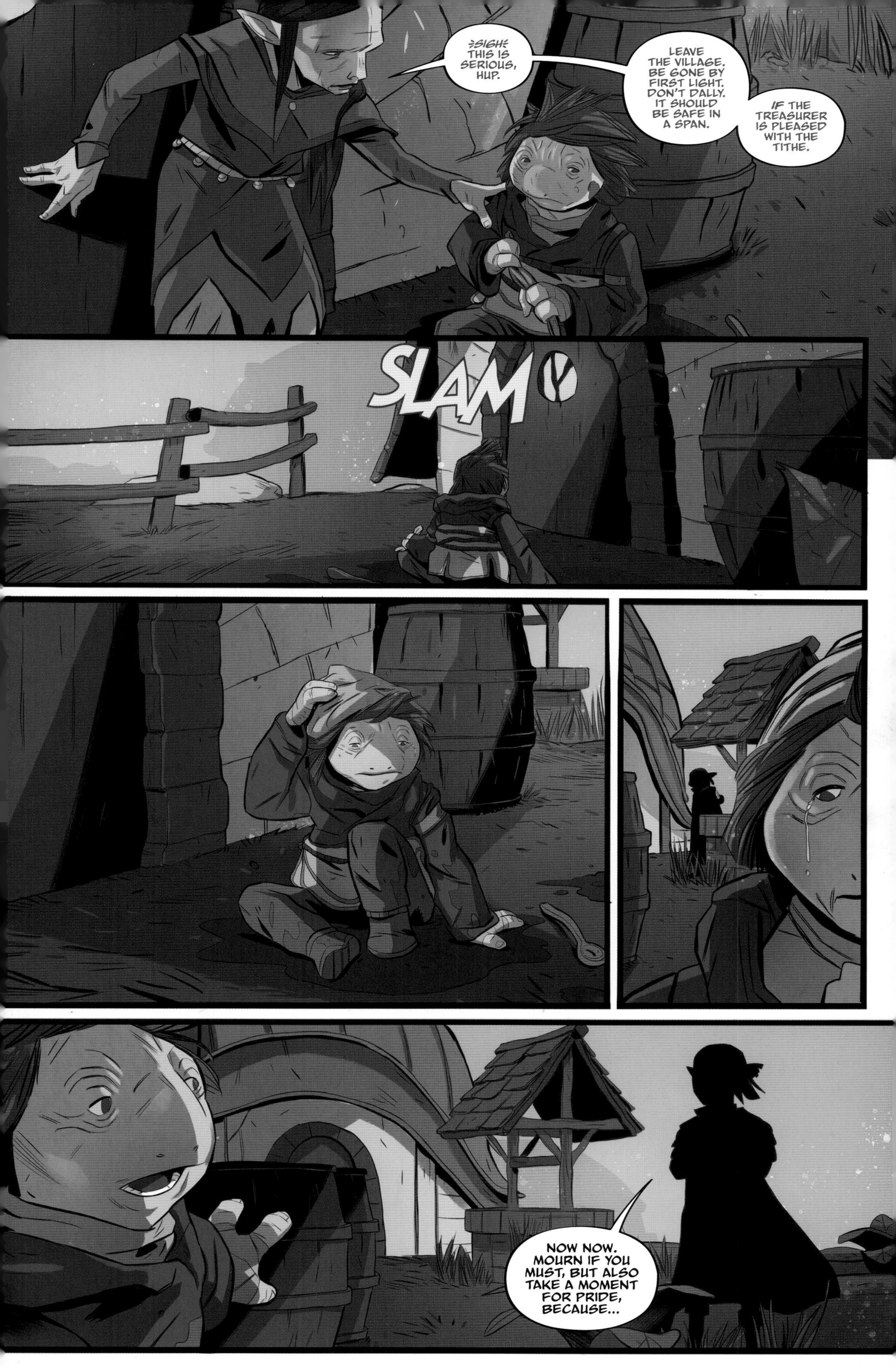
SIGH THIS IS SERIOUS, HUP.
LEAVE THE VILLAGE. BE GONE BY FIRST LIGHT. DON'T DALLY. IT SHOULD BE SAFE IN A SPAN.
IF THE TREASURER IS PLEASED WITH THE TITHE.
SLAM
NOW NOW. MOURN IF YOU MUST, BUT ALSO TAKE A MOMENT FOR PRIDE, BECAUSE...

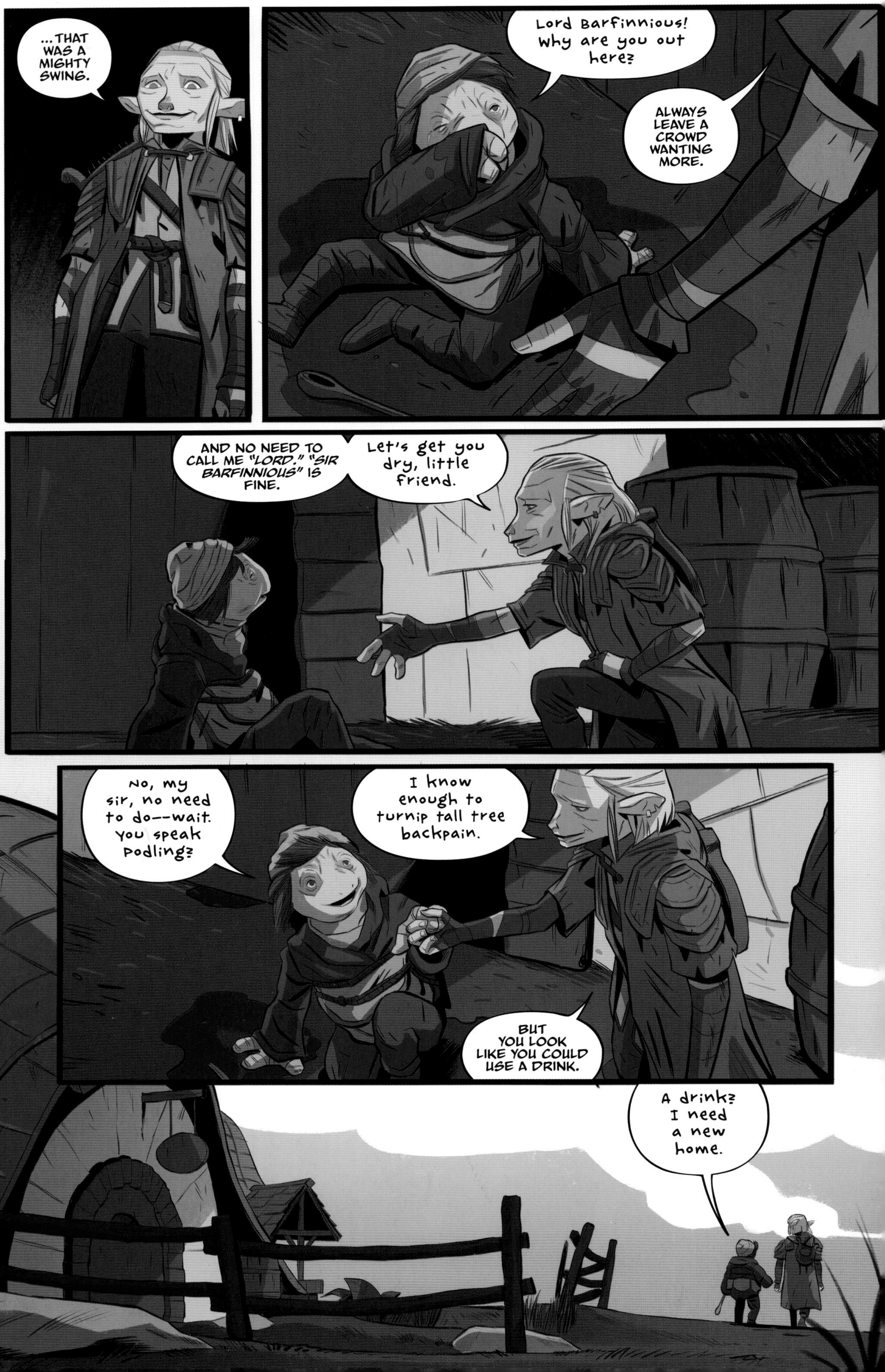
...THAT WAS A MIGHTY SWING.
Lord Barfinnious! Why are you out here?
ALWAYS LEAVE A CROWD WANTING MORE.
AND NO NEED TO CALL ME "LORD." "SIR BARFINNIOUS" IS FINE.
Let's get you dry, little friend.
No, my sir, no need to do--wait. You speak Podling?
I know enough to turnip tall tree backpain.
BUT YOU LOOK LIKE YOU COULD USE A DRINK.
A drink? I need a new home.

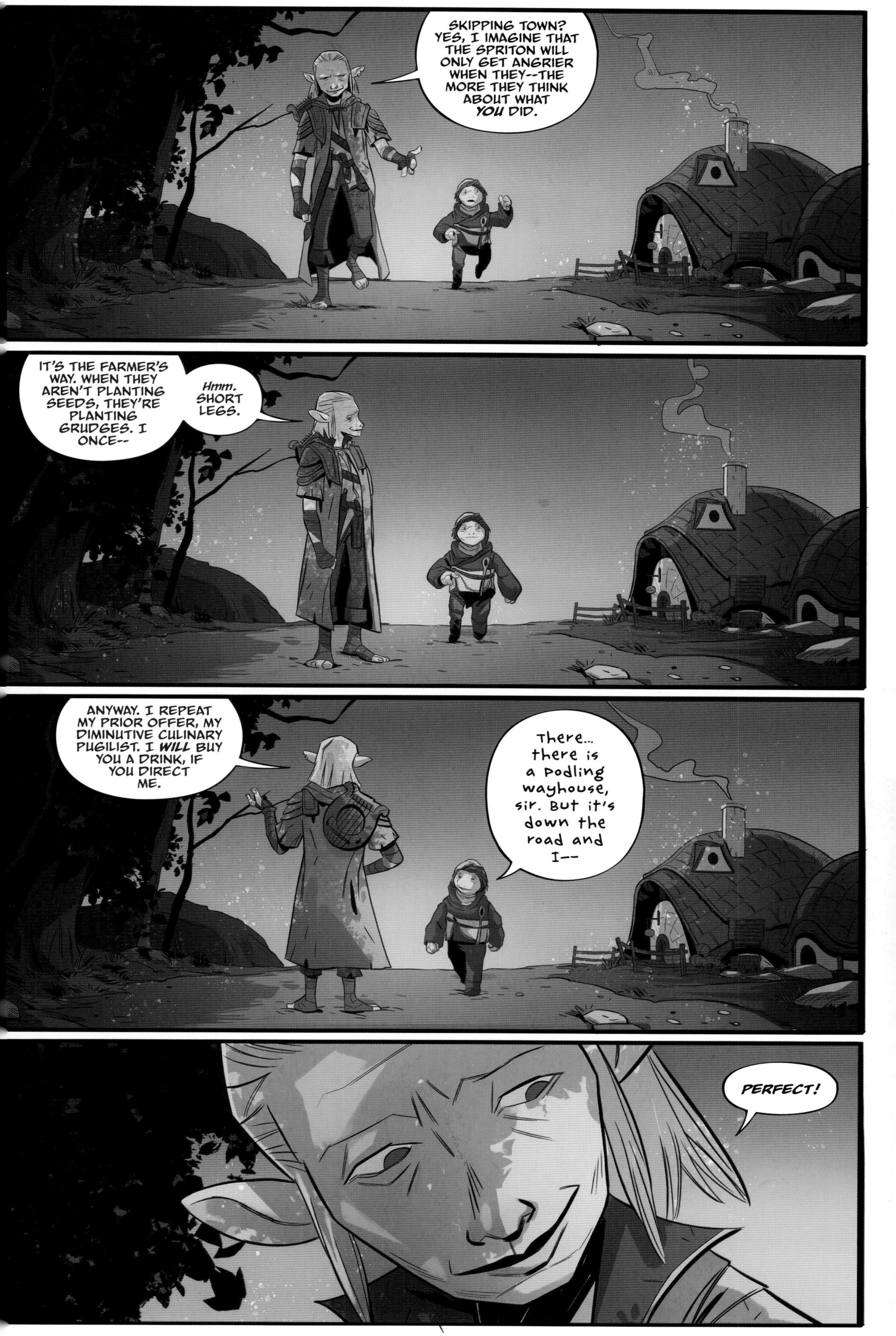
SKIPPING TOWN? YES, I IMAGINE THAT THE SPRITON WILL ONLY GET ANGRIER WHEN THEY--THE MORE THEY THINK ABOUT WHAT *YOU* DID.
IT'S THE FARMER'S WAY. WHEN THEY AREN'T PLANTING SEEDS, THEY'RE PLANTING GRUDGES. I ONCE--
Hmm. SHORT LEGS.
ANYWAY. I REPEAT MY PRIOR OFFER, MY DIMINUTIVE CULINARY PUGILIST. I *WILL* BUY YOU A DRINK, IF YOU DIRECT ME.
There... there is a Podling wayhouse, sir. But it's down the road and I--
PERFECT!

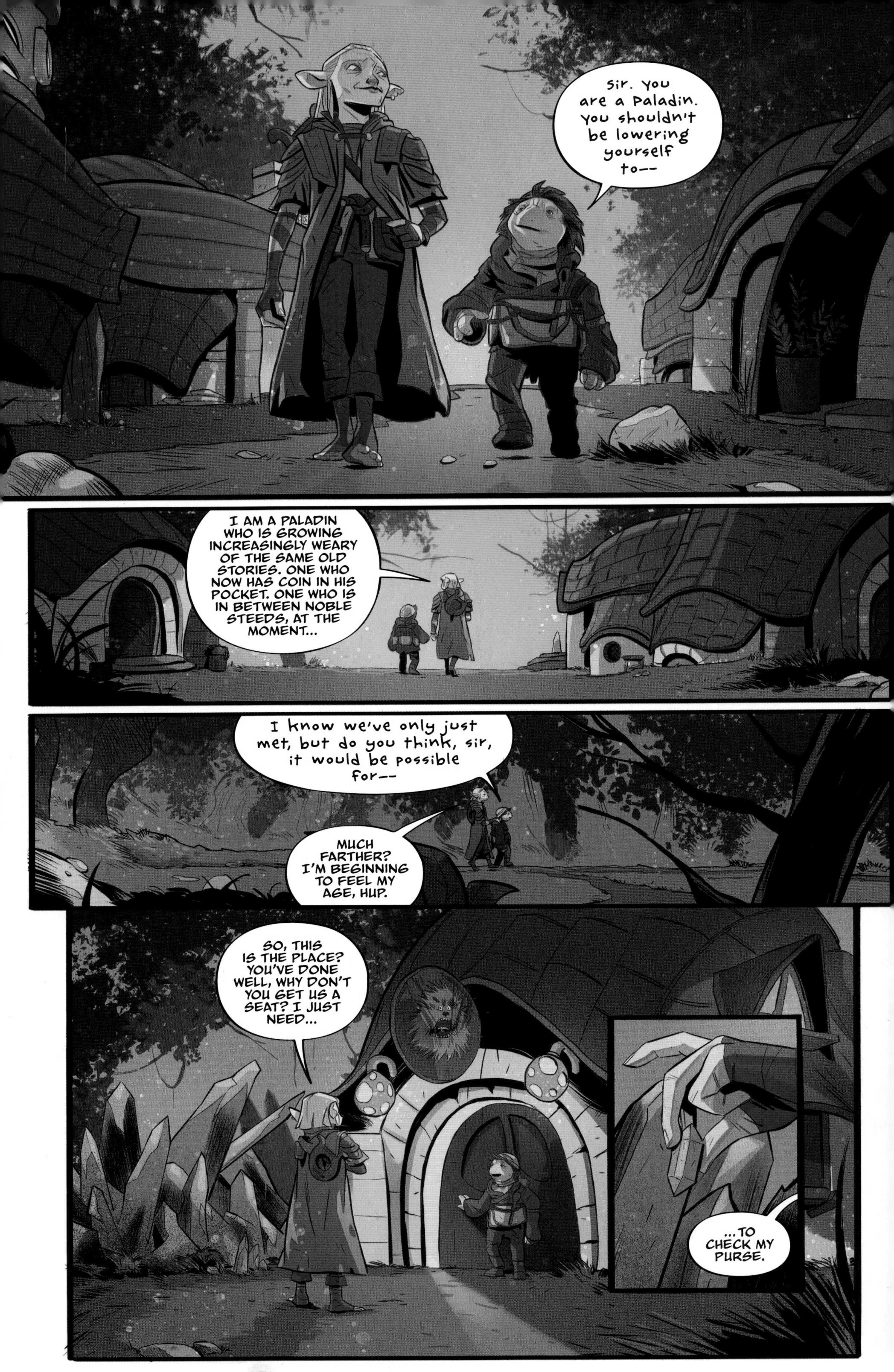
Sir. You are a Paladin. You shouldn't be lowering yourself to--
I AM A PALADIN WHO IS GROWING INCREASINGLY WEARY OF THE SAME OLD STORIES. ONE WHO NOW HAS COIN IN HIS POCKET. ONE WHO IS IN BETWEEN NOBLE STEEDS, AT THE MOMENT...
I know we've only just met, but do you think, sir, it would be possible for--
MUCH FARTHER? I'M BEGINNING TO FEEL MY AGE, HUP.
SO, THIS IS THE PLACE? YOU'VE DONE WELL, WHY DON'T YOU GET US A SEAT? I JUST NEED...
...TO CHECK MY PURSE.

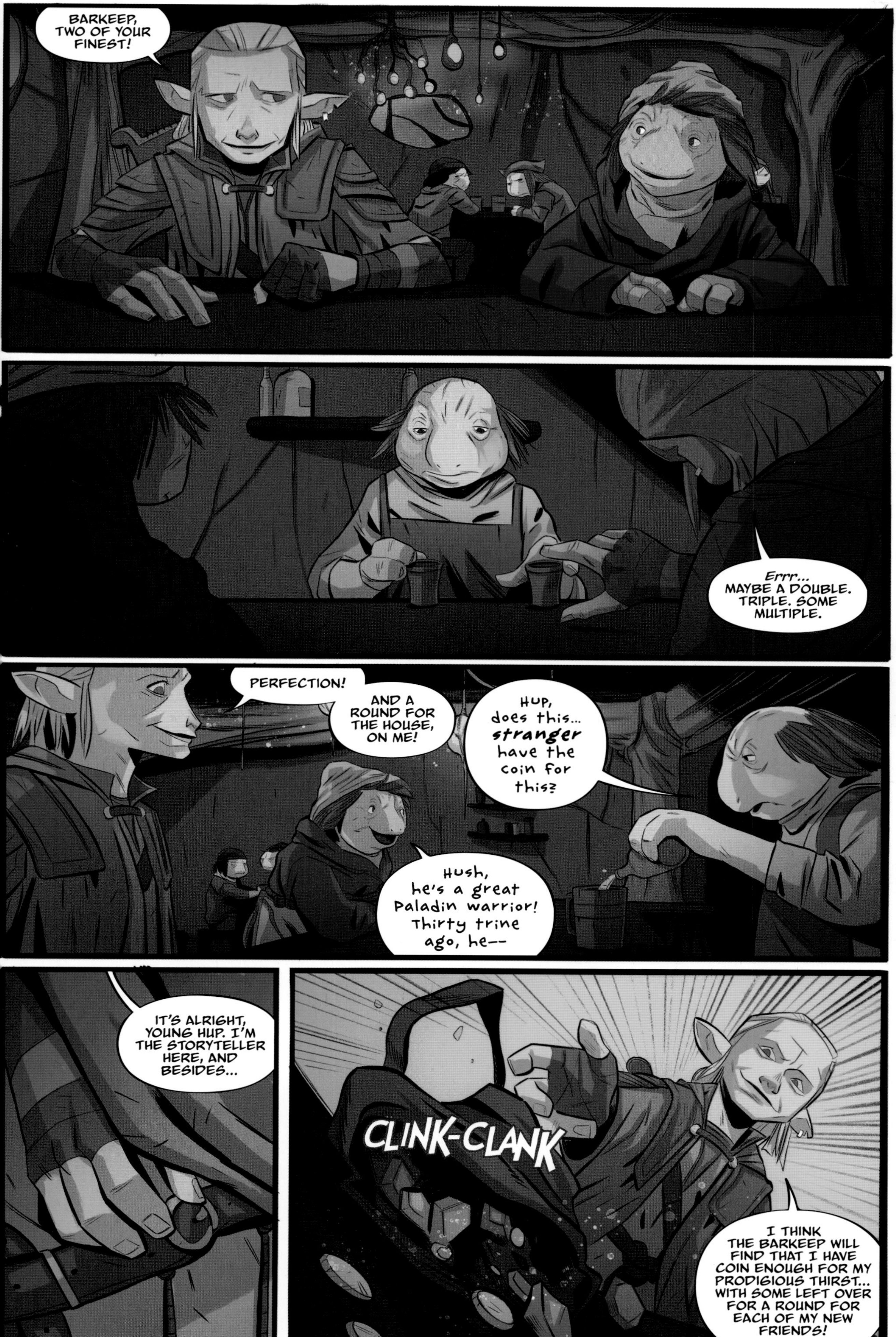
BARKEEP, TWO OF YOUR FINEST!
Errr... MAYBE A DOUBLE. TRIPLE. SOME MULTIPLE.
PERFECTION!
AND A ROUND FOR THE HOUSE, ON ME!
Hup, does this... stranger have the coin for this?
Hush, he's a great Paladin warrior! Thirty trine ago, he--
IT'S ALRIGHT, YOUNG HUP. I'M THE STORYTELLER HERE, AND BESIDES...
CLINK-CLANK
I THINK THE BARKEEP WILL FIND THAT I HAVE COIN ENOUGH FOR MY PRODIGIOUS THIRST... WITH SOME LEFT OVER FOR A ROUND FOR EACH OF MY NEW FRIENDS!

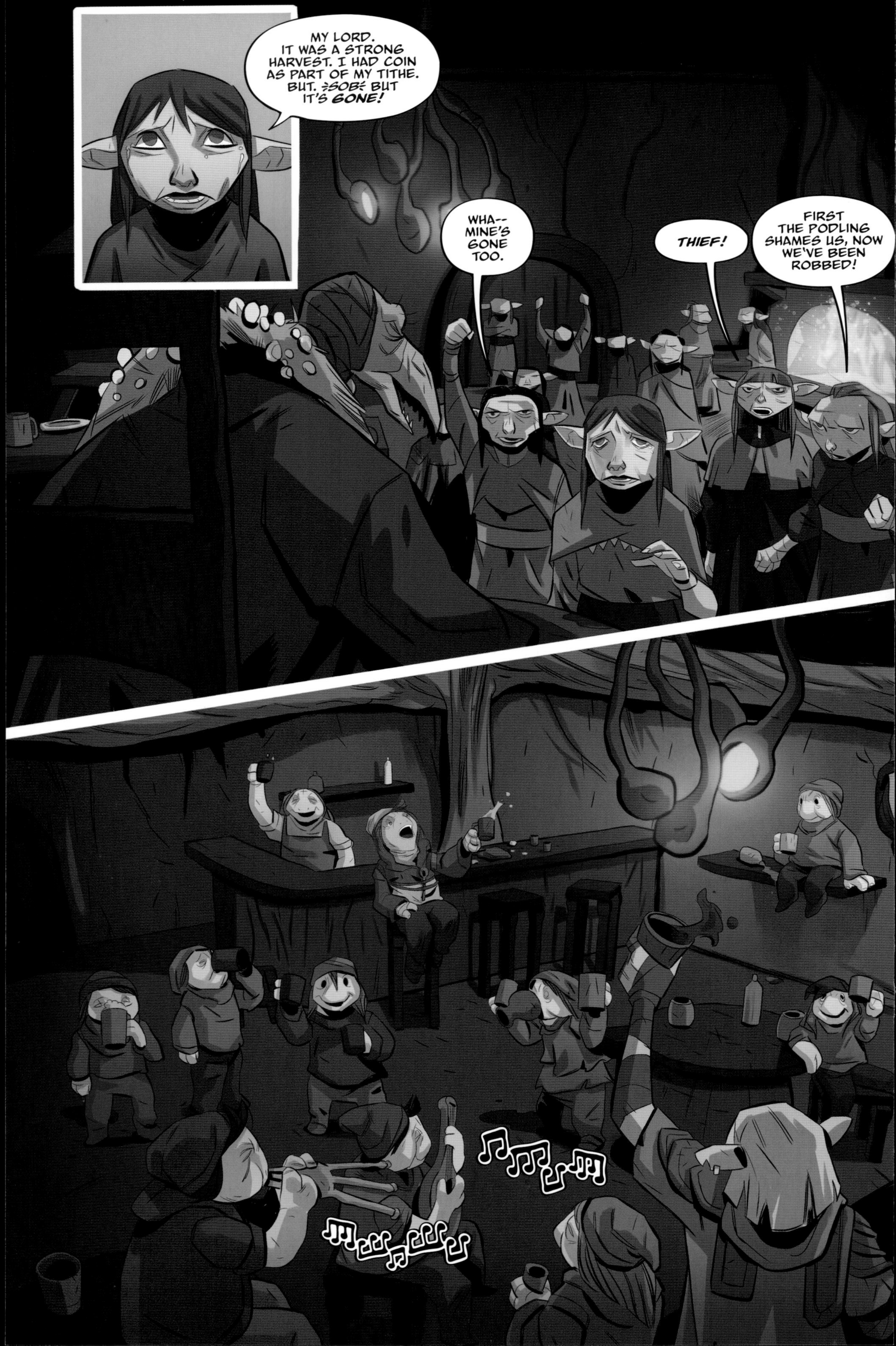
MY LORD. IT WAS A STRONG HARVEST. I HAD COIN AS PART OF MY TITHE. BUT. ≈SOB≈ BUT IT'S GONE!
WHA-- MINE'S GONE TOO.
THIEF!
FIRST THE PODLING SHAMES US, NOW WE'VE BEEN ROBBED!

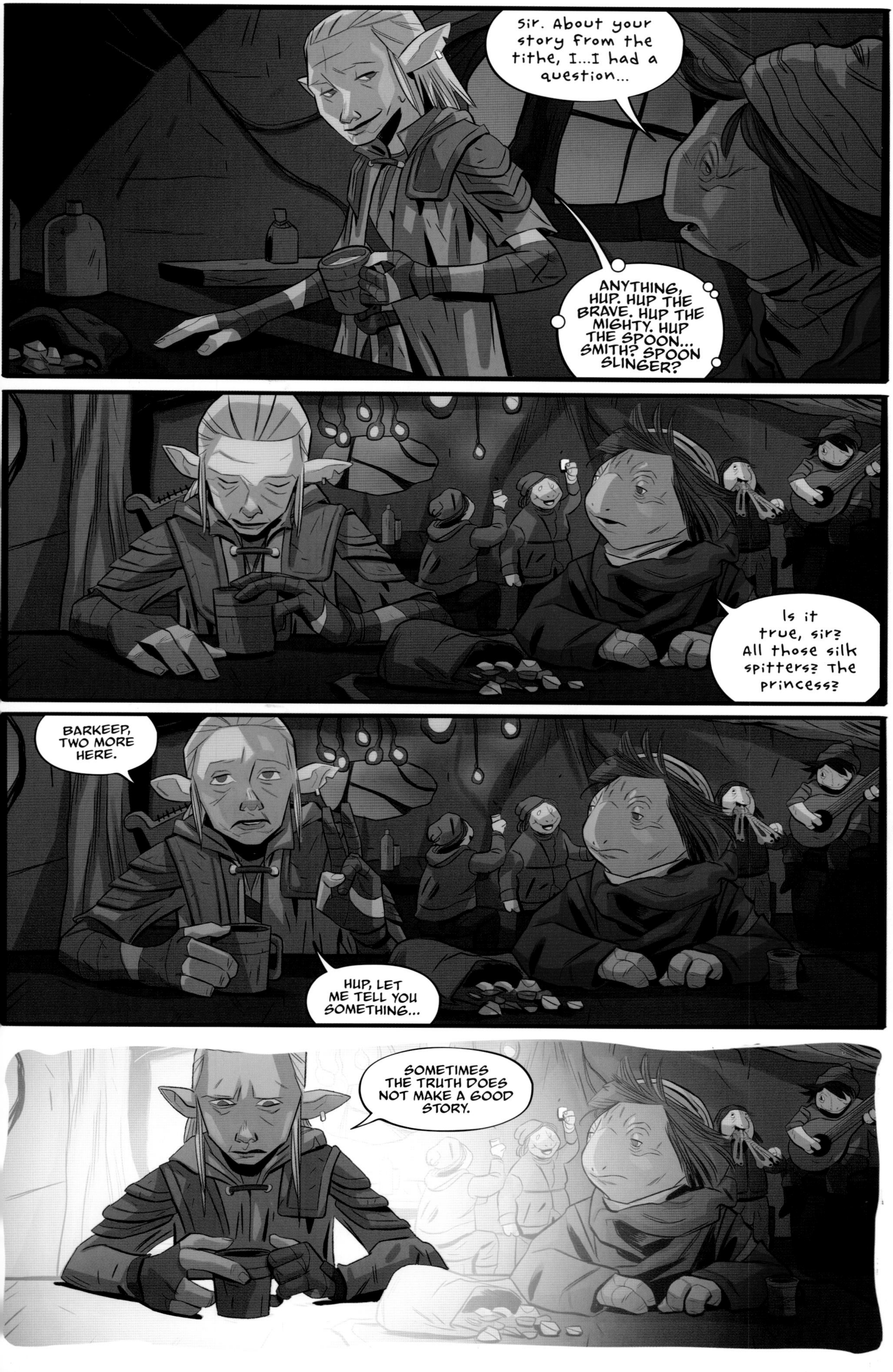
Sir. About your story from the tithe, I...I had a question...
ANYTHING, HUP. HUP THE BRAVE. HUP THE MIGHTY. HUP THE SPOON... SMITH? SPOON SLINGER?
Is it true, sir? All those silk spitters? The princess?
BARKEEP, TWO MORE HERE.
HUP, LET ME TELL YOU SOMETHING...
SOMETIMES THE TRUTH DOES NOT MAKE A GOOD STORY.

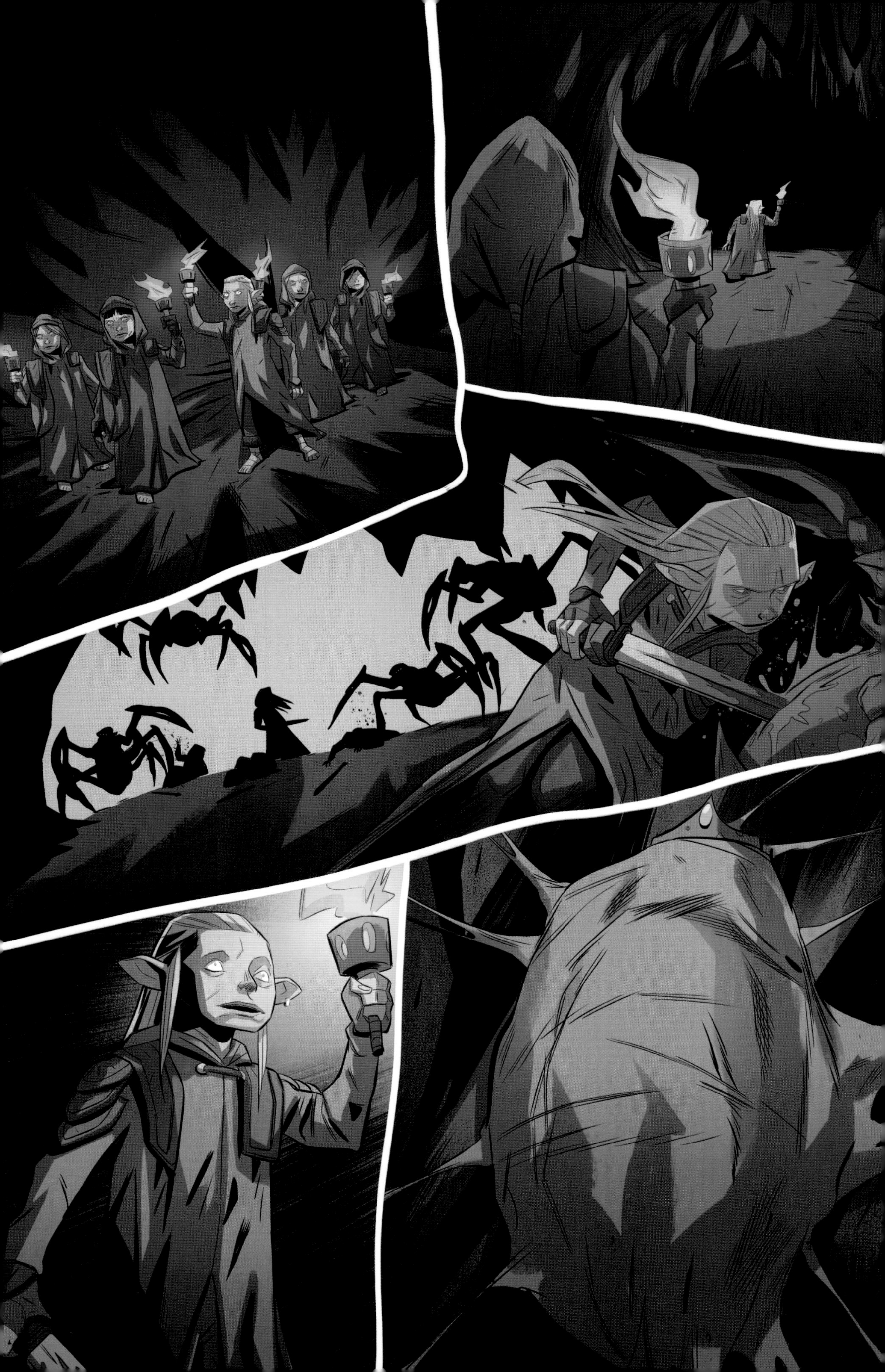

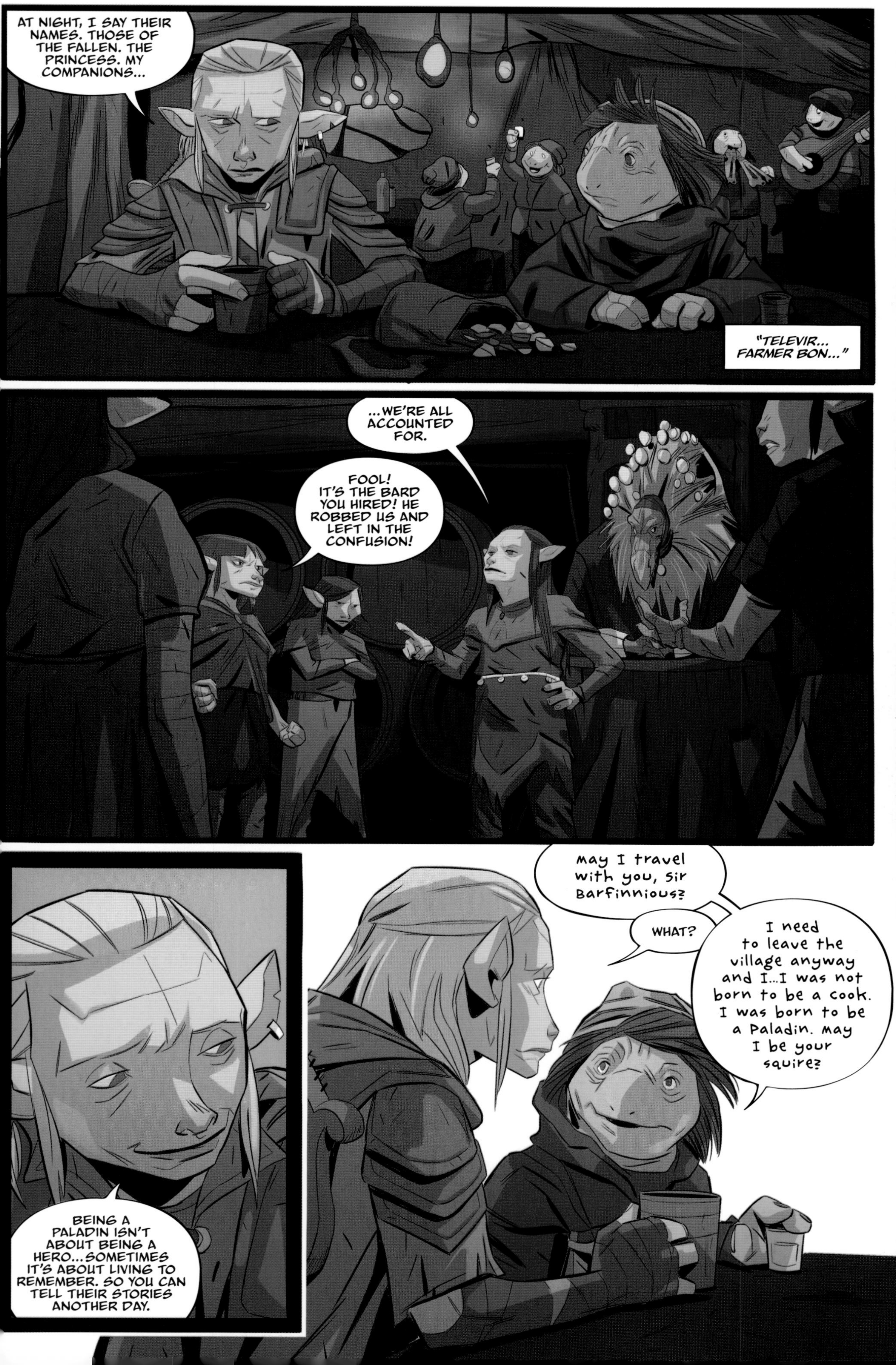
AT NIGHT, I SAY THEIR NAMES. THOSE OF THE FALLEN. THE PRINCESS. MY COMPANIONS...
"TELEVIR... FARMER BON..."
...WE'RE ALL ACCOUNTED FOR.
FOOL! IT'S THE BARD YOU HIRED! HE ROBBED US AND LEFT IN THE CONFUSION!
may I travel with you, sir Barfinnious?
WHAT?
I need to leave the village anyway and I...I was not born to be a cook. I was born to be a Paladin. may I be your squire?
BEING A PALADIN ISN'T ABOUT BEING A HERO...SOMETIMES IT'S ABOUT LIVING TO REMEMBER. SO YOU CAN TELL THEIR STORIES ANOTHER DAY.

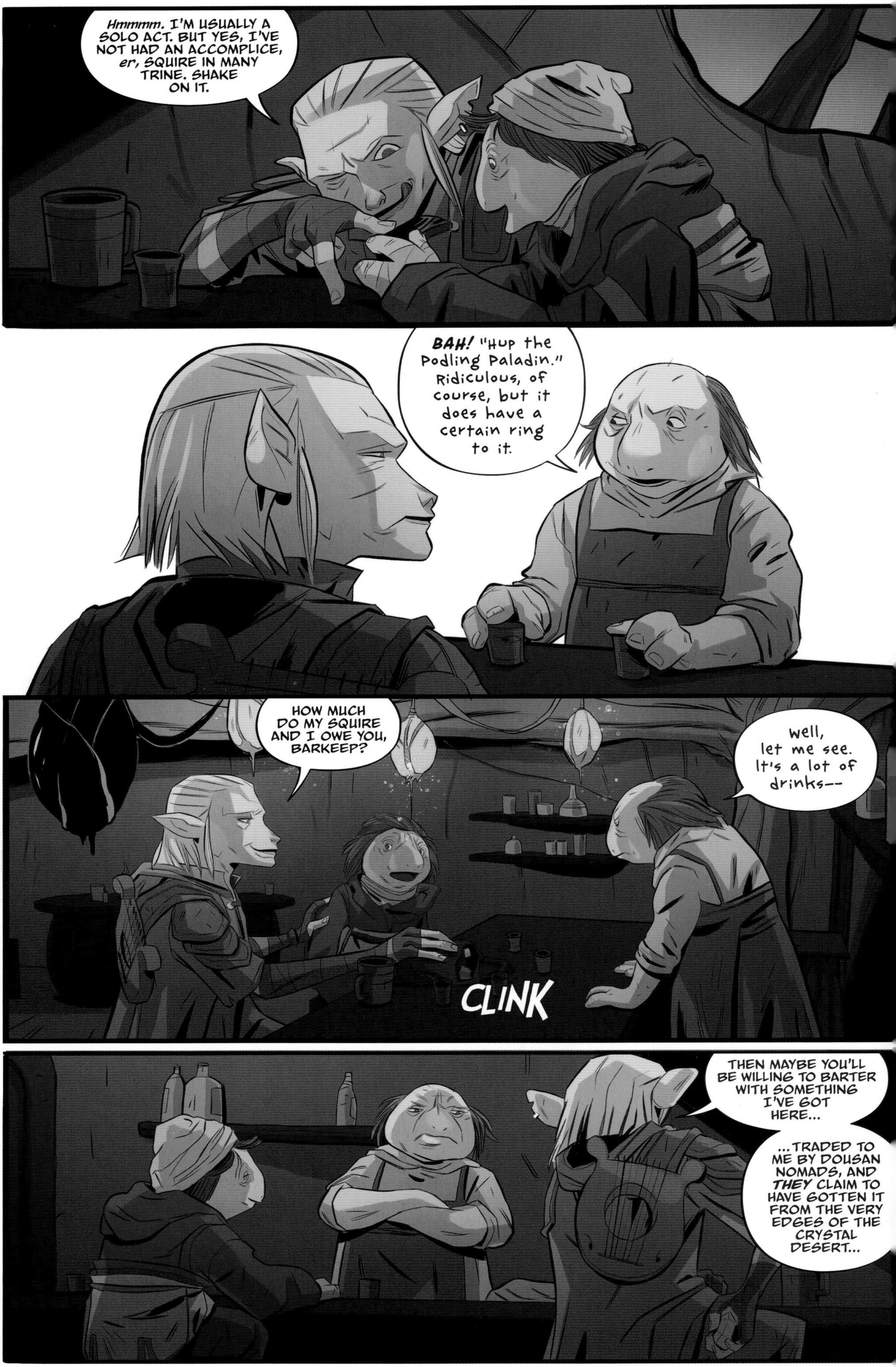
Hmmmm. I'M USUALLY A SOLO ACT. BUT YES, I'VE NOT HAD AN ACCOMPLICE, er, SQUIRE IN MANY TRINE. SHAKE ON IT.
BAH! "Hup the Podling Paladin." Ridiculous, of course, but it does have a certain ring to it.
HOW MUCH DO MY SQUIRE AND I OWE YOU, BARKEEP?
Well, let me see. It's a lot of drinks--
CLINK
THEN MAYBE YOU'LL BE WILLING TO BARTER WITH SOMETHING I'VE GOT HERE...
...TRADED TO ME BY DOUSAN NOMADS, AND THEY CLAIM TO HAVE GOTTEN IT FROM THE VERY EDGES OF THE CRYSTAL DESERT...

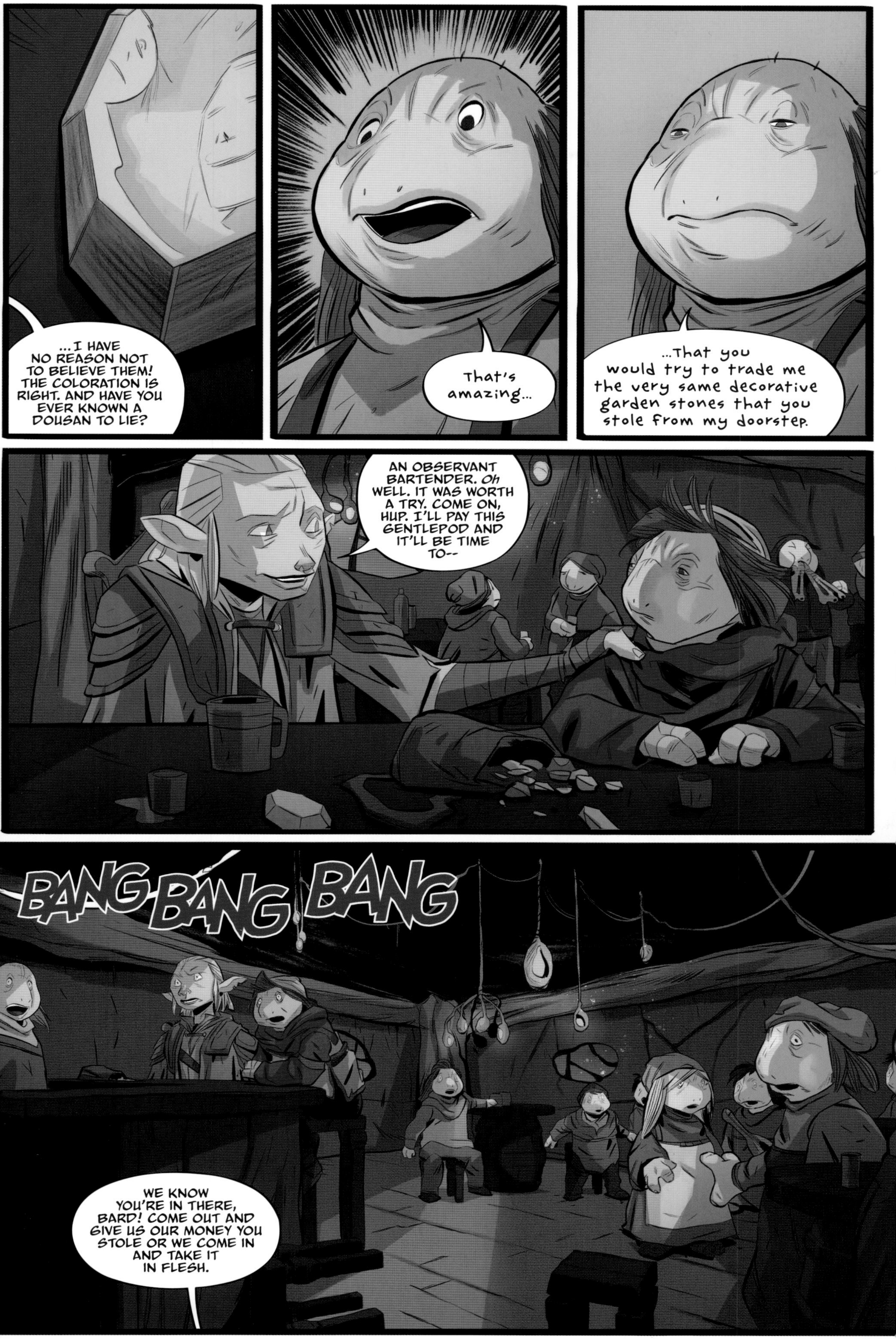
...I HAVE NO REASON NOT TO BELIEVE THEM! THE COLORATION IS RIGHT. AND HAVE YOU EVER KNOWN A DOUSAN TO LIE?
That's amazing...
...That you would try to trade me the very same decorative garden stones that you stole from my doorstep.
AN OBSERVANT BARTENDER. Oh WELL. IT WAS WORTH A TRY. COME ON, HUP. I'LL PAY THIS GENTLEPOD AND IT'LL BE TIME TO--
BANG BANG BANG
WE KNOW YOU'RE IN THERE, BARD! COME OUT AND GIVE US OUR MONEY YOU STOLE OR WE COME IN AND TAKE IT IN FLESH.

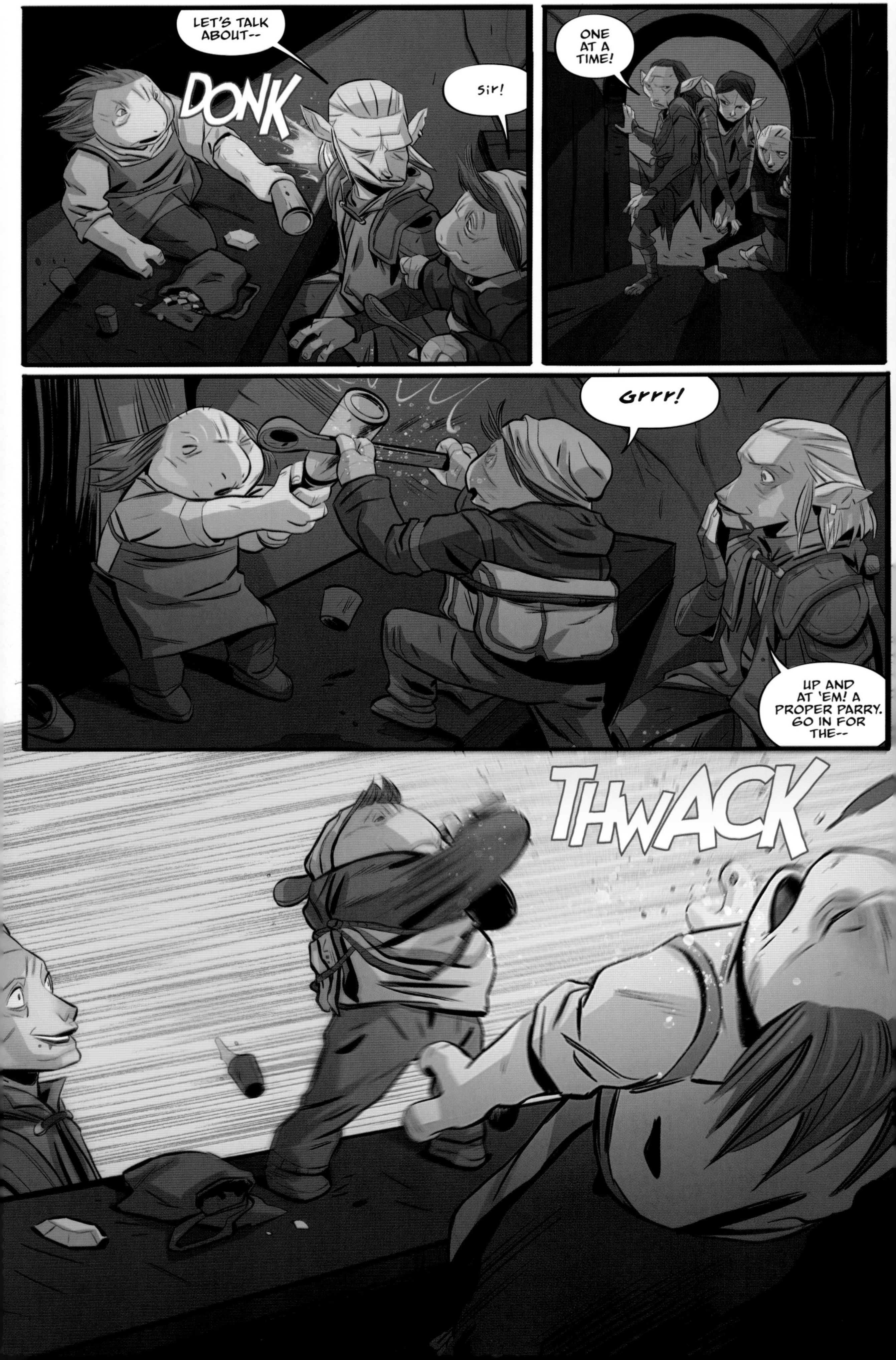
LET'S TALK ABOUT--
DONK
sir!
ONE AT A TIME!
Grrr!
UP AND AT 'EM! A PROPER PARRY. GO IN FOR THE--
THWACK

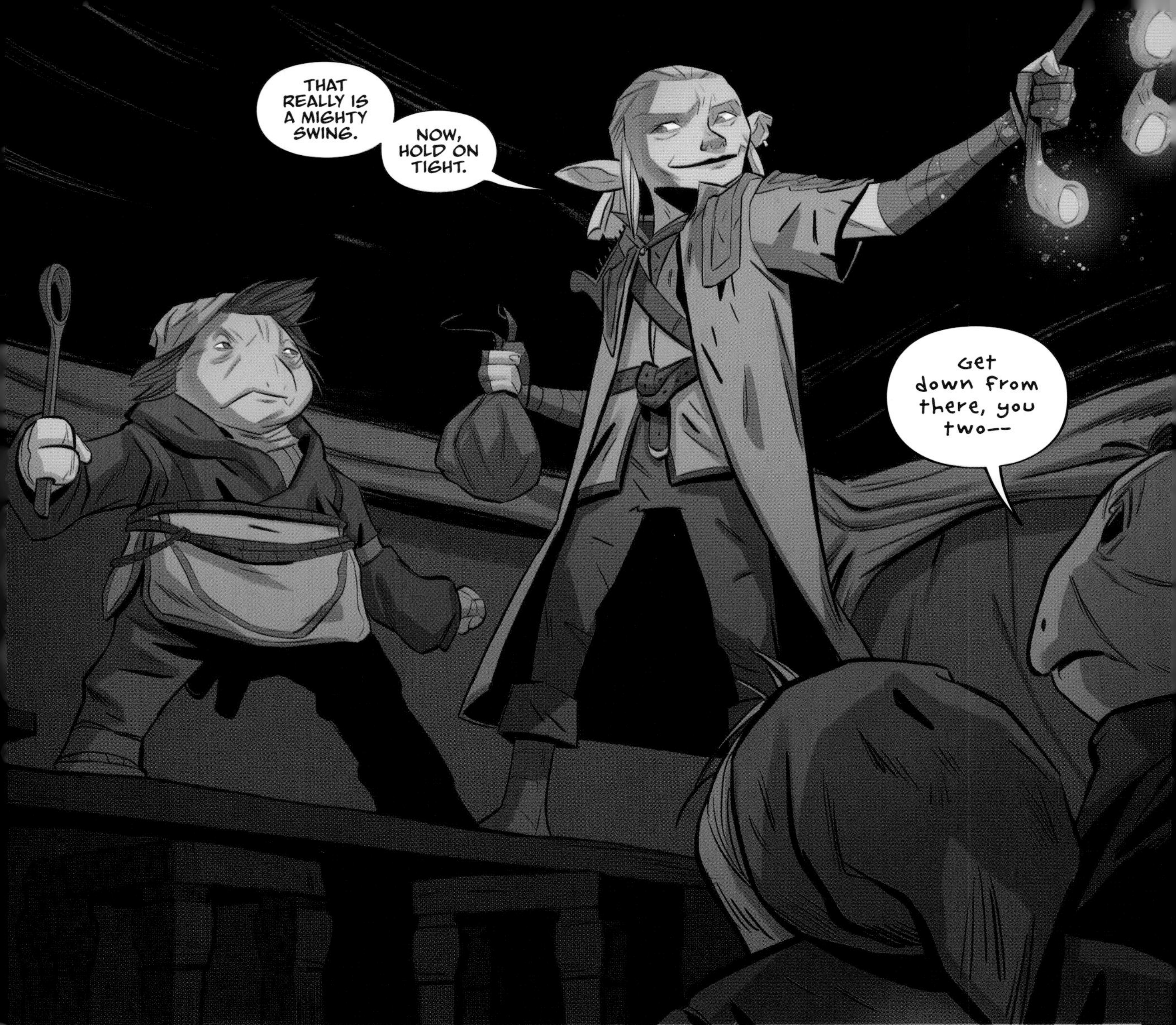
THAT REALLY IS A MIGHTY SWING.
NOW, HOLD ON TIGHT.
Get down from there, you two--

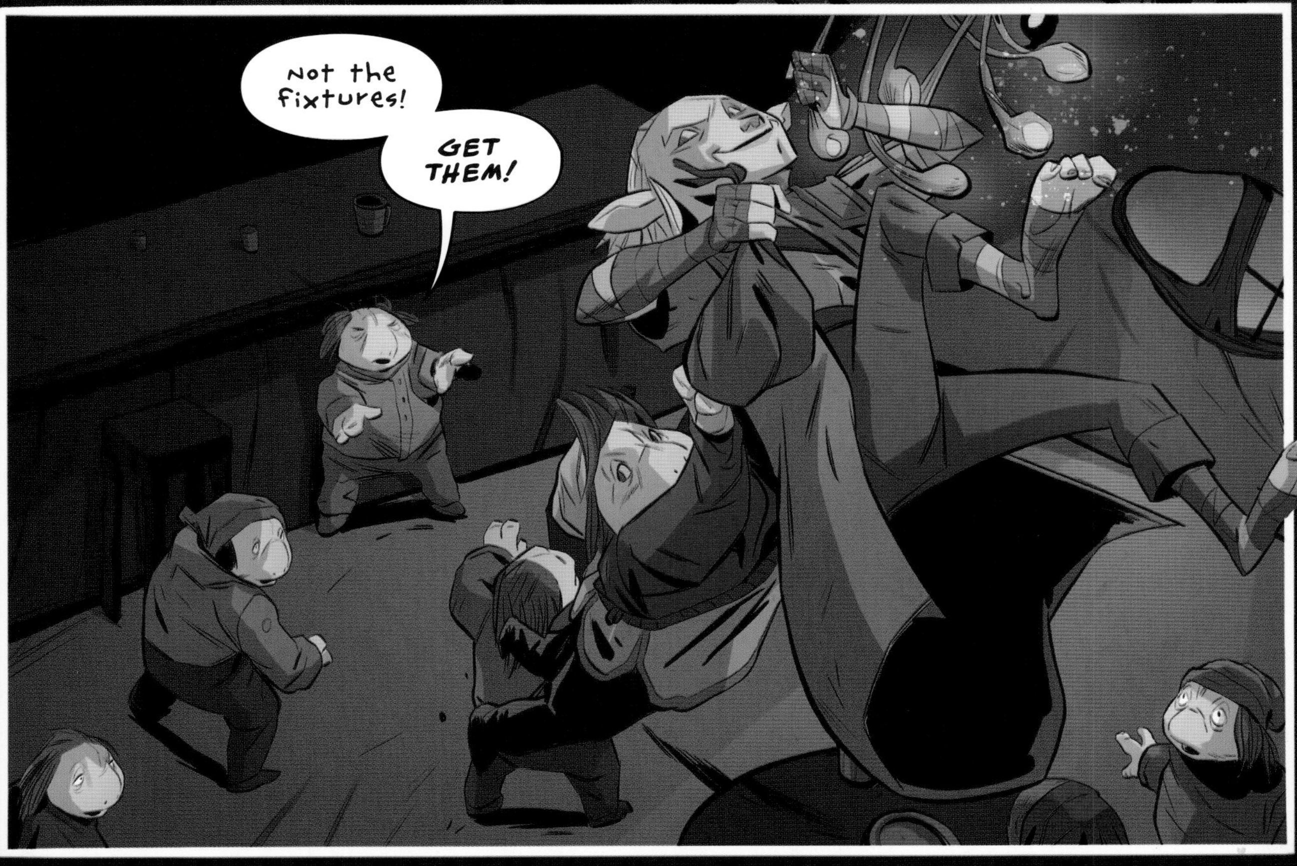
Not the fixtures!
GET THEM!

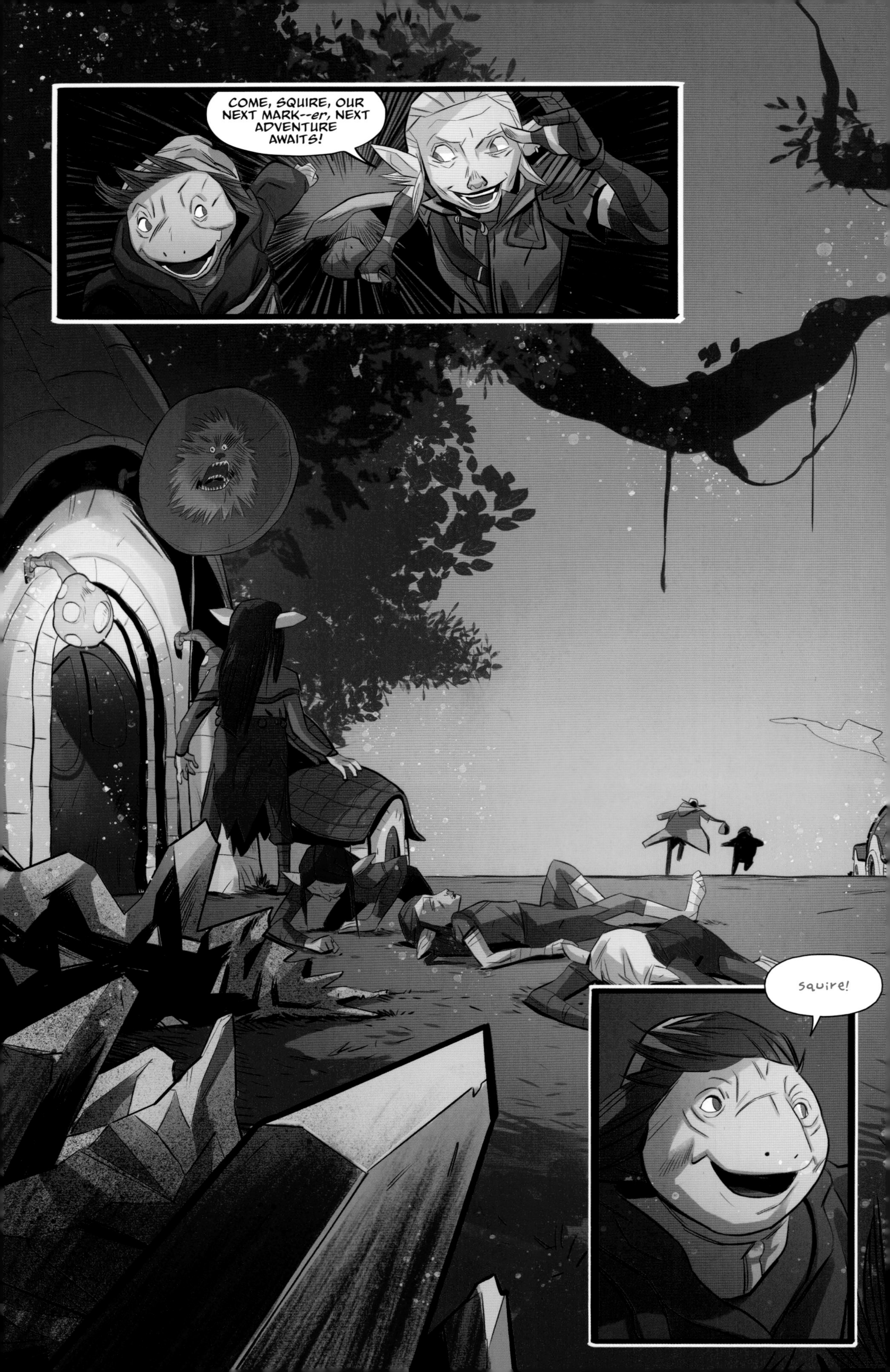
COME, SQUIRE, OUR NEXT MARK--*er*, NEXT ADVENTURE AWAITS!
squire!

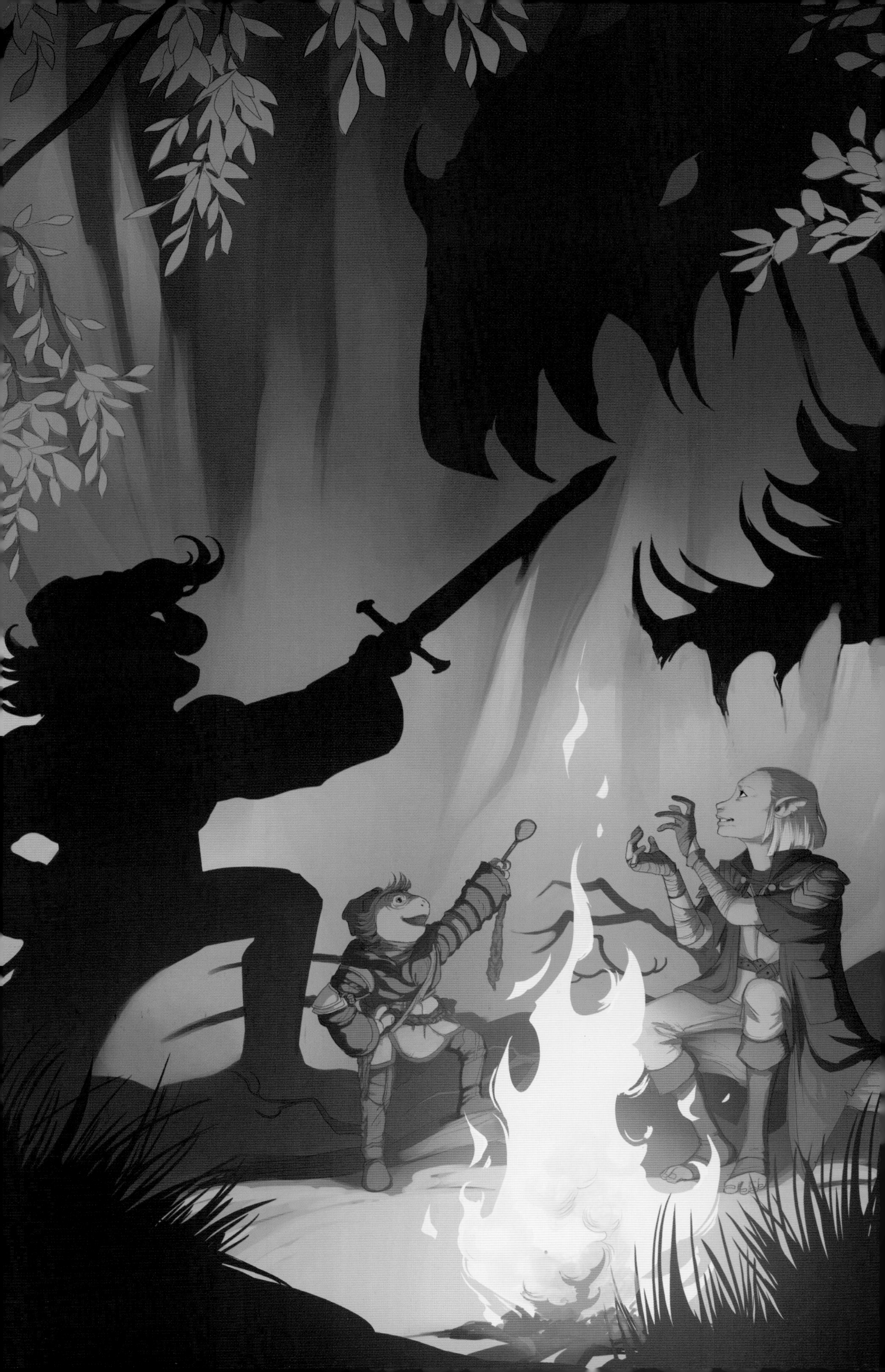

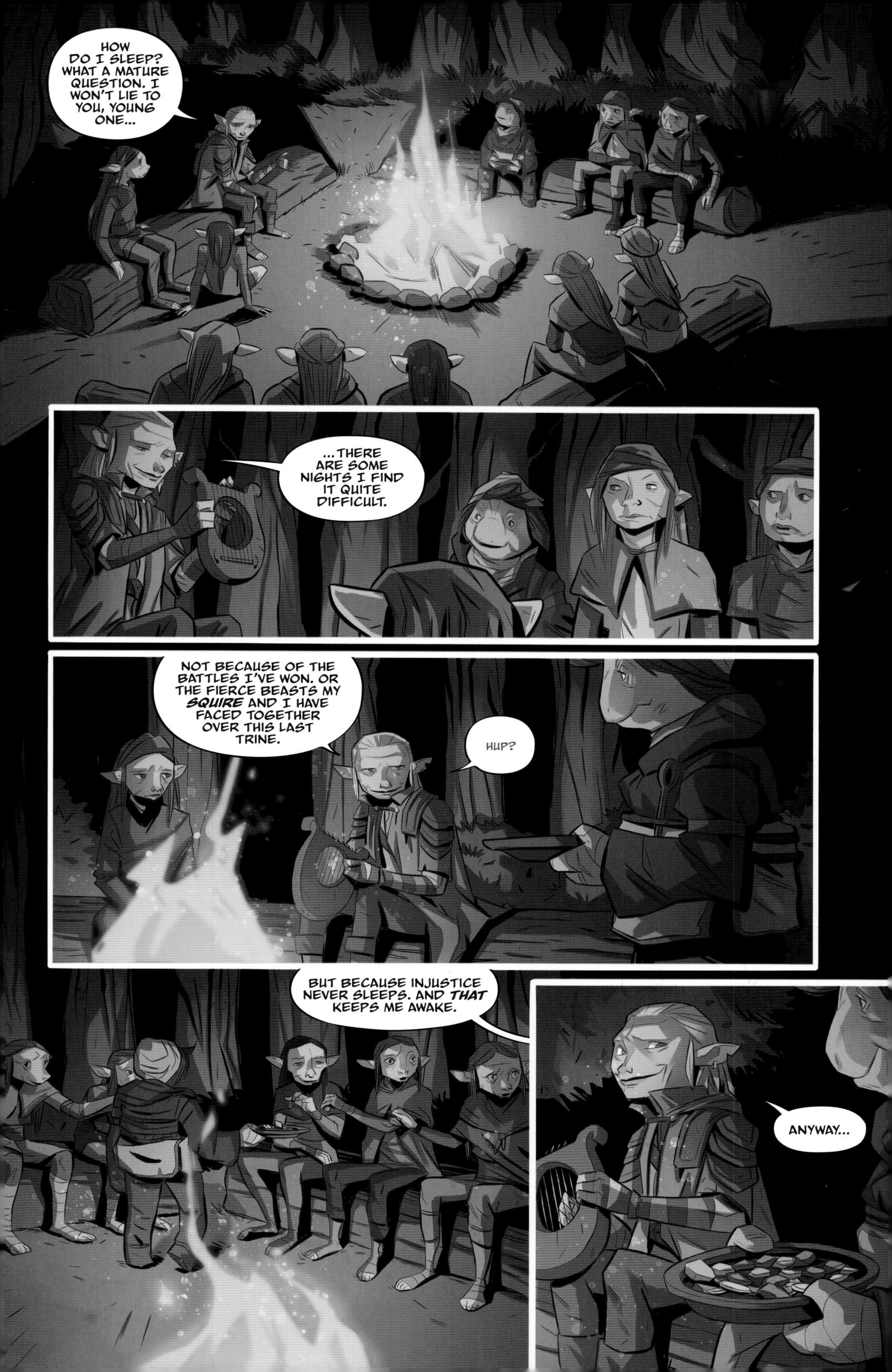
HOW DO I SLEEP? WHAT A MATURE QUESTION. I WON'T LIE TO YOU, YOUNG ONE...
...THERE ARE SOME NIGHTS I FIND IT QUITE DIFFICULT.
NOT BECAUSE OF THE BATTLES I'VE WON. OR THE FIERCE BEASTS MY *SQUIRE* AND I HAVE FACED TOGETHER OVER THIS LAST TRINE.
HUP?
BUT BECAUSE INJUSTICE NEVER SLEEPS. AND *THAT* KEEPS ME AWAKE.
ANYWAY...

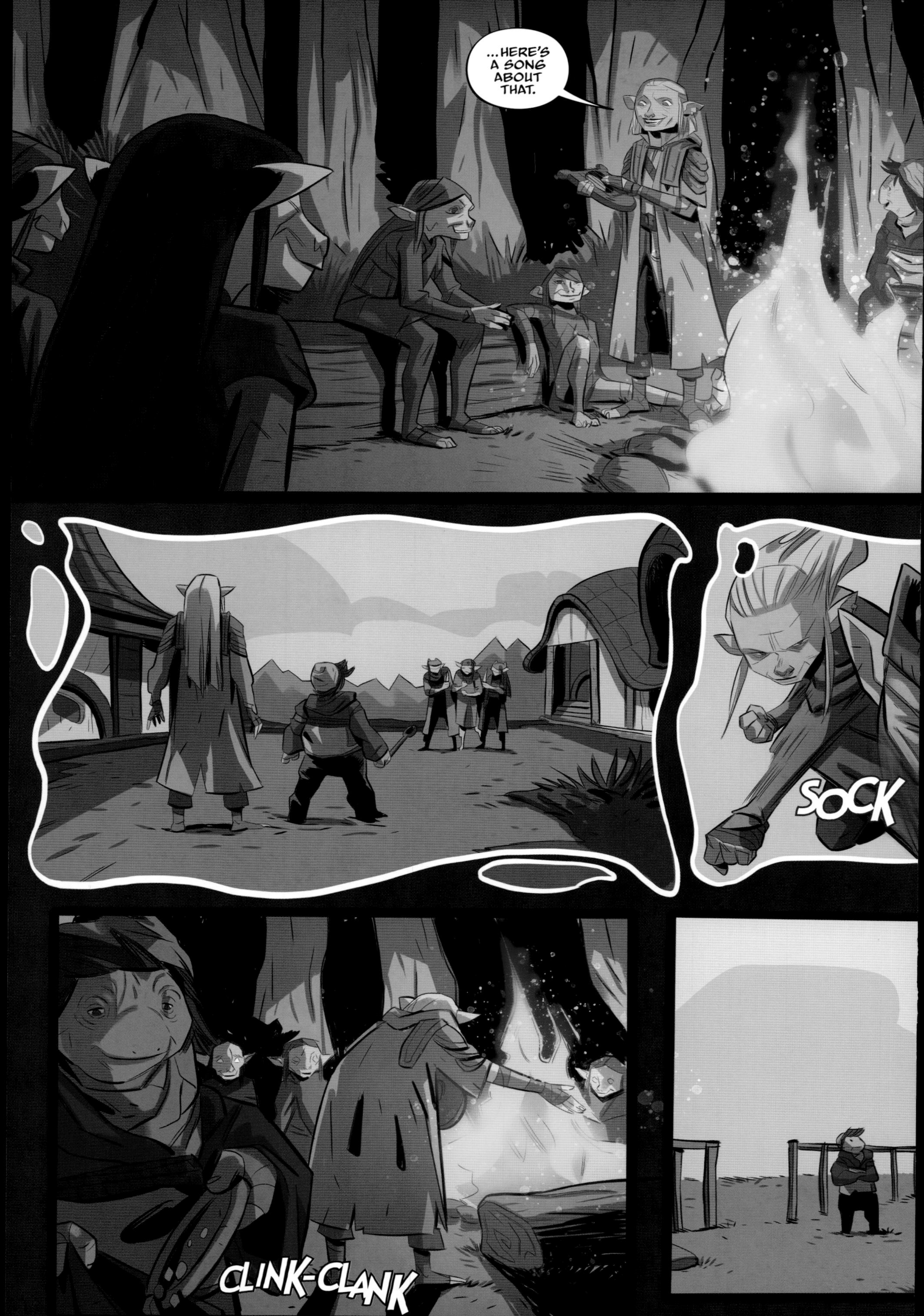
...HERE'S A SONG ABOUT THAT.
SOCK
CLINK-CLANK

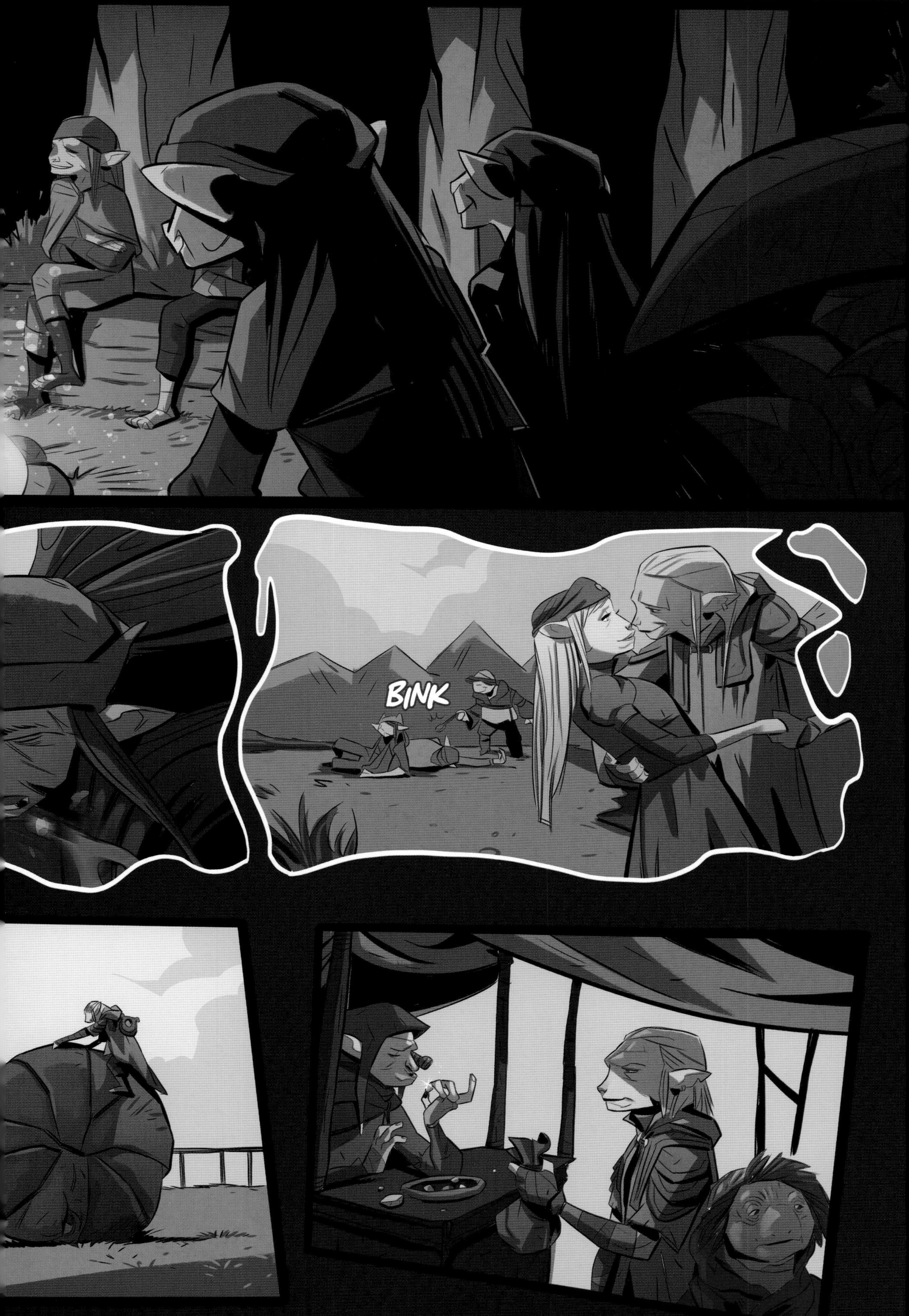
BINK

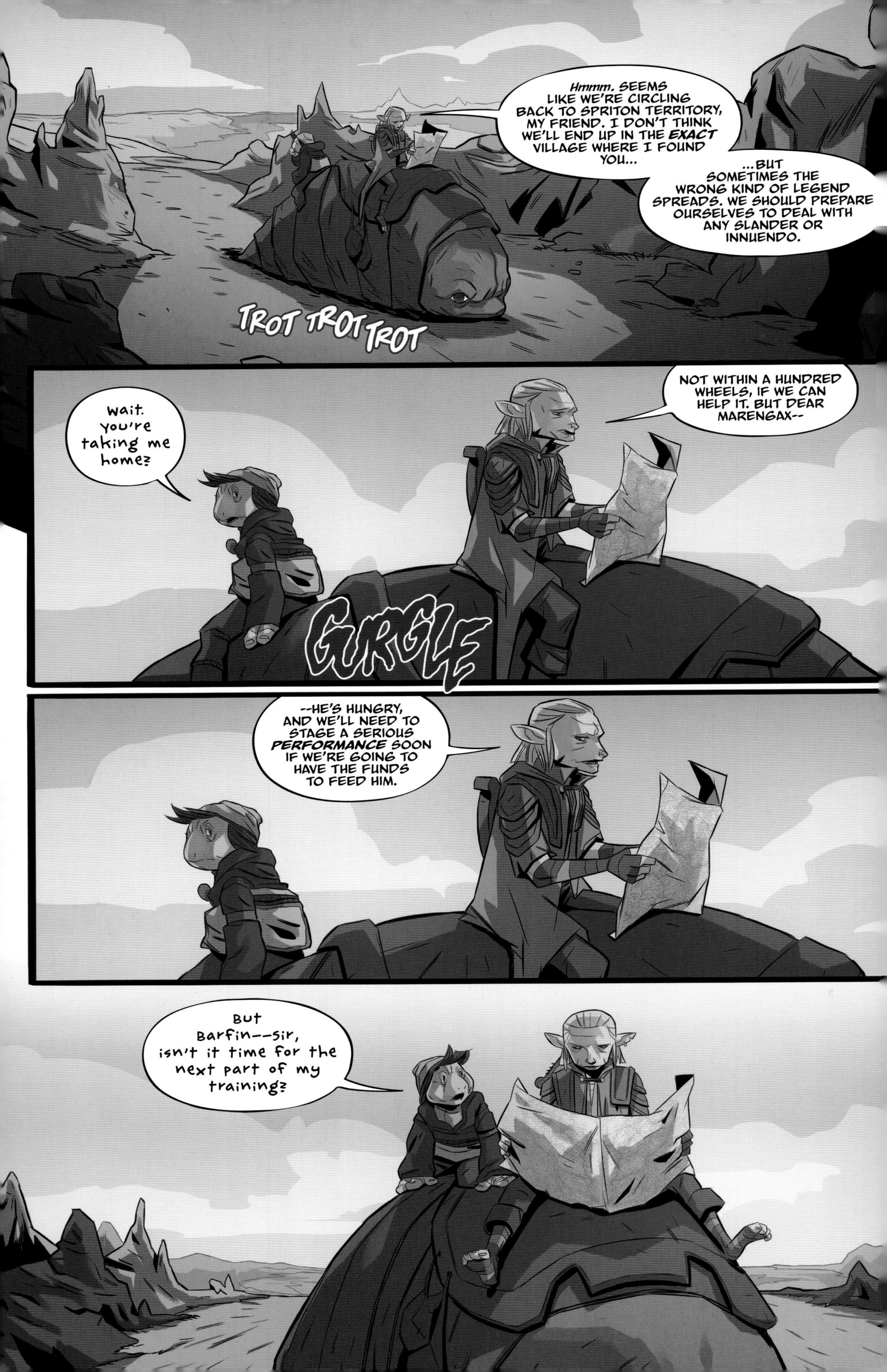
Hmmm. SEEMS LIKE WE'RE CIRCLING BACK TO SPRITON TERRITORY, MY FRIEND. I DON'T THINK WE'LL END UP IN THE EXACT VILLAGE WHERE I FOUND YOU...
...BUT SOMETIMES THE WRONG KIND OF LEGEND SPREADS. WE SHOULD PREPARE OURSELVES TO DEAL WITH ANY SLANDER OR INNUENDO.
TROT TROT TROT
Wait. You're taking me home?
NOT WITHIN A HUNDRED WHEELS, IF WE CAN HELP IT. BUT DEAR MARENGAX--
GURGLE
--HE'S HUNGRY, AND WE'LL NEED TO STAGE A SERIOUS PERFORMANCE SOON IF WE'RE GOING TO HAVE THE FUNDS TO FEED HIM.
But Barfin--sir, isn't it time for the next part of my training?

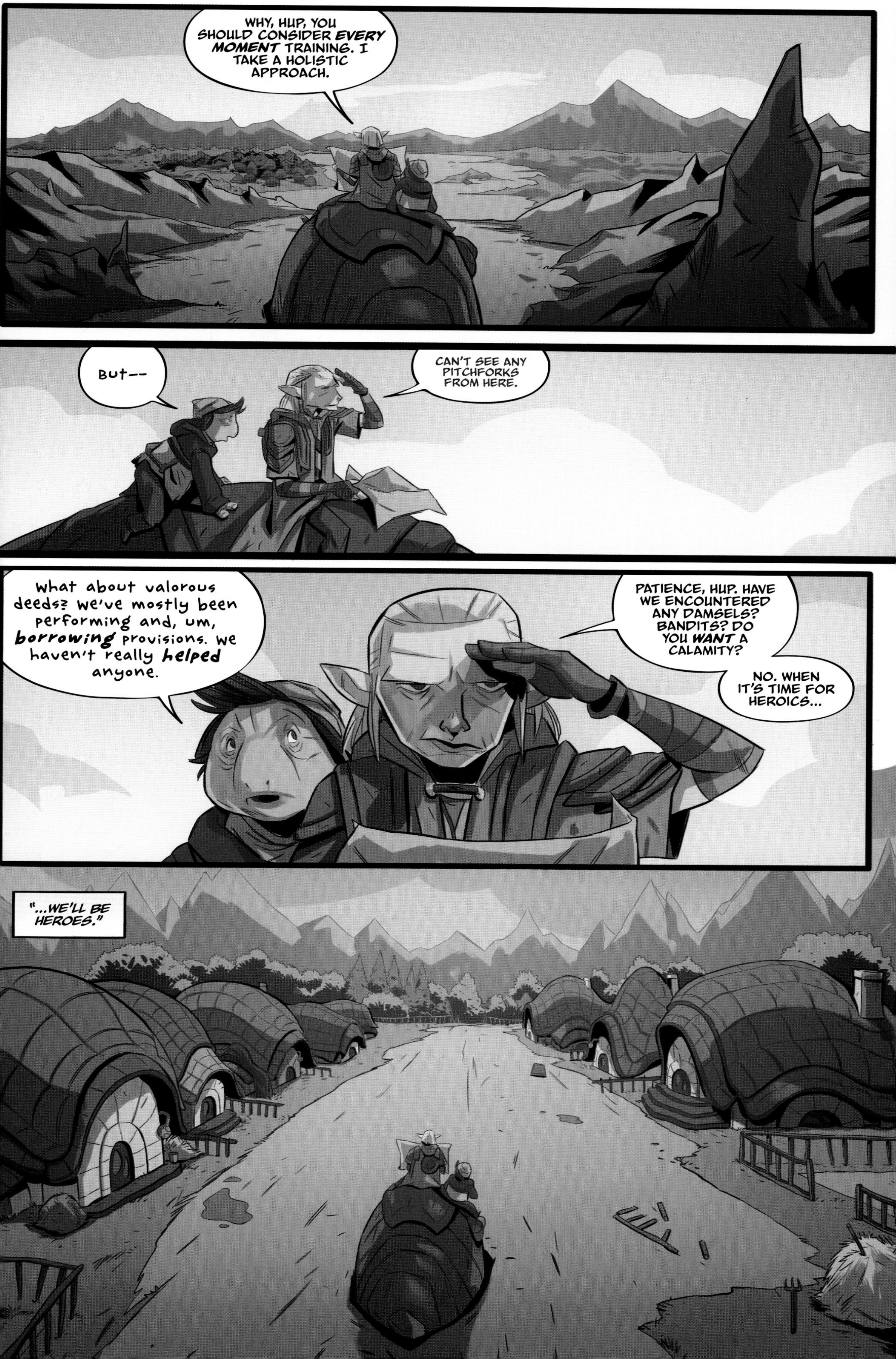
WHY, HUP, YOU SHOULD CONSIDER EVERY MOMENT TRAINING. I TAKE A HOLISTIC APPROACH.
But--
CAN'T SEE ANY PITCHFORKS FROM HERE.
What about valorous deeds? We've mostly been performing and, um, borrowing provisions. We haven't really helped anyone.
PATIENCE, HUP. HAVE WE ENCOUNTERED ANY DAMSELS? BANDITS? DO YOU WANT A CALAMITY?
NO. WHEN IT'S TIME FOR HEROICS...
"...WE'LL BE HEROES."

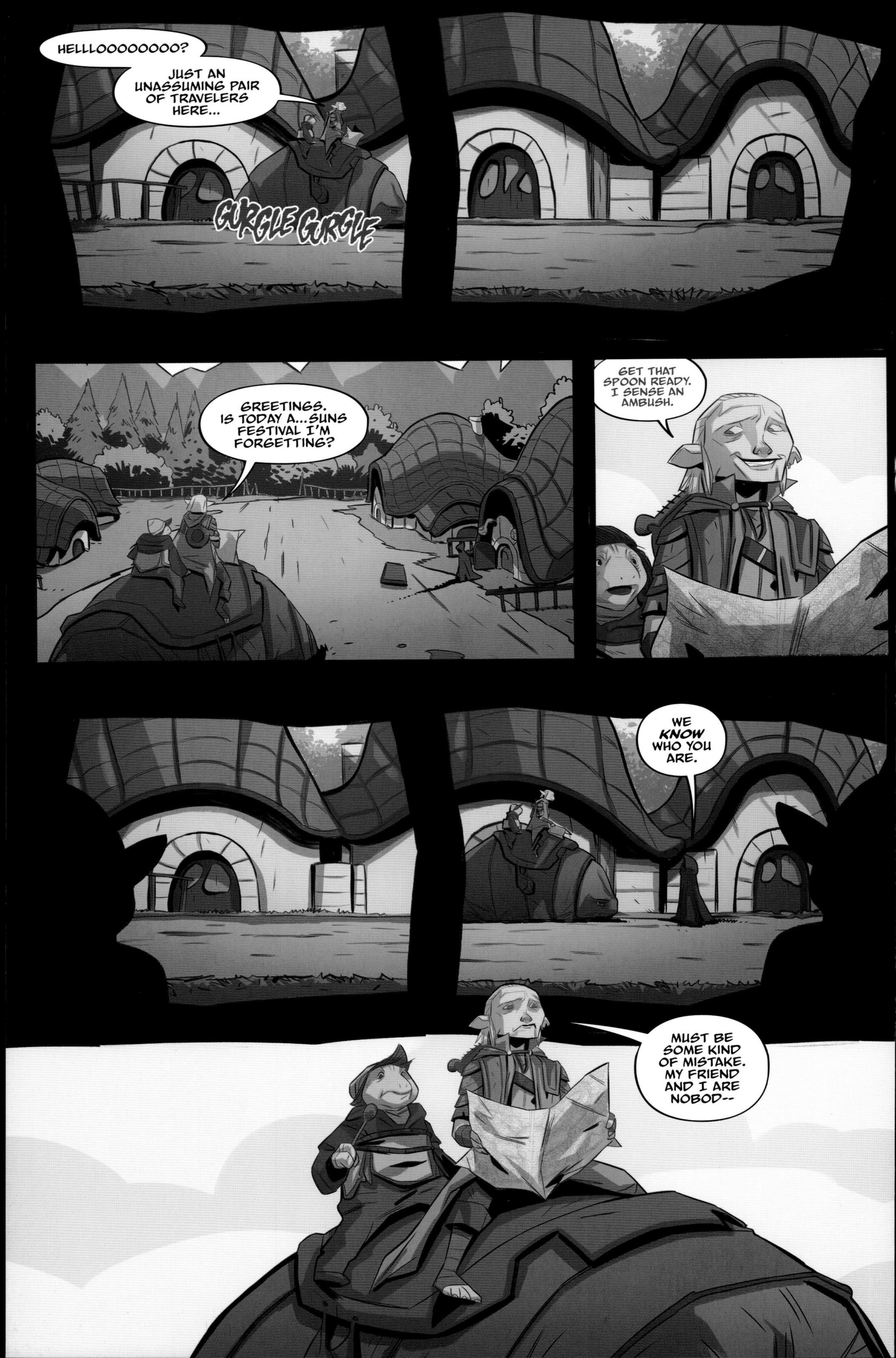
HELLLOOOOOOOO?
JUST AN UNASSUMING PAIR OF TRAVELERS HERE...
GURGLE GURGLE
GREETINGS. IS TODAY A...SUNS FESTIVAL I'M FORGETTING?
GET THAT SPOON READY. I SENSE AN AMBUSH.
WE KNOW WHO YOU ARE.
MUST BE SOME KIND OF MISTAKE. MY FRIEND AND I ARE NOBOD--

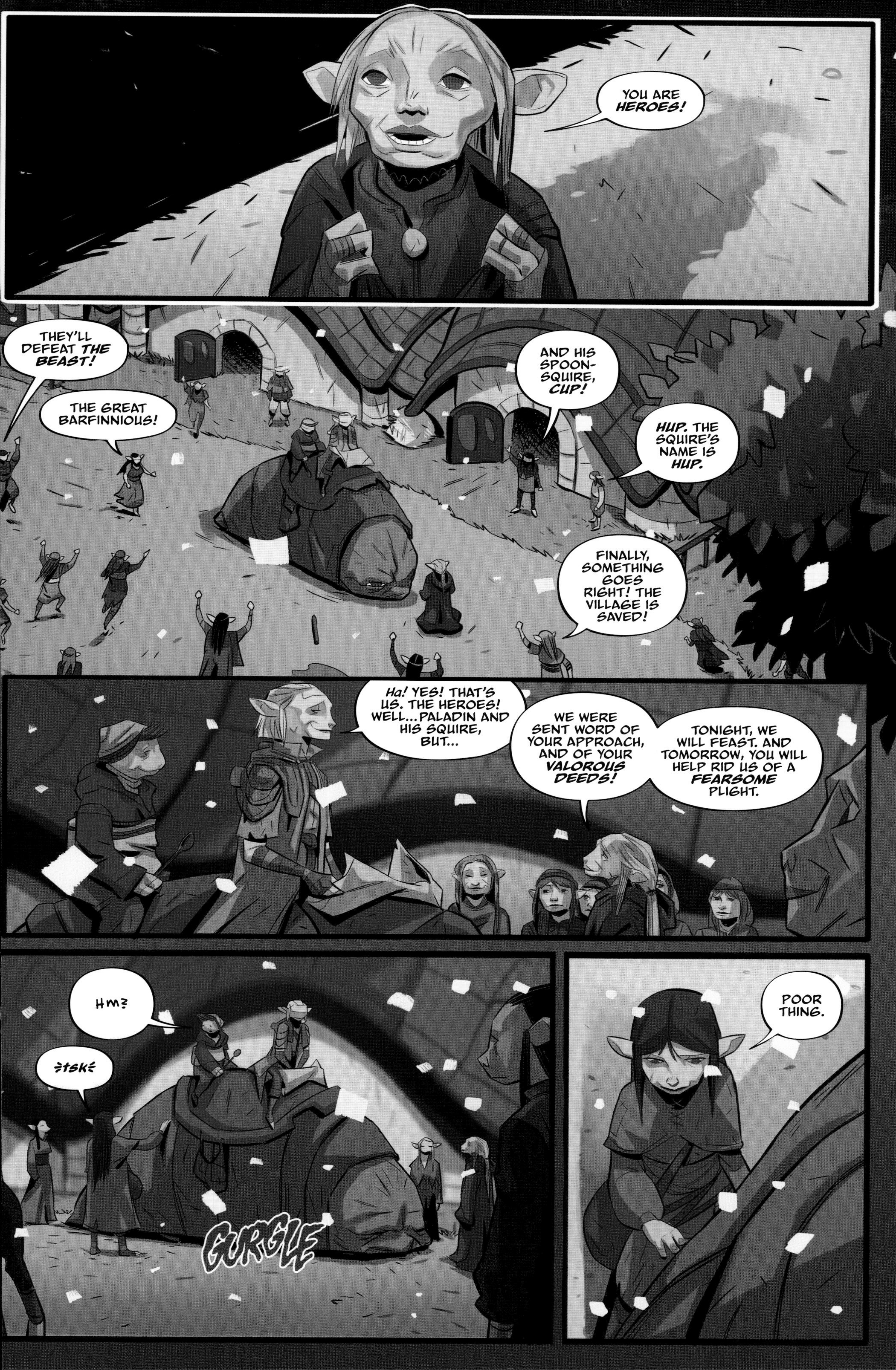
YOU ARE HEROES!
THEY'LL DEFEAT THE BEAST!
THE GREAT BARFINNIOUS!
AND HIS SPOON-SQUIRE, CUP!
HUP. THE SQUIRE'S NAME IS HUP.
FINALLY, SOMETHING GOES RIGHT! THE VILLAGE IS SAVED!
Ha! YES! THAT'S US. THE HEROES! WELL...PALADIN AND HIS SQUIRE, BUT...
WE WERE SENT WORD OF YOUR APPROACH, AND OF YOUR VALOROUS DEEDS!
TONIGHT, WE WILL FEAST. AND TOMORROW, YOU WILL HELP RID US OF A FEARSOME PLIGHT.
Hm?
tsk
GURGLE
POOR THING.

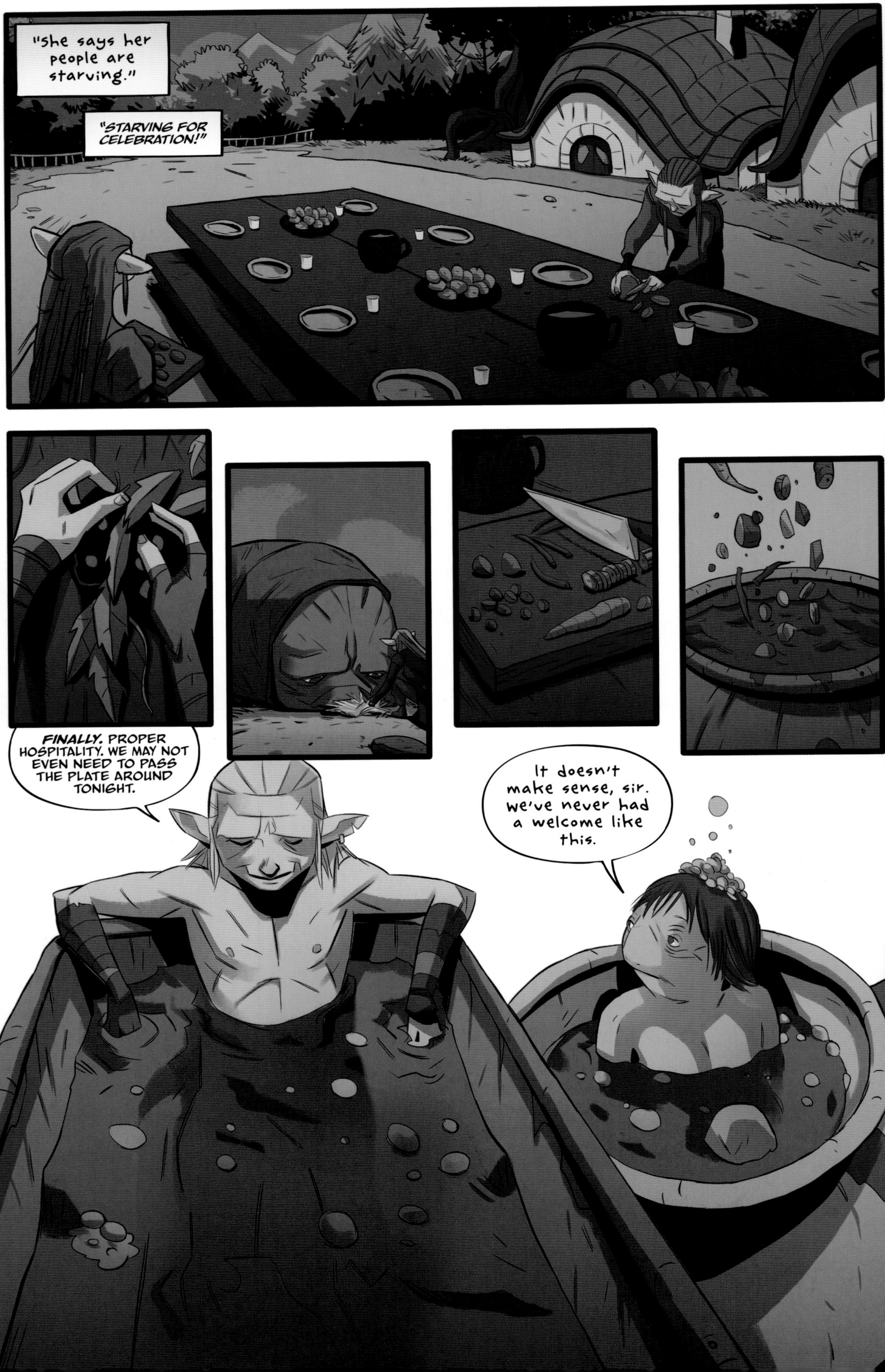
"she says her people are starving."
"STARVING FOR CELEBRATION!"
FINALLY. PROPER HOSPITALITY. WE MAY NOT EVEN NEED TO PASS THE PLATE AROUND TONIGHT.
It doesn't make sense, sir. we've never had a welcome like this.

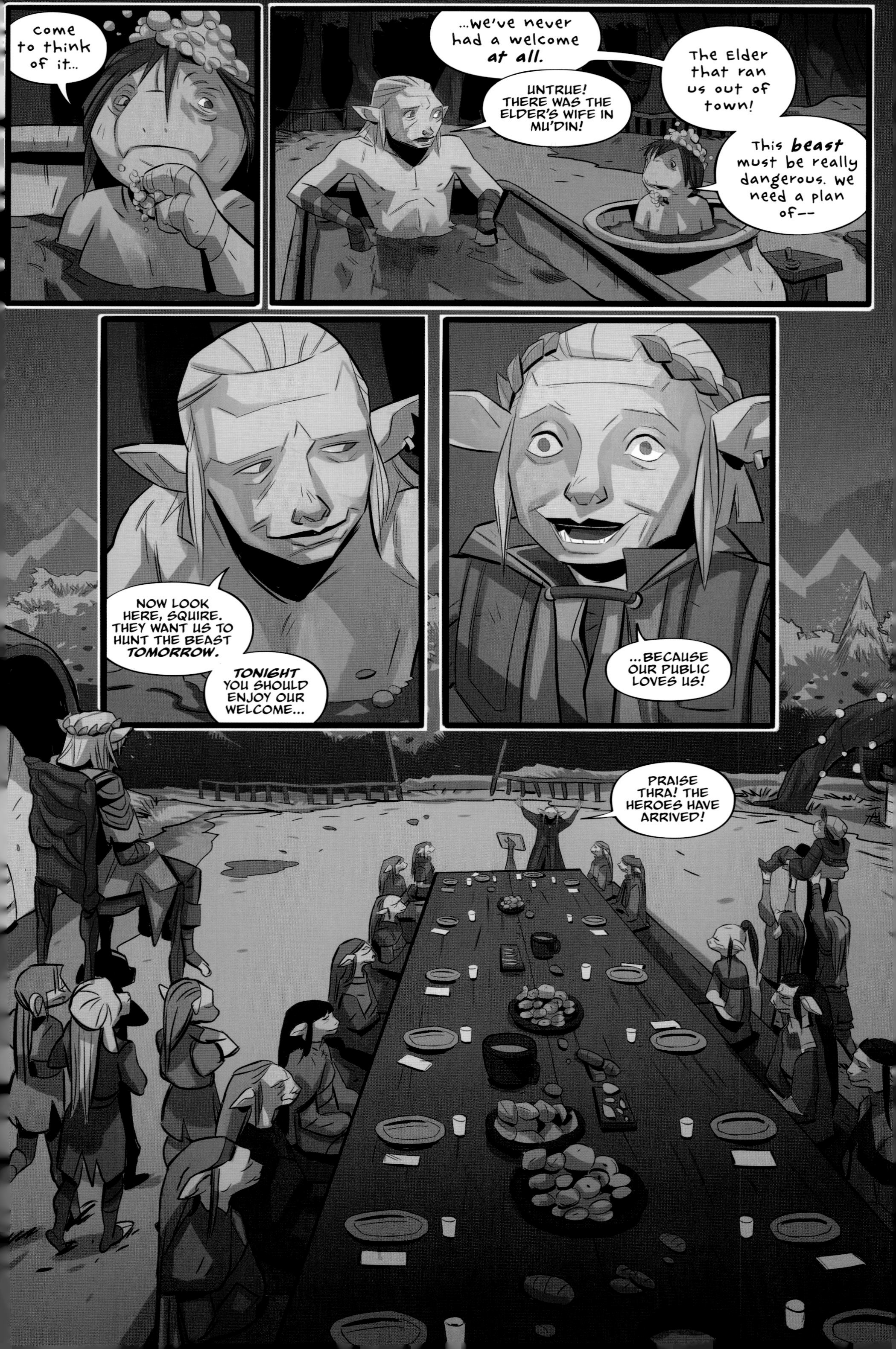
come to think of it...
...we've never had a welcome *at all.*
UNTRUE! THERE WAS THE ELDER'S WIFE IN MU'DIN!
The Elder that ran us out of town!
This **beast** must be really dangerous. we need a plan of--
NOW LOOK HERE, SQUIRE. THEY WANT US TO HUNT THE BEAST ***TOMORROW.***
TONIGHT YOU SHOULD ENJOY OUR WELCOME...
...BECAUSE OUR PUBLIC LOVES US!
PRAISE THRA! THE HEROES HAVE ARRIVED!

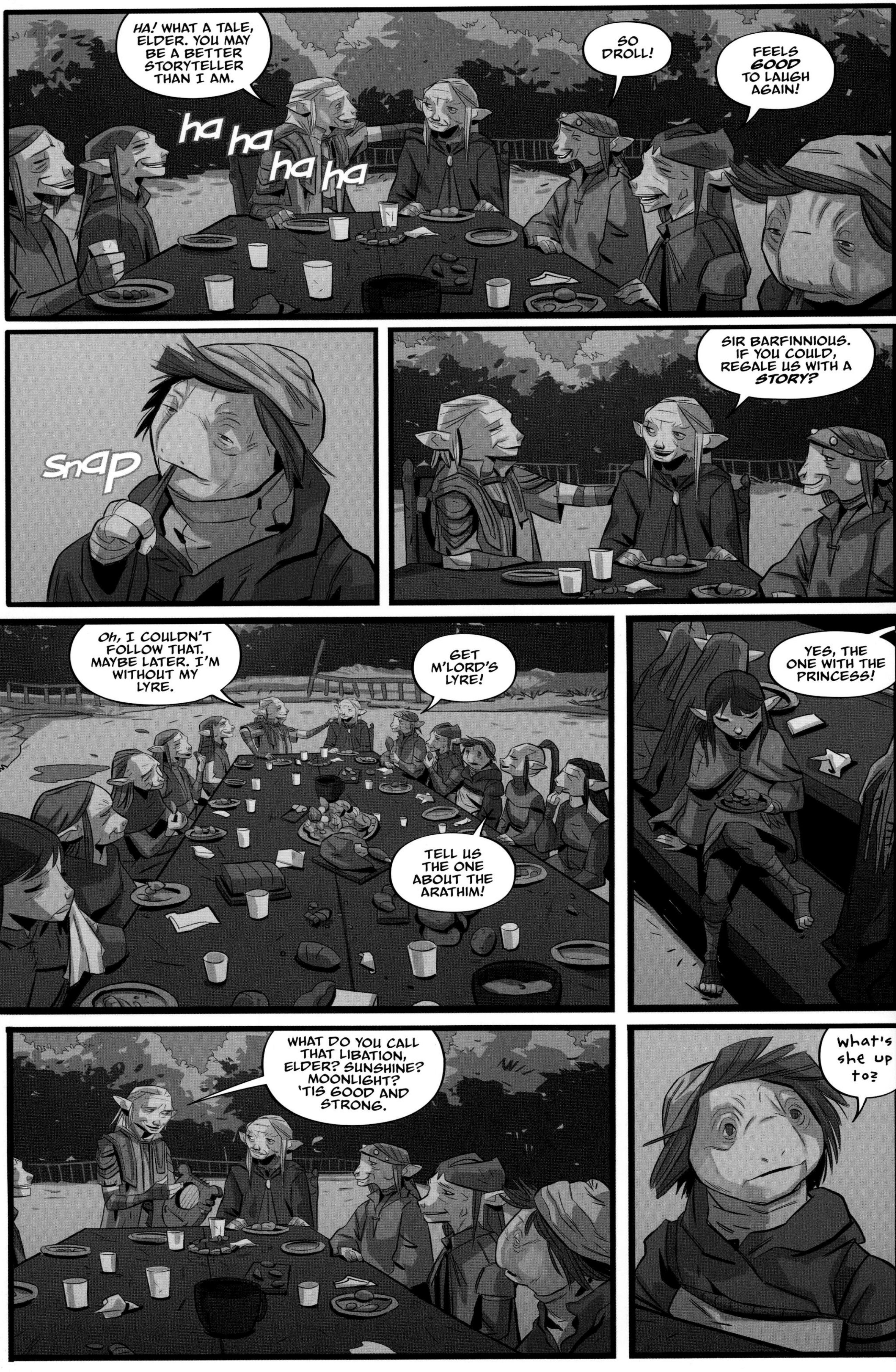
HA! WHAT A TALE, ELDER. YOU MAY BE A BETTER STORYTELLER THAN I AM.
ha ha ha ha
SO DROLL!
FEELS GOOD TO LAUGH AGAIN!
snap
SIR BARFINNIOUS. IF YOU COULD, REGALE US WITH A STORY?
Oh, I COULDN'T FOLLOW THAT. MAYBE LATER. I'M WITHOUT MY LYRE.
GET M'LORD'S LYRE!
TELL US THE ONE ABOUT THE ARATHIM!
YES, THE ONE WITH THE PRINCESS!
WHAT DO YOU CALL THAT LIBATION, ELDER? SUNSHINE? MOONLIGHT? 'TIS GOOD AND STRONG.
What's she up to?

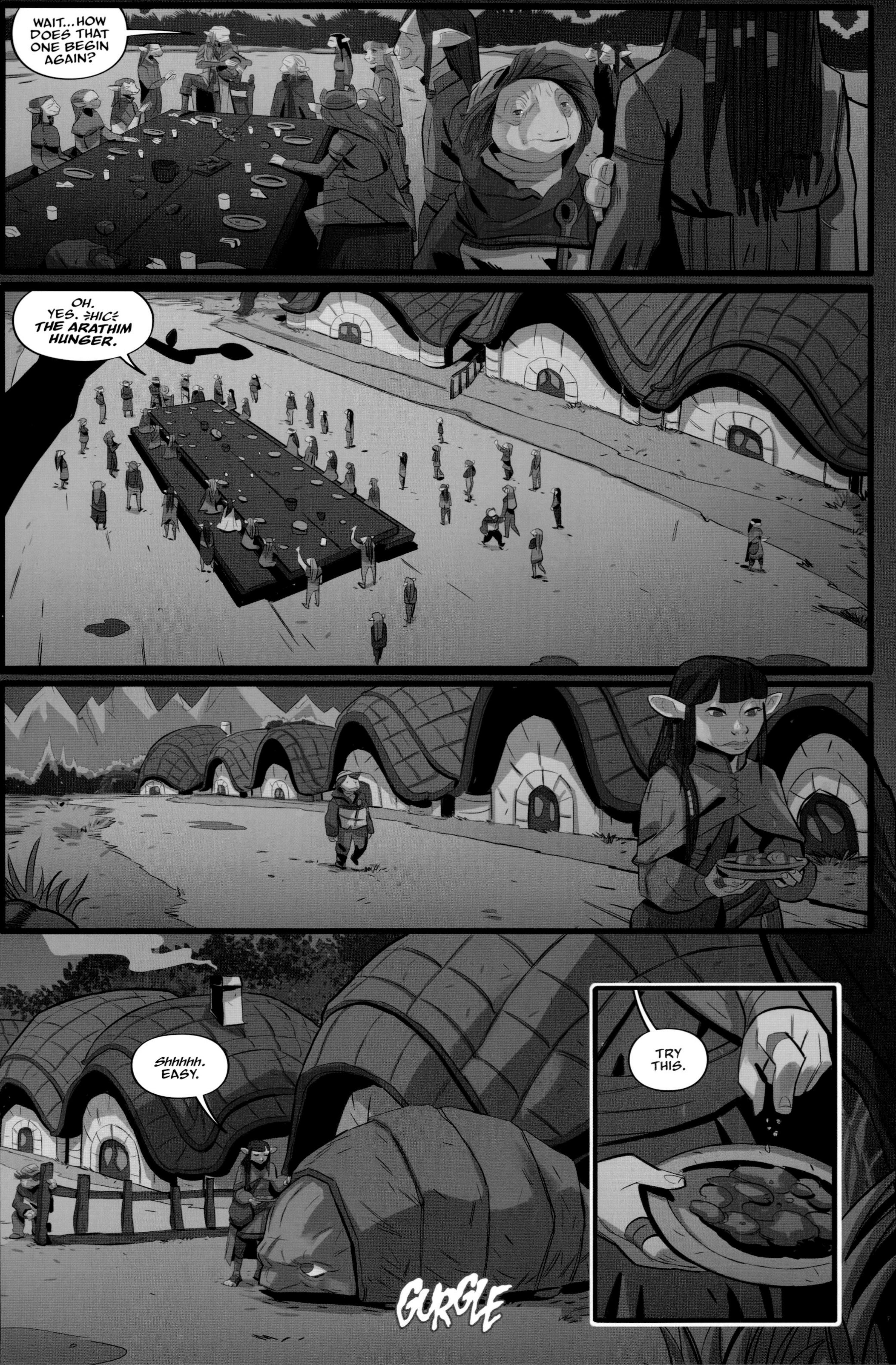
WAIT...HOW DOES THAT ONE BEGIN AGAIN?
OH. YES. HIC THE ARATHIM HUNGER.
Shhhhh. EASY.
TRY THIS.
GURGLE

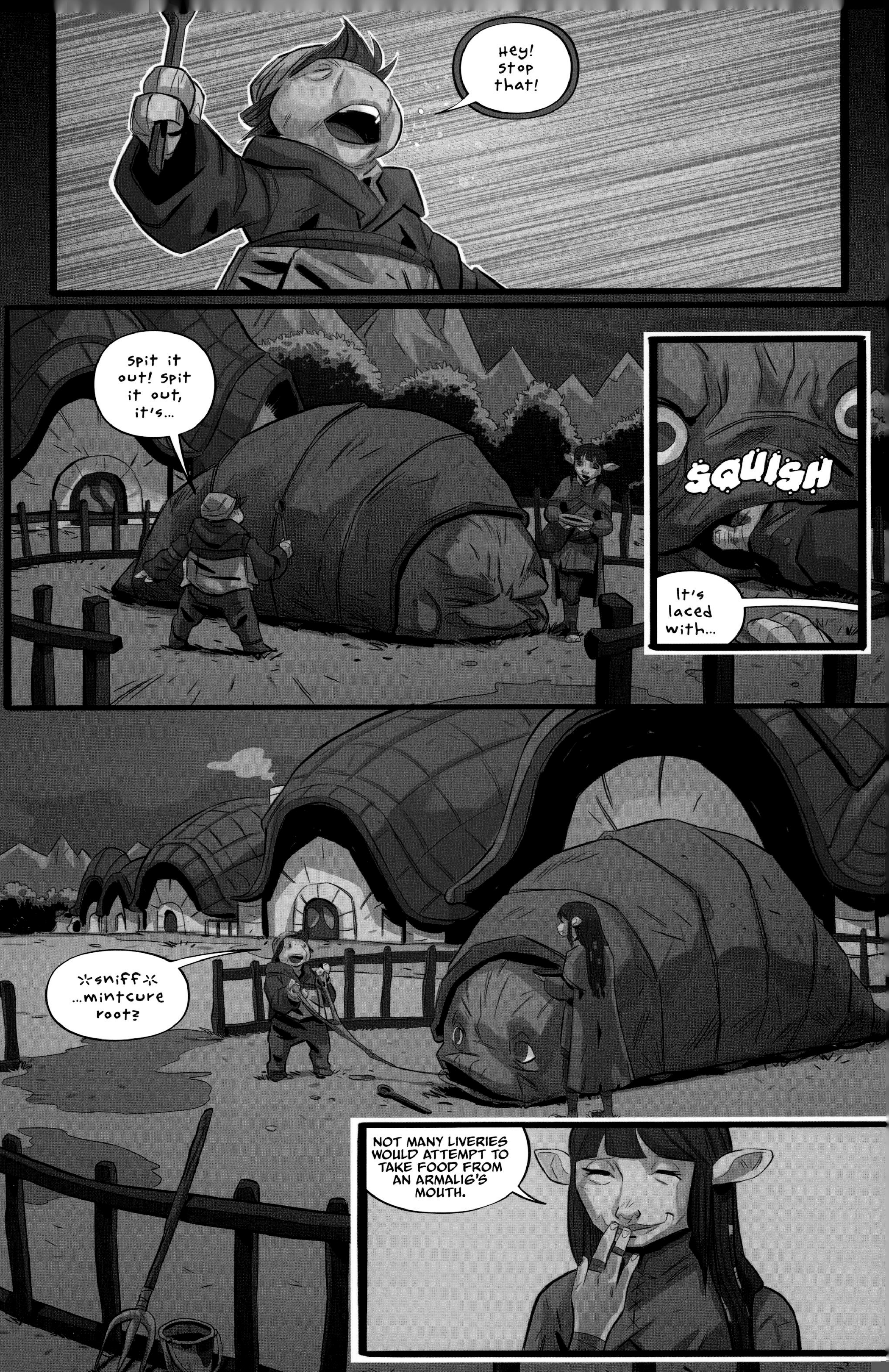
Hey! Stop that!
Spit it out! Spit it out, it's...
SQUISH
It's laced with...
sniff ...mintcure root?
NOT MANY LIVERIES WOULD ATTEMPT TO TAKE FOOD FROM AN ARMALIG'S MOUTH.

HE'S VERY... BLOATED. THE MINTCURE ROOT WILL HELP. IT--

--is supposed to be good for digestion. I used it for garnish back when I was...

MUNCH MUNCH

...back when I was a chef.

I--I'M SORRY. I DON'T SPEAK PODLING. I ONLY UNDERSTAND A FEW WORDS.

squeeeeaaakPPFFF

FTTTT

≥COUGH≥ I'M VEARA. I'M THE TOWN HEALER. AND A BUSY ONE, THESE DAYS...

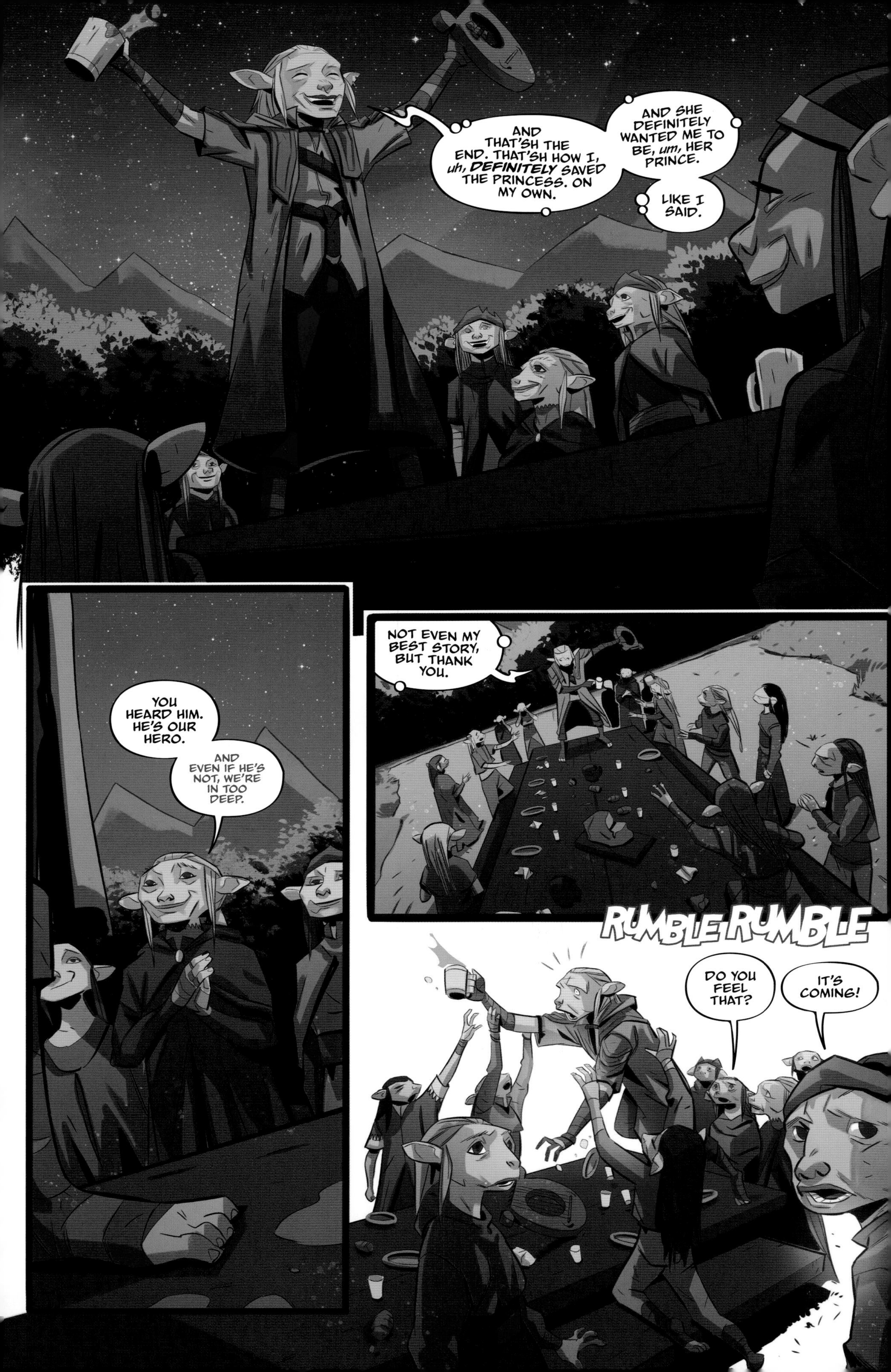
AND THAT'SH THE END. THAT'SH HOW I, *uh,* **DEFINITELY** SAVED THE PRINCESS. ON MY OWN.
AND SHE DEFINITELY WANTED ME TO BE, *um,* HER PRINCE.
LIKE I SAID.
YOU HEARD HIM. HE'S OUR HERO.
AND EVEN IF HE'S NOT, WE'RE IN TOO DEEP.
NOT EVEN MY BEST STORY, BUT THANK YOU.
RUMBLE RUMBLE
DO YOU FEEL THAT?
IT'S COMING!

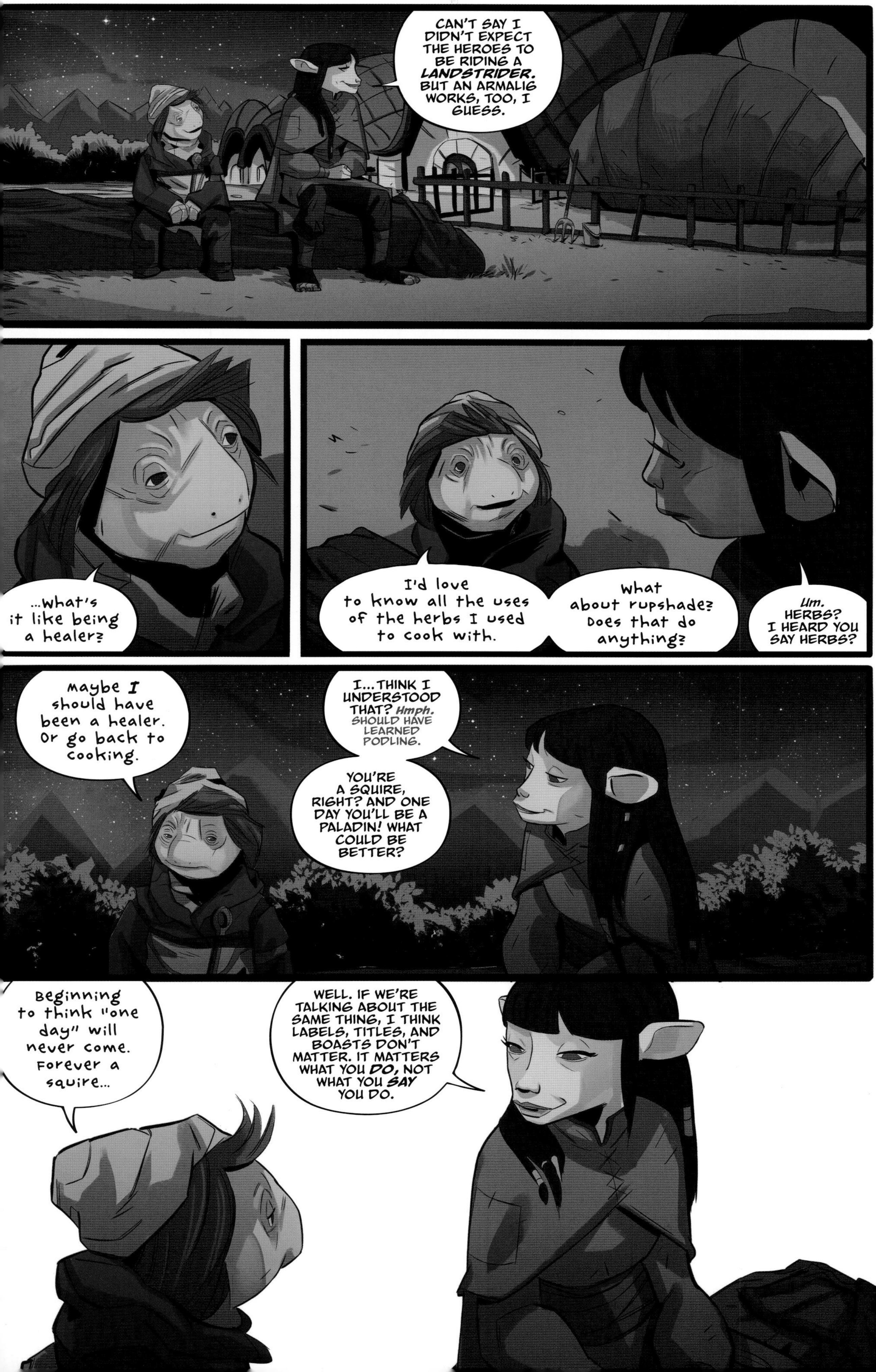
CAN'T SAY I DIDN'T EXPECT THE HEROES TO BE RIDING A LANDSTRIDER. BUT AN ARMALIG WORKS, TOO, I GUESS.
...What's it like being a healer?
I'd love to know all the uses of the herbs I used to cook with.
What about rupshade? Does that do anything?
Um. HERBS? I HEARD YOU SAY HERBS?
Maybe I should have been a healer. Or go back to cooking.
I... THINK I UNDERSTOOD THAT? Hmph. SHOULD HAVE LEARNED PODLING.
YOU'RE A SQUIRE, RIGHT? AND ONE DAY YOU'LL BE A PALADIN! WHAT COULD BE BETTER?
Beginning to think "one day" will never come. Forever a squire...
WELL. IF WE'RE TALKING ABOUT THE SAME THING, I THINK LABELS, TITLES, AND BOASTS DON'T MATTER. IT MATTERS WHAT YOU DO, NOT WHAT YOU SAY YOU DO.

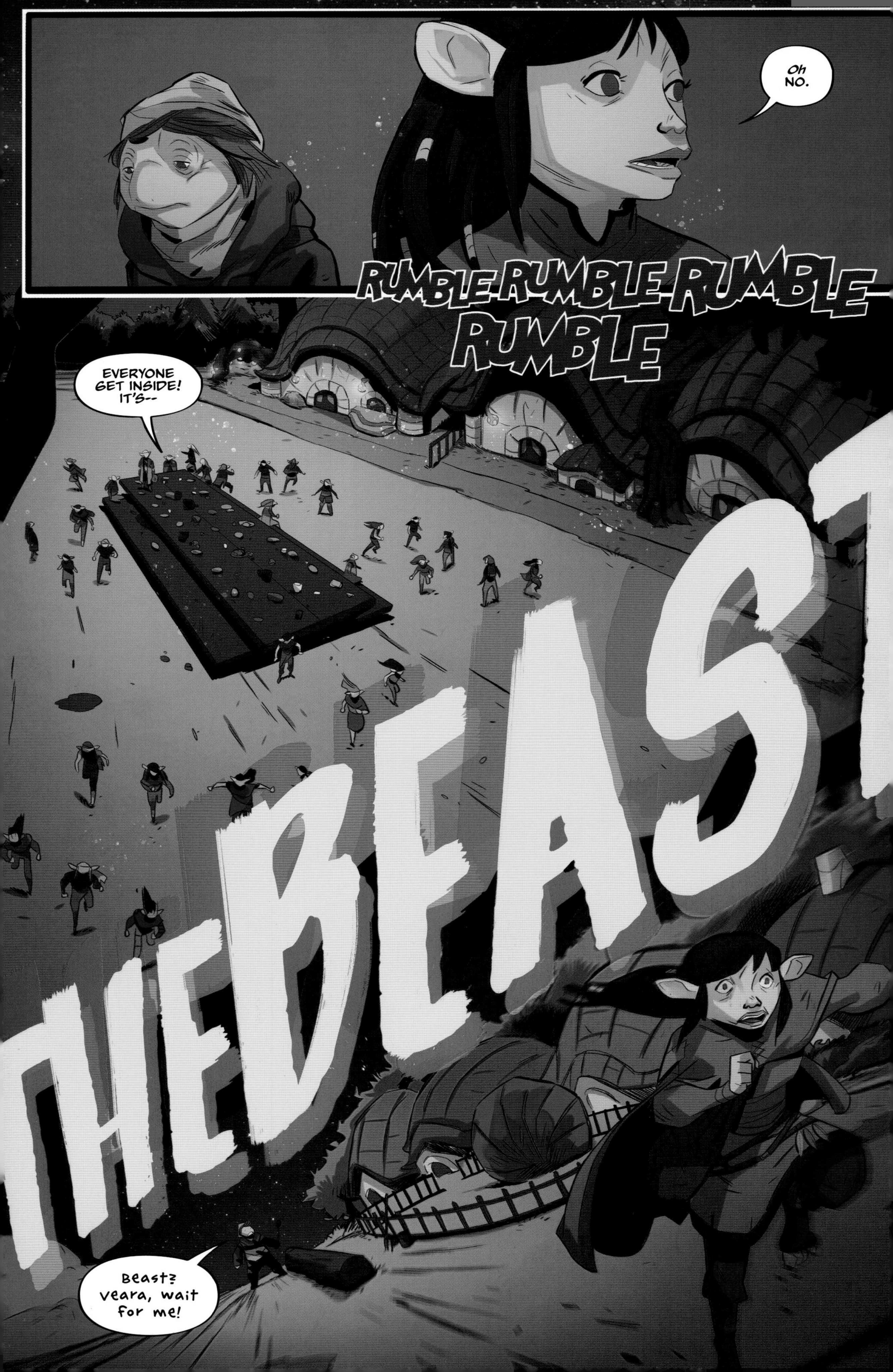
Oh NO.
RUMBLE RUMBLE RUMBLE RUMBLE
EVERYONE GET INSIDE! IT'S--
THE BEAST
Beast? Veara, wait for me!

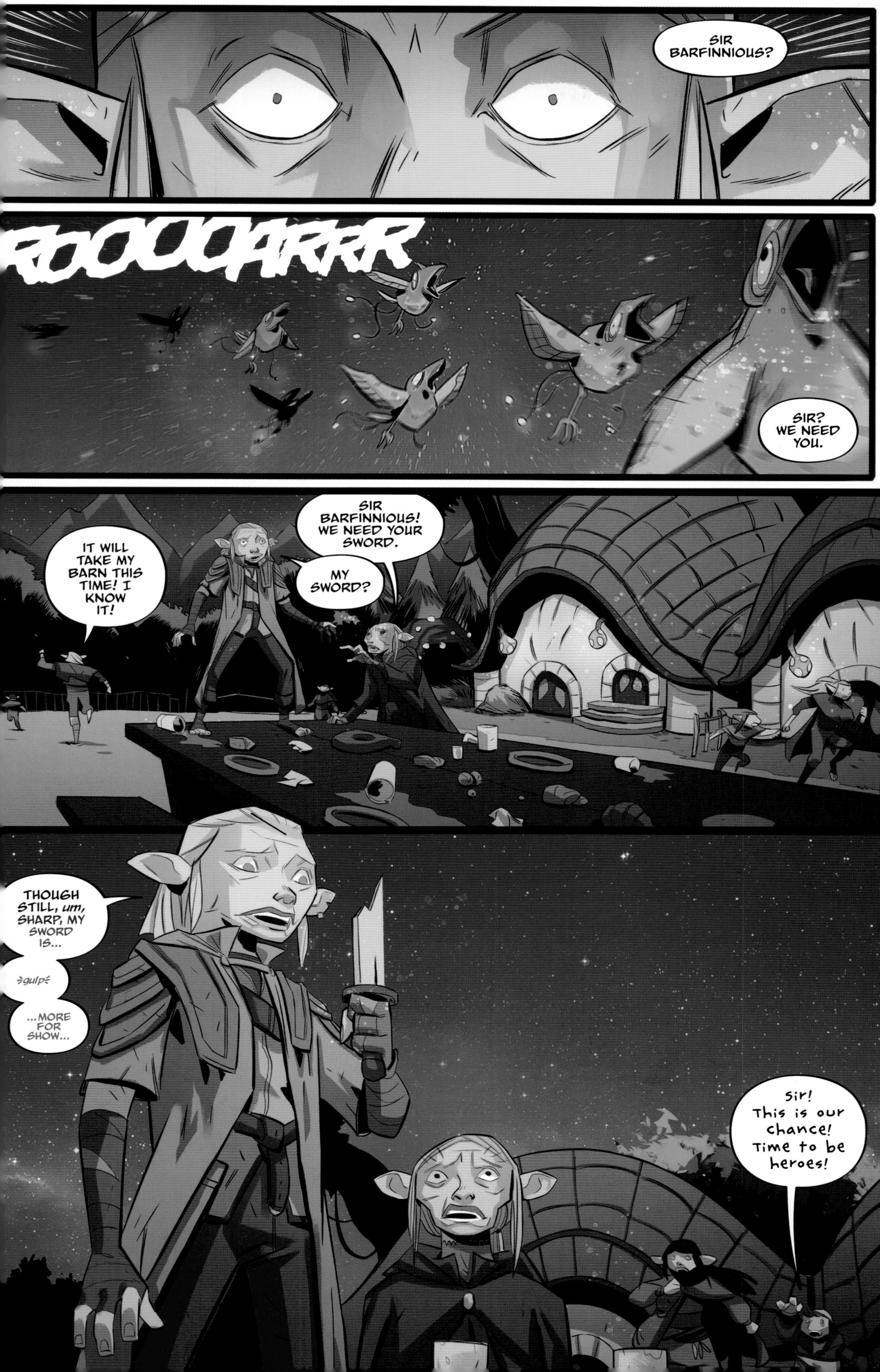

SIR BARFINNIOUS?
ROOOOARRR
SIR? WE NEED YOU.
IT WILL TAKE MY BARN THIS TIME! I KNOW IT!
SIR BARFINNIOUS! WE NEED YOUR SWORD.
MY SWORD?
THOUGH STILL, *um*, SHARP, MY SWORD IS...
gulp
...MORE FOR SHOW...
Sir! This is our chance! Time to be heroes!

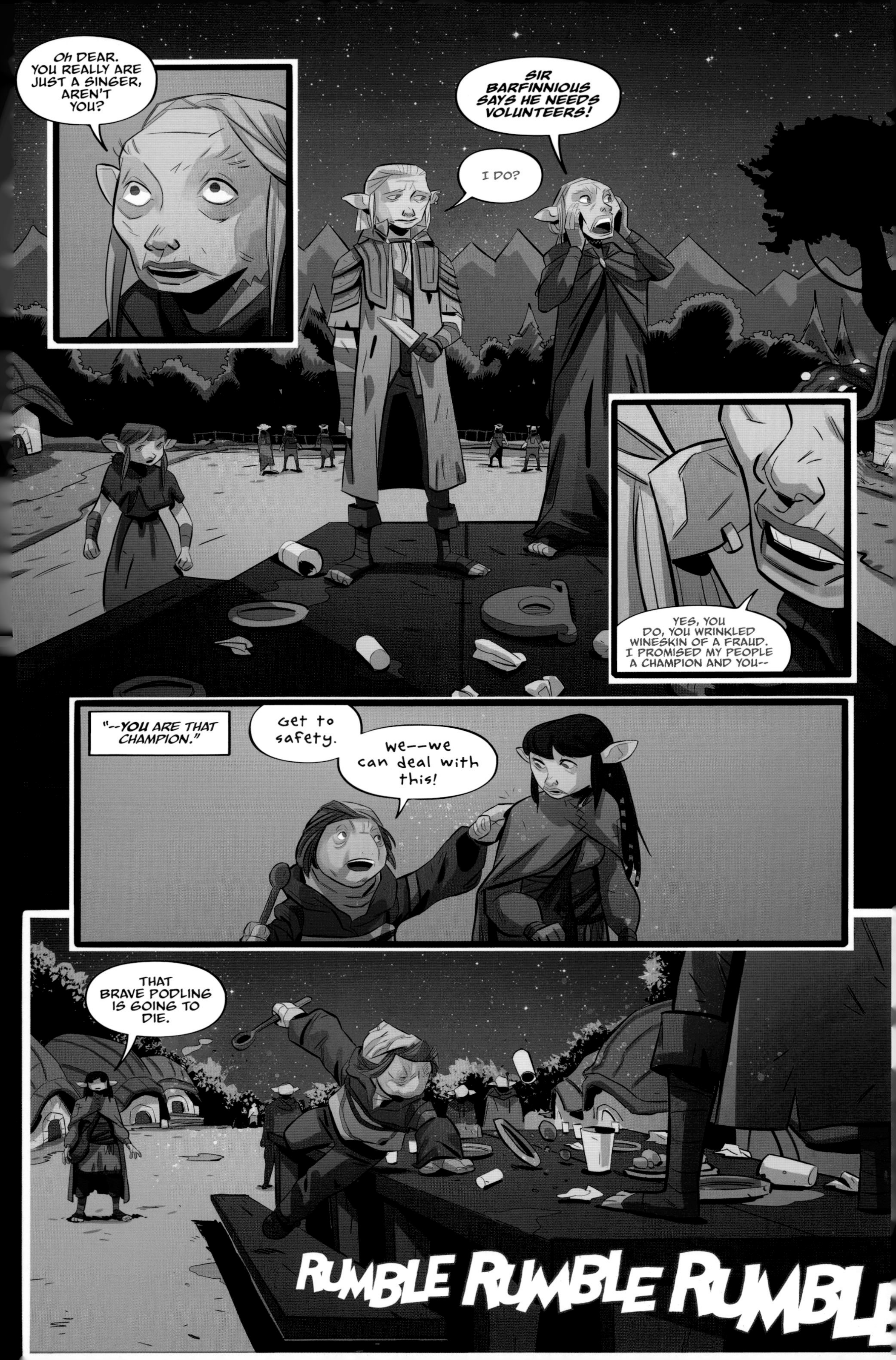
Oh DEAR. YOU REALLY ARE JUST A SINGER, AREN'T YOU?
SIR BARFINNIOUS SAYS HE NEEDS VOLUNTEERS!
I DO?
YES, YOU DO, YOU WRINKLED WINESKIN OF A FRAUD. I PROMISED MY PEOPLE A CHAMPION AND YOU--
"--YOU ARE THAT CHAMPION."
Get to safety.
we--we can deal with this!
THAT BRAVE PODLING IS GOING TO DIE.
RUMBLE RUMBLE RUMBLE

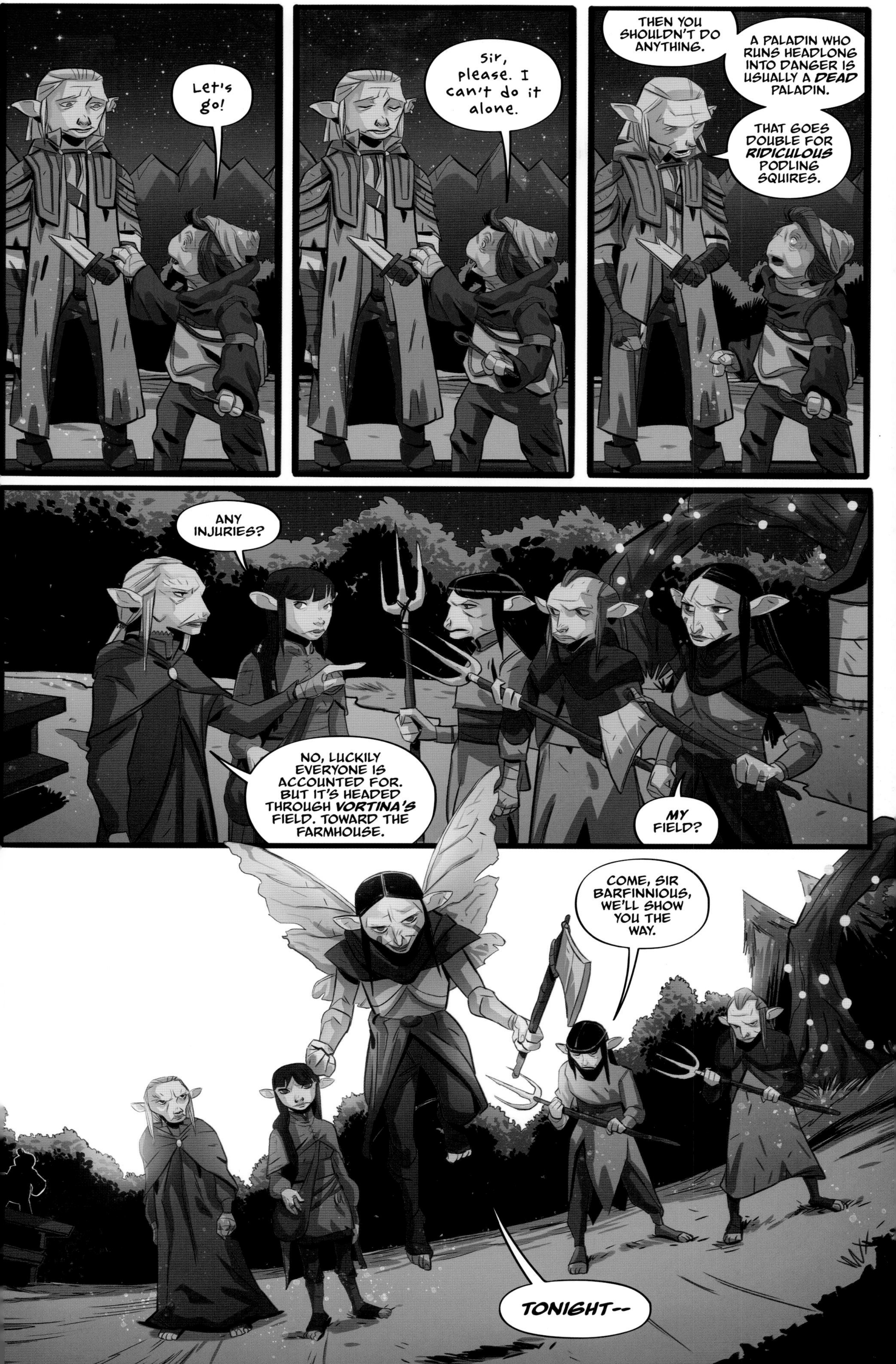
Let's go!
Sir, please. I can't do it alone.
THEN YOU SHOULDN'T DO ANYTHING.
A PALADIN WHO RUNS HEADLONG INTO DANGER IS USUALLY A *DEAD* PALADIN.
THAT GOES DOUBLE FOR *RIDICULOUS* PODLING SQUIRES.
ANY INJURIES?
NO, LUCKILY EVERYONE IS ACCOUNTED FOR. BUT IT'S HEADED THROUGH *VORTINA'S* FIELD. TOWARD THE FARMHOUSE.
MY FIELD?
COME, SIR BARFINNIOUS, WE'LL SHOW YOU THE WAY.
TONIGHT--

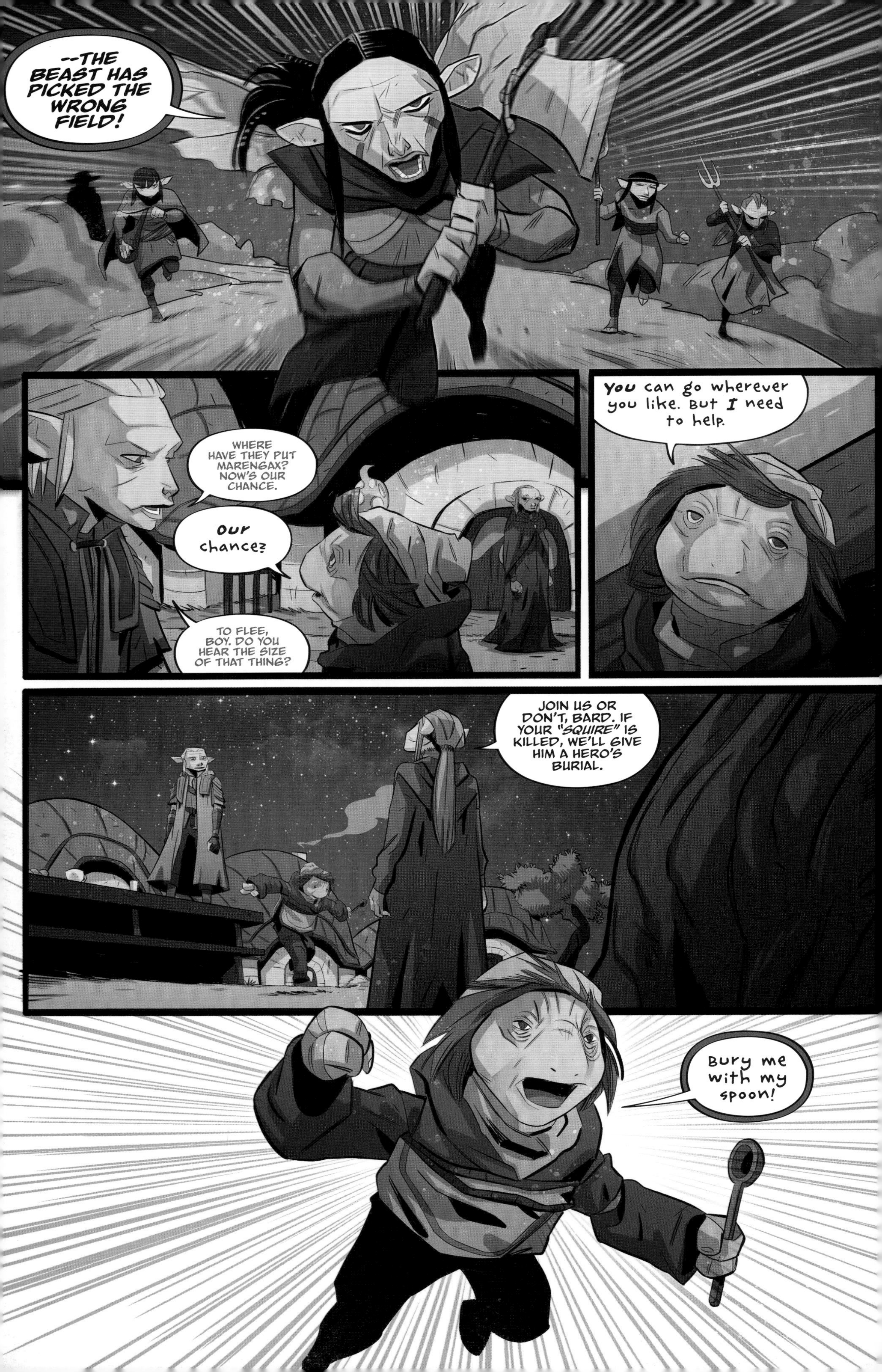
--THE BEAST HAS PICKED THE WRONG FIELD!
WHERE HAVE THEY PUT MARENGAX? NOW'S OUR CHANCE.
Our chance?
TO FLEE, BOY. DO YOU HEAR THE SIZE OF THAT THING?
You can go wherever you like. But I need to help.
JOIN US OR DON'T, BARD. IF YOUR "SQUIRE" IS KILLED, WE'LL GIVE HIM A HERO'S BURIAL.
Bury me with my spoon!

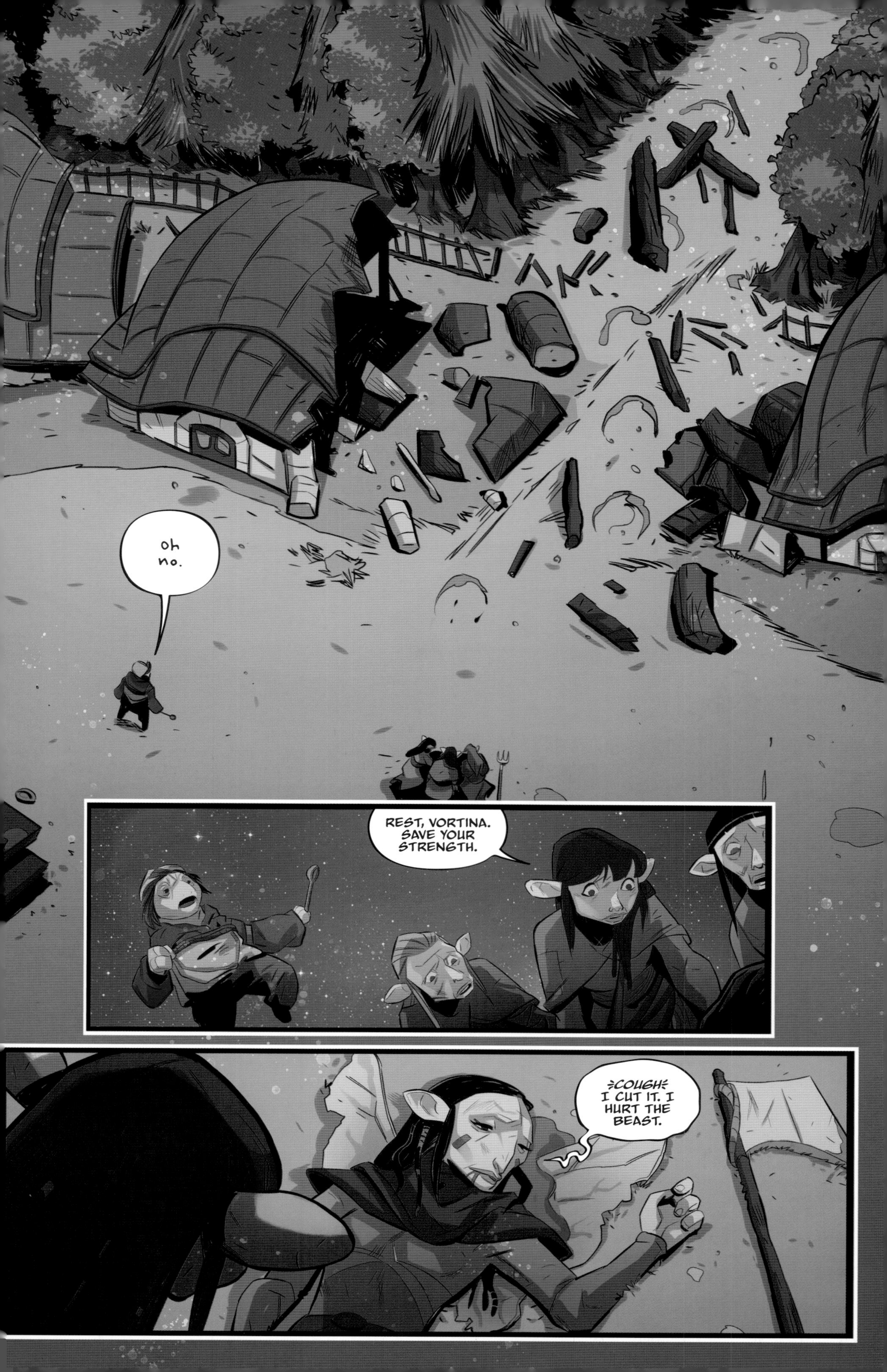
oh no.
REST, VORTINA. SAVE YOUR STRENGTH.
COUGH I CUT IT. I HURT THE BEAST.

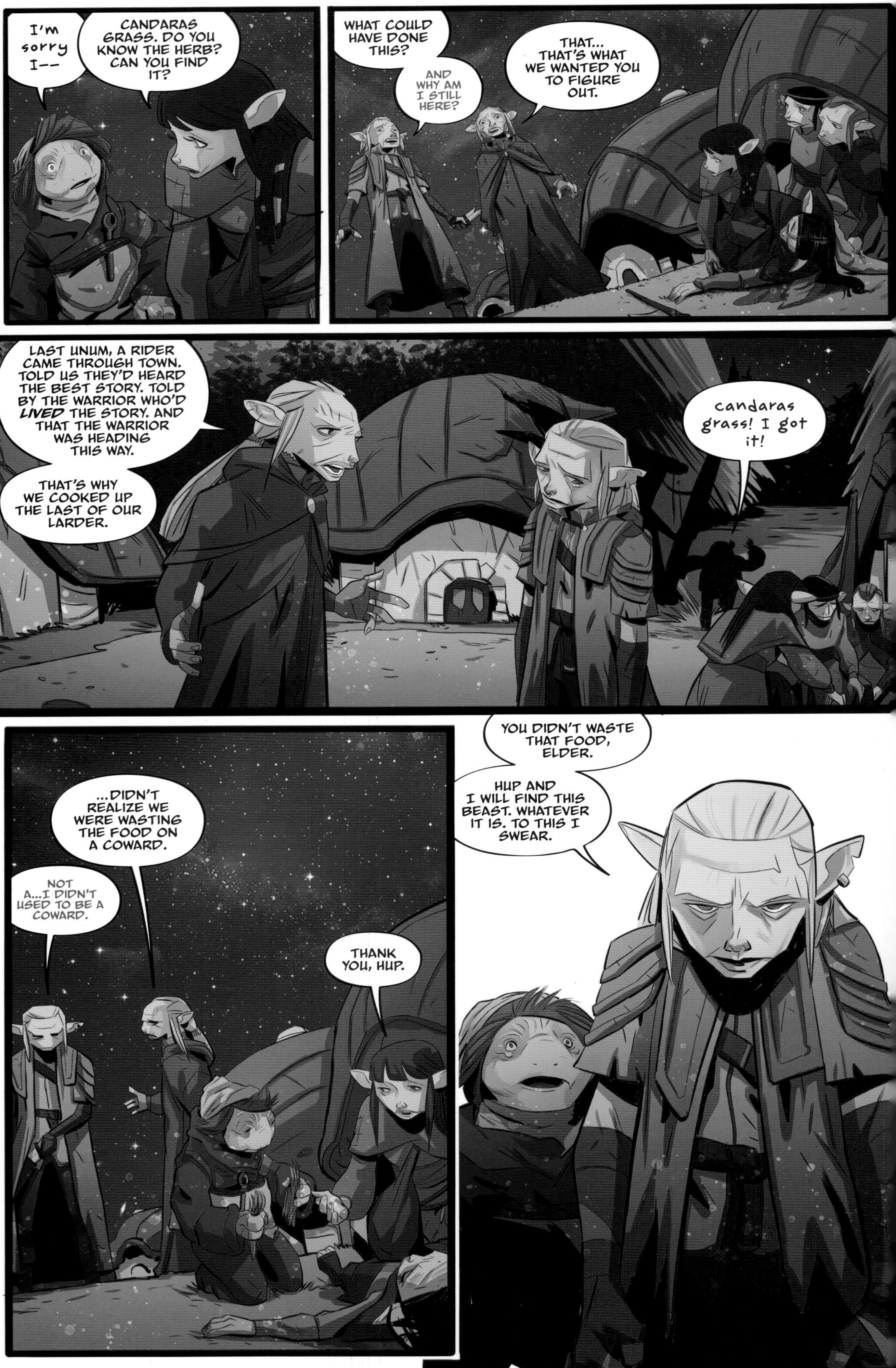
I'm sorry I--
CANDARAS GRASS. DO YOU KNOW THE HERB? CAN YOU FIND IT?
WHAT COULD HAVE DONE THIS?
AND WHY AM I STILL HERE?
THAT... THAT'S WHAT WE WANTED YOU TO FIGURE OUT.
LAST UNUM, A RIDER CAME THROUGH TOWN. TOLD US THEY'D HEARD THE BEST STORY. TOLD BY THE WARRIOR WHO'D *LIVED* THE STORY. AND THAT THE WARRIOR WAS HEADING THIS WAY.
THAT'S WHY WE COOKED UP THE LAST OF OUR LARDER.
candaras grass! I got it!
...DIDN'T REALIZE WE WERE WASTING THE FOOD ON A COWARD.
NOT A...I DIDN'T USED TO BE A COWARD.
THANK YOU, HUP.
YOU DIDN'T WASTE THAT FOOD, ELDER.
HUP AND I WILL FIND THIS BEAST. WHATEVER IT IS. TO THIS I SWEAR.

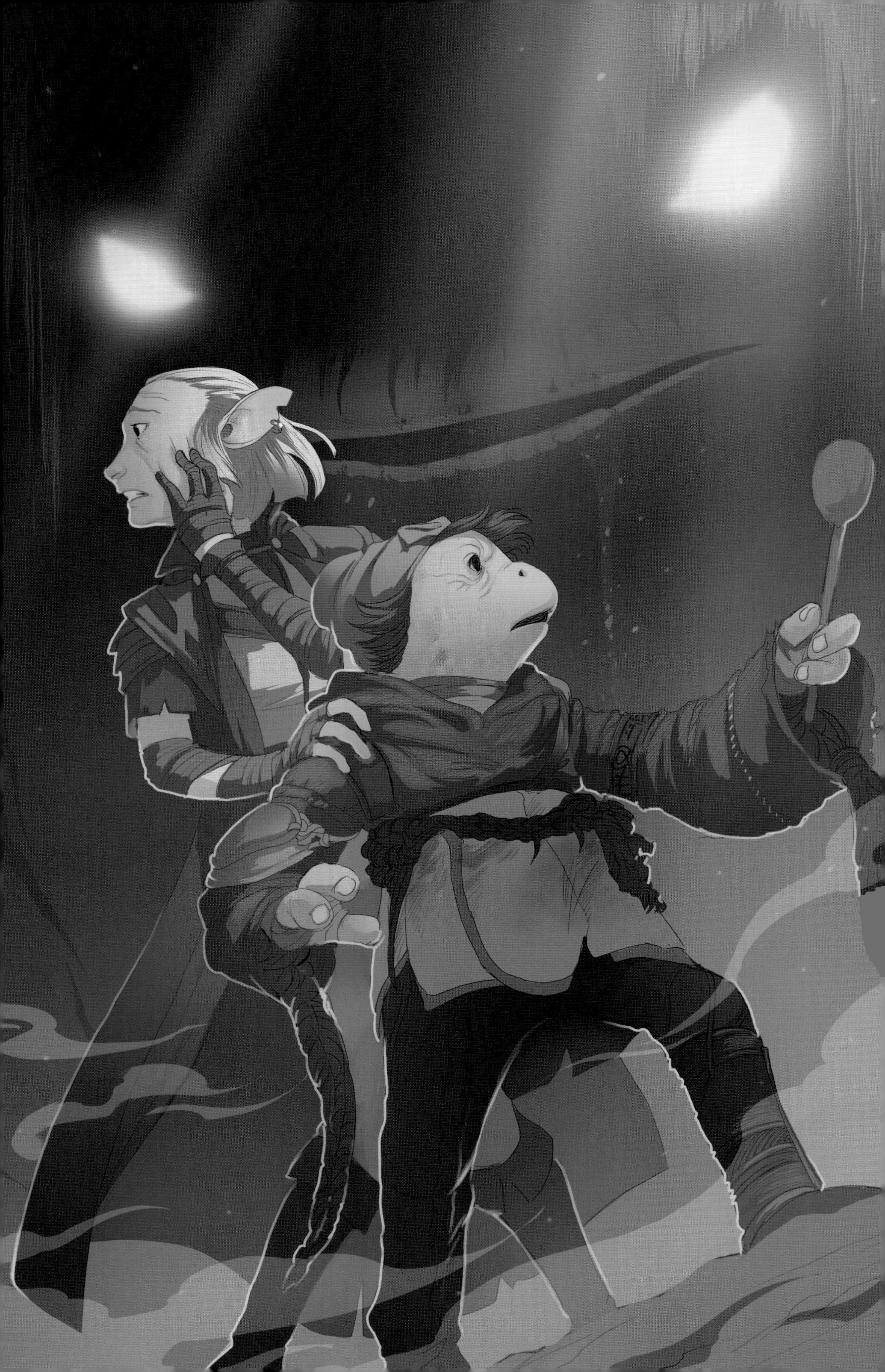

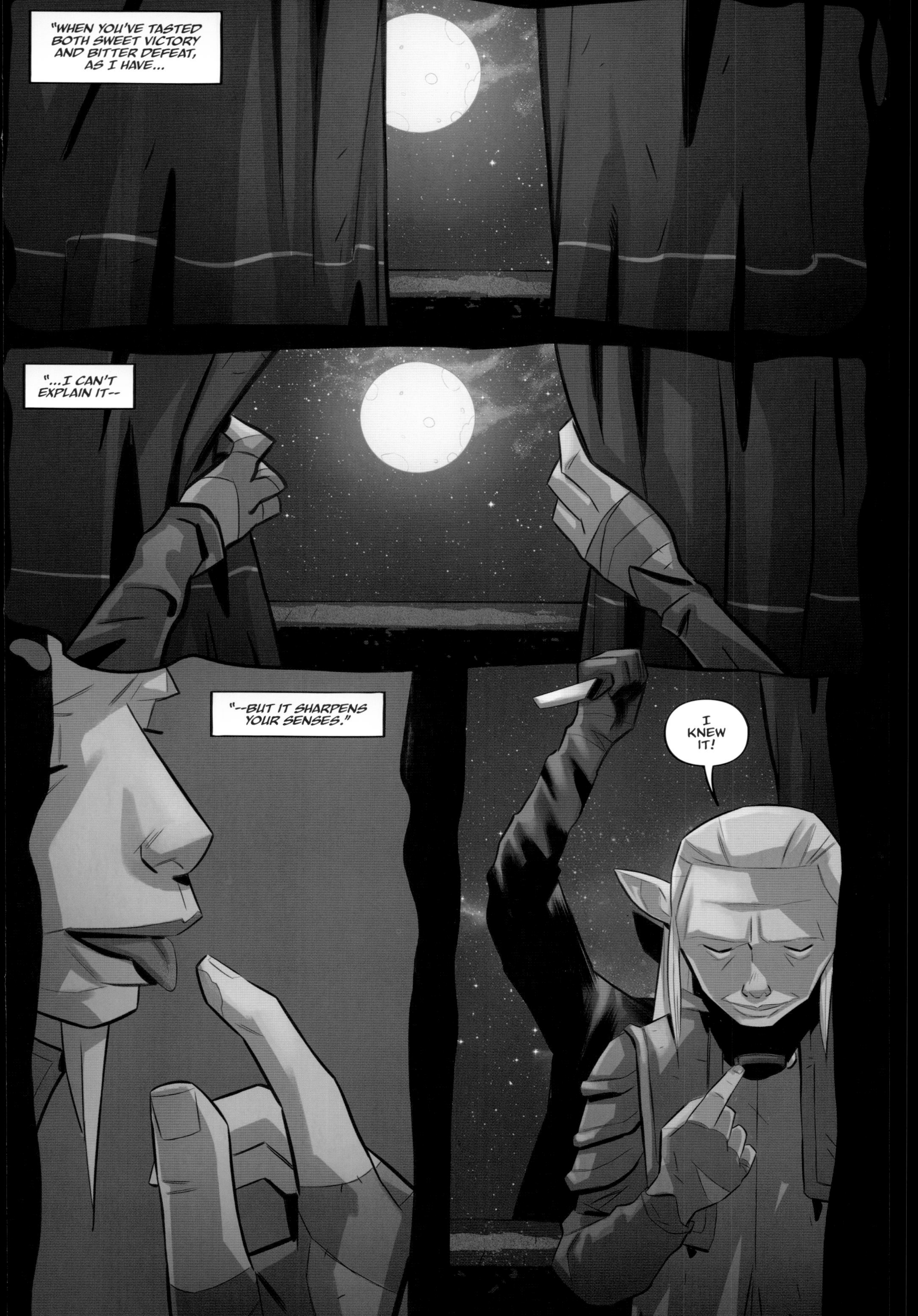
"WHEN YOU'VE TASTED BOTH SWEET VICTORY AND BITTER DEFEAT, AS I HAVE...
"...I CAN'T EXPLAIN IT--
"--BUT IT SHARPENS YOUR SENSES."
I KNEW IT!

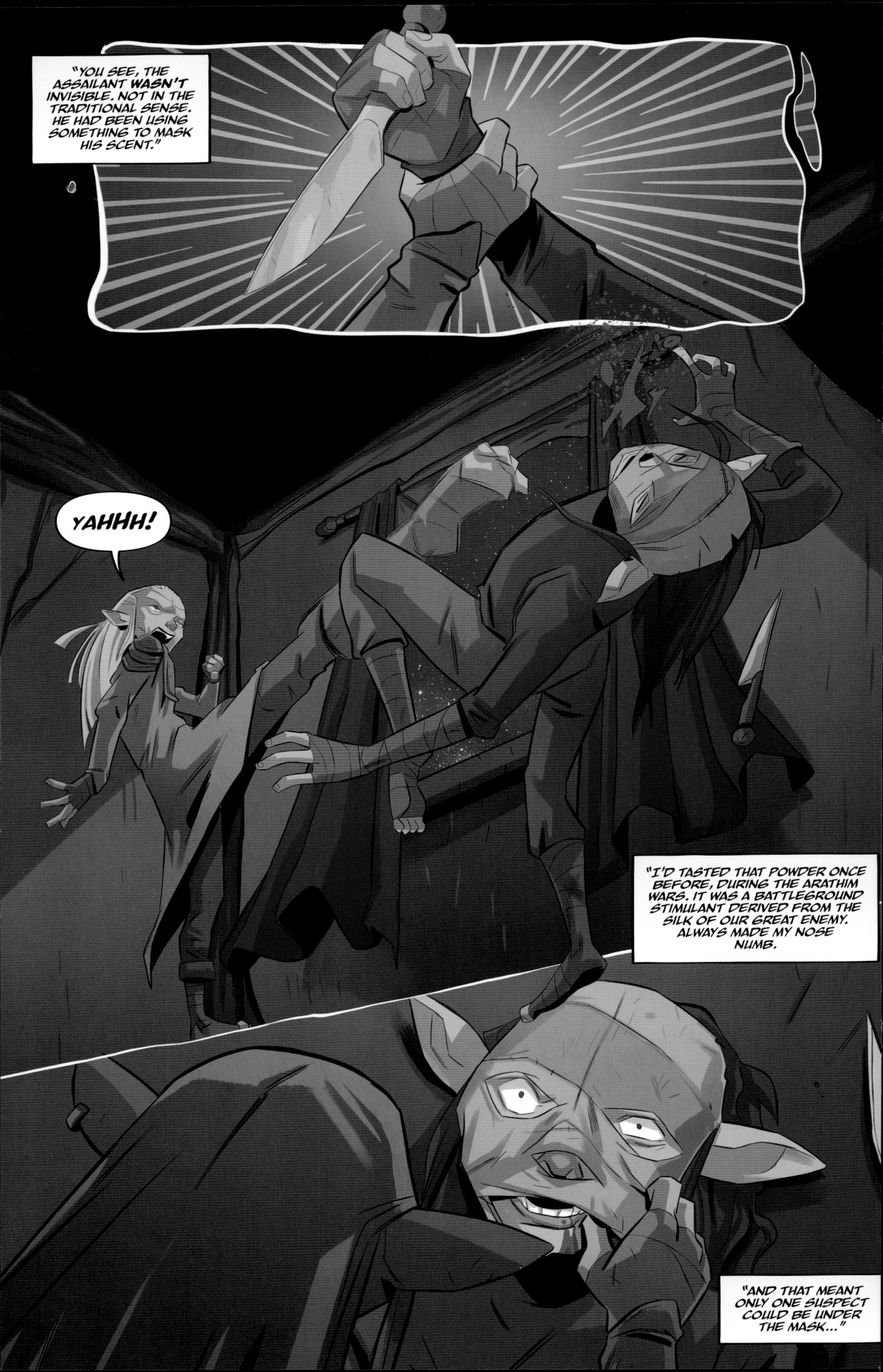
"YOU SEE, THE ASSAILANT WASN'T INVISIBLE. NOT IN THE TRADITIONAL SENSE. HE HAD BEEN USING SOMETHING TO MASK HIS SCENT."
YAHHH!
"I'D TASTED THAT POWDER ONCE BEFORE, DURING THE ARATHIM WARS. IT WAS A BATTLEGROUND STIMULANT DERIVED FROM THE SILK OF OUR GREAT ENEMY. ALWAYS MADE MY NOSE NUMB.
"AND THAT MEANT ONLY ONE SUSPECT COULD BE UNDER THE MASK..."

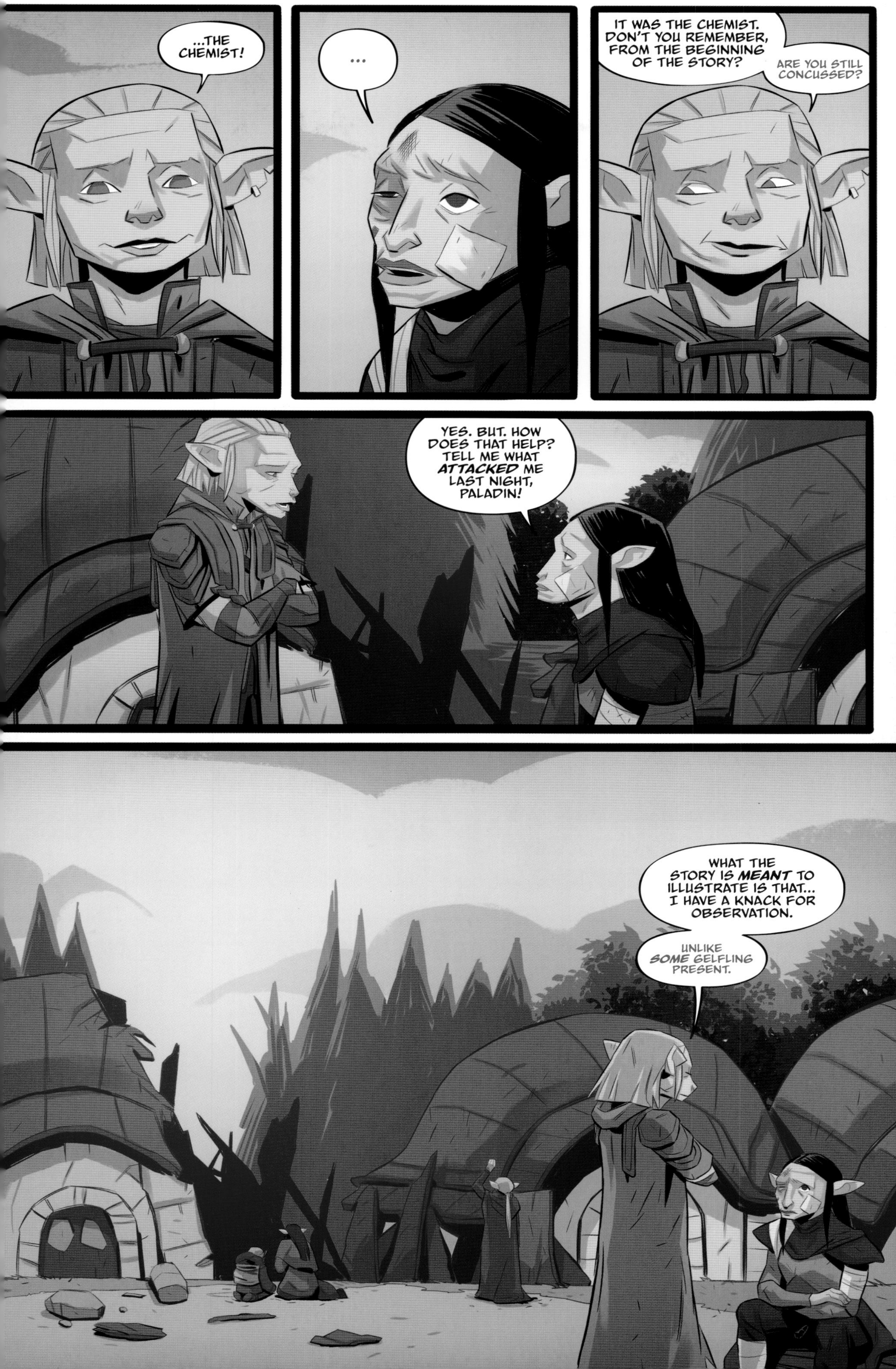
...THE CHEMIST!
...
IT WAS THE CHEMIST. DON'T YOU REMEMBER, FROM THE BEGINNING OF THE STORY?
ARE YOU STILL CONCUSSED?
YES. BUT. HOW DOES THAT HELP? TELL ME WHAT ATTACKED ME LAST NIGHT, PALADIN!
WHAT THE STORY IS MEANT TO ILLUSTRATE IS THAT... I HAVE A KNACK FOR OBSERVATION.
UNLIKE SOME GELFLING PRESENT.

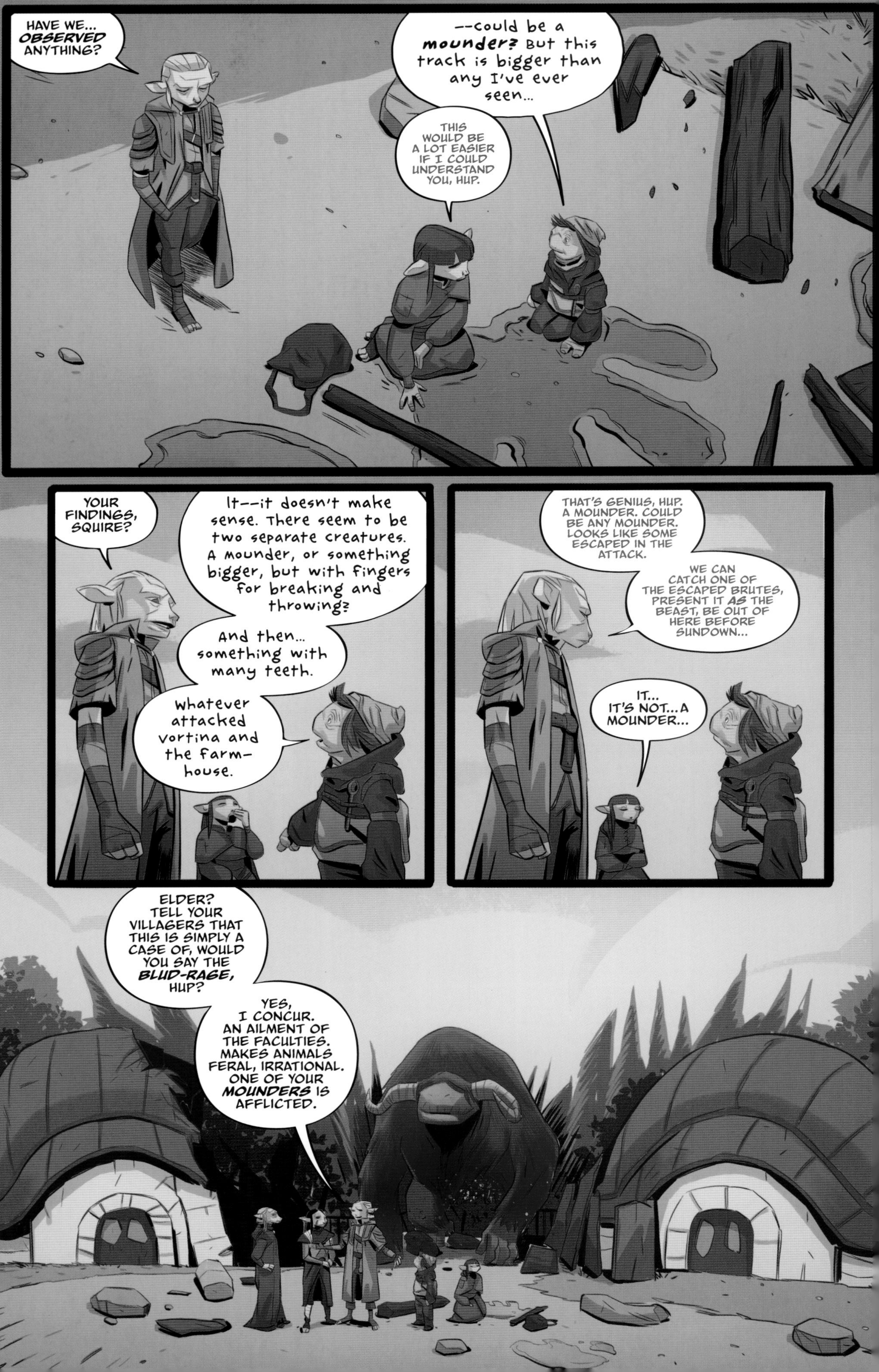
HAVE WE... OBSERVED ANYTHING?
--could be a mounder? But this track is bigger than any I've ever seen...
THIS WOULD BE A LOT EASIER IF I COULD UNDERSTAND YOU, HUP.
YOUR FINDINGS, SQUIRE?
It--it doesn't make sense. There seem to be two separate creatures. A mounder, or something bigger, but with fingers for breaking and throwing?
And then... something with many teeth.
Whatever attacked Vortina and the farm-house.
THAT'S GENIUS, HUP. A MOUNDER. COULD BE ANY MOUNDER. LOOKS LIKE SOME ESCAPED IN THE ATTACK.
WE CAN CATCH ONE OF THE ESCAPED BRUTES, PRESENT IT AS THE BEAST, BE OUT OF HERE BEFORE SUNDOWN...
IT... IT'S NOT...A MOUNDER...
ELDER? TELL YOUR VILLAGERS THAT THIS IS SIMPLY A CASE OF, WOULD YOU SAY THE BLUD-RAGE, HUP?
YES, I CONCUR. AN AILMENT OF THE FACULTIES. MAKES ANIMALS FERAL, IRRATIONAL. ONE OF YOUR MOUNDERS IS AFFLICTED.

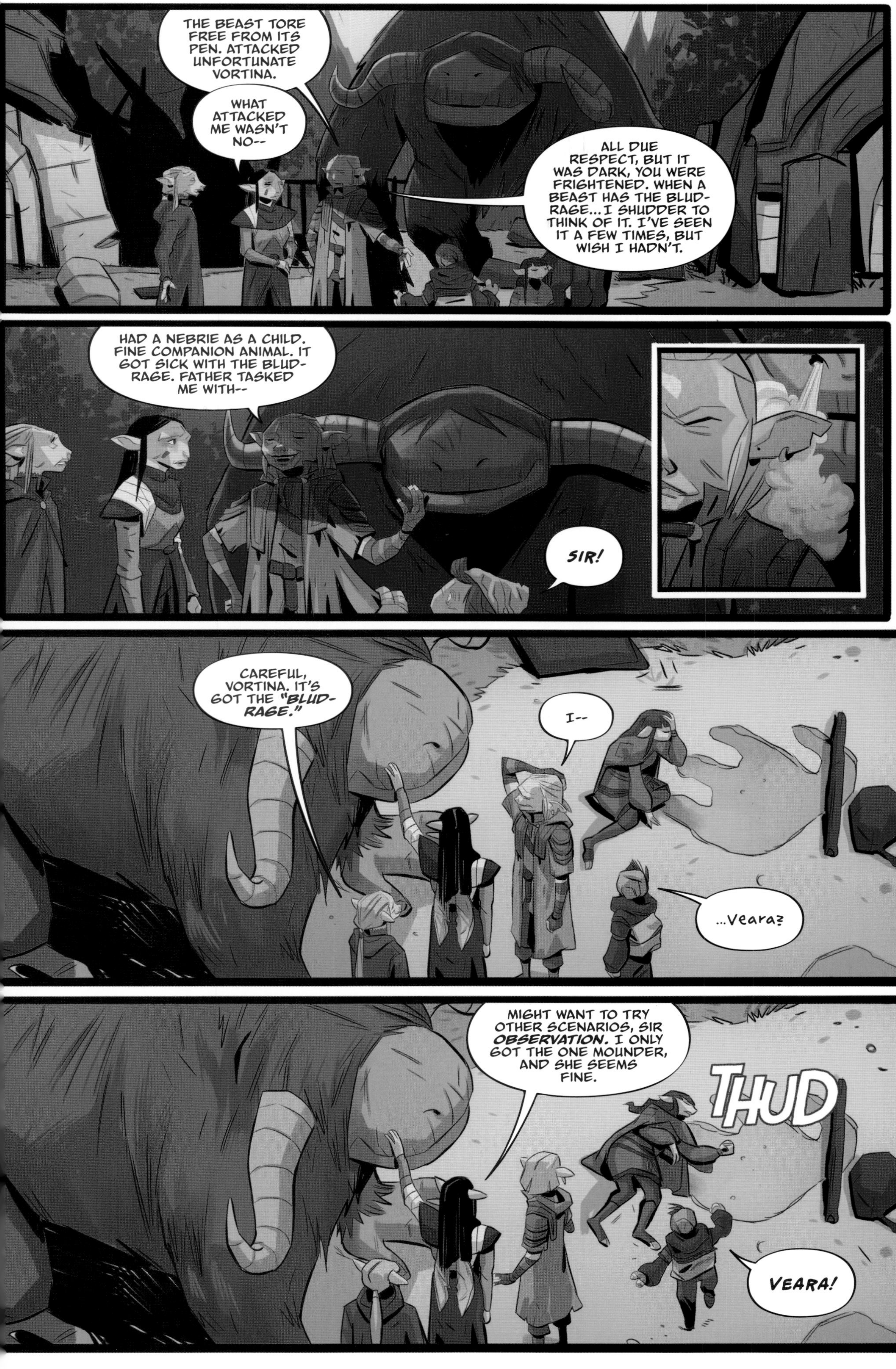
THE BEAST TORE FREE FROM ITS PEN. ATTACKED UNFORTUNATE VORTINA.
WHAT ATTACKED ME WASN'T NO--
ALL DUE RESPECT, BUT IT WAS DARK, YOU WERE FRIGHTENED. WHEN A BEAST HAS THE BLUD-RAGE... I SHUDDER TO THINK OF IT. I'VE SEEN IT A FEW TIMES, BUT WISH I HADN'T.
HAD A NEBRIE AS A CHILD. FINE COMPANION ANIMAL. IT GOT SICK WITH THE BLUD-RAGE. FATHER TASKED ME WITH--
SIR!
CAREFUL, VORTINA. IT'S GOT THE "BLUD-RAGE."
I--
...Veara?
MIGHT WANT TO TRY OTHER SCENARIOS, SIR OBSERVATION. I ONLY GOT THE ONE MOUNDER, AND SHE SEEMS FINE.
THUD
VEARA!

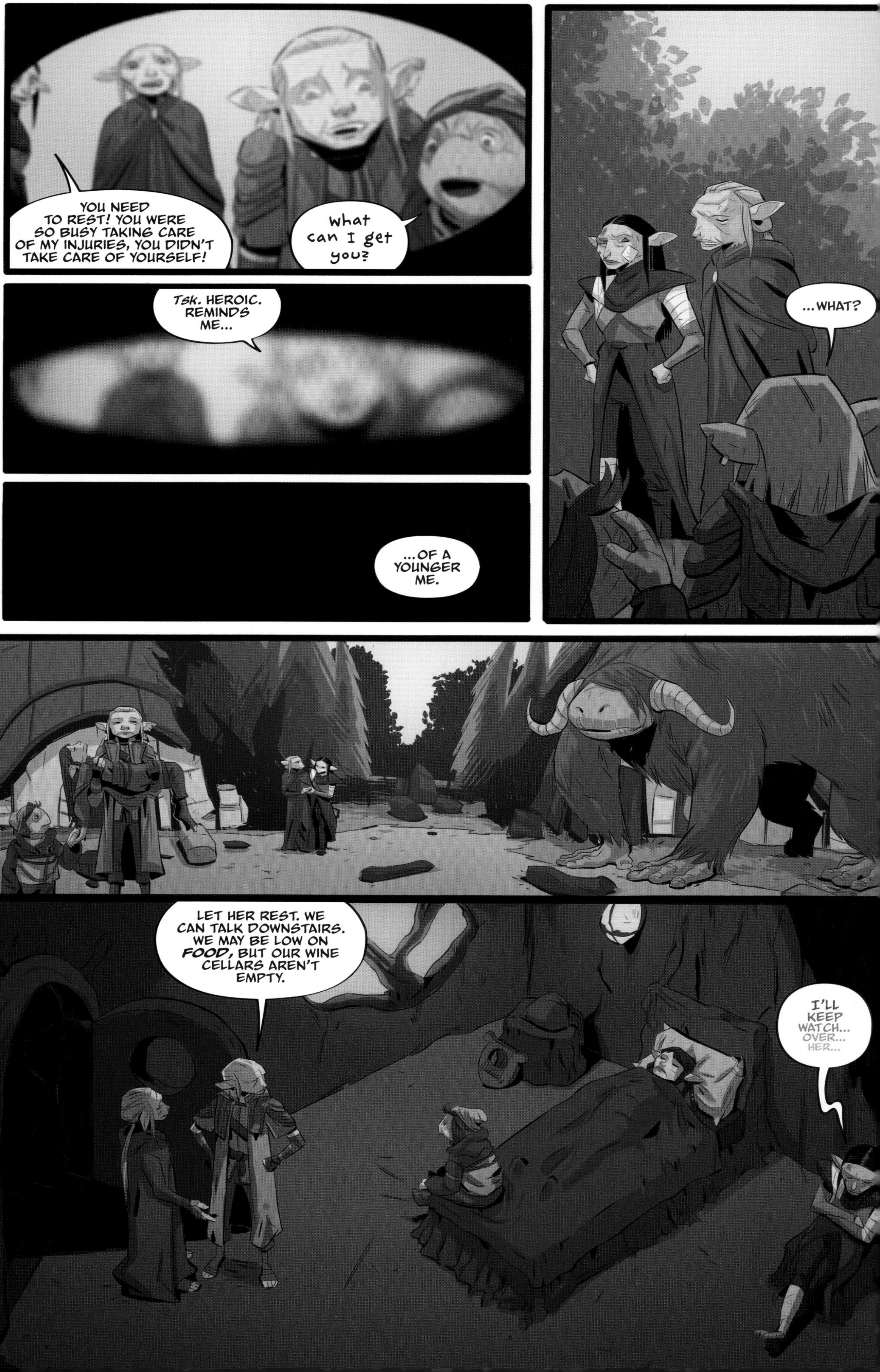
YOU NEED TO REST! YOU WERE SO BUSY TAKING CARE OF MY INJURIES, YOU DIDN'T TAKE CARE OF YOURSELF!
What can I get you?
Tsk. HEROIC. REMINDS ME...
...OF A YOUNGER ME.
...WHAT?
LET HER REST. WE CAN TALK DOWNSTAIRS. WE MAY BE LOW ON FOOD, BUT OUR WINE CELLARS AREN'T EMPTY.
I'LL KEEP WATCH... OVER... HER...

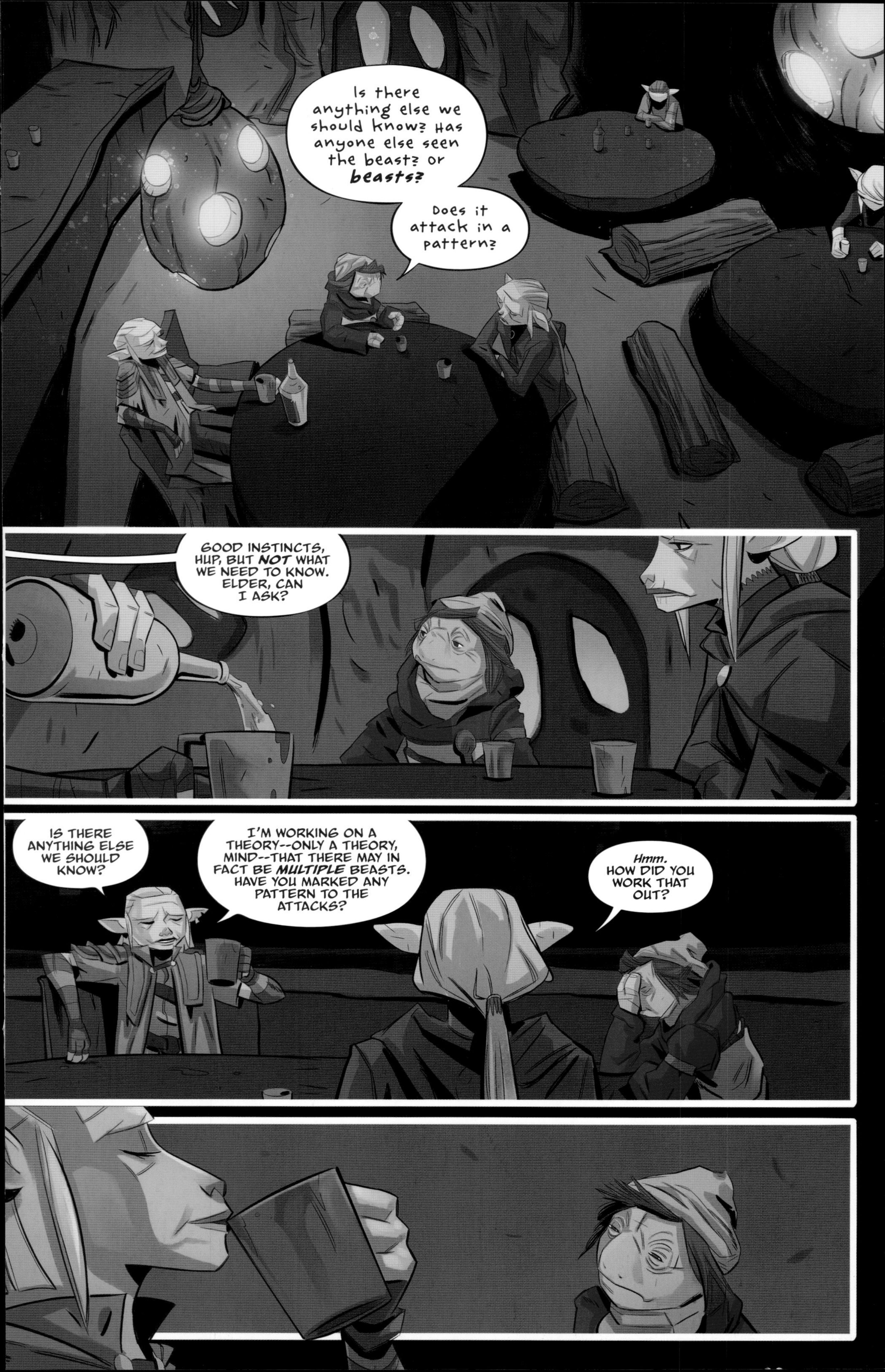
Is there anything else we should know? Has anyone else seen the beast? Or *beasts?*
Does it attack in a pattern?
GOOD INSTINCTS, HUP, BUT *NOT* WHAT WE NEED TO KNOW. ELDER, CAN I ASK?
IS THERE ANYTHING ELSE WE SHOULD KNOW?
I'M WORKING ON A THEORY--ONLY A THEORY, MIND--THAT THERE MAY IN FACT BE *MULTIPLE* BEASTS. HAVE YOU MARKED ANY PATTERN TO THE ATTACKS?
Hmm. HOW DID YOU WORK THAT OUT?

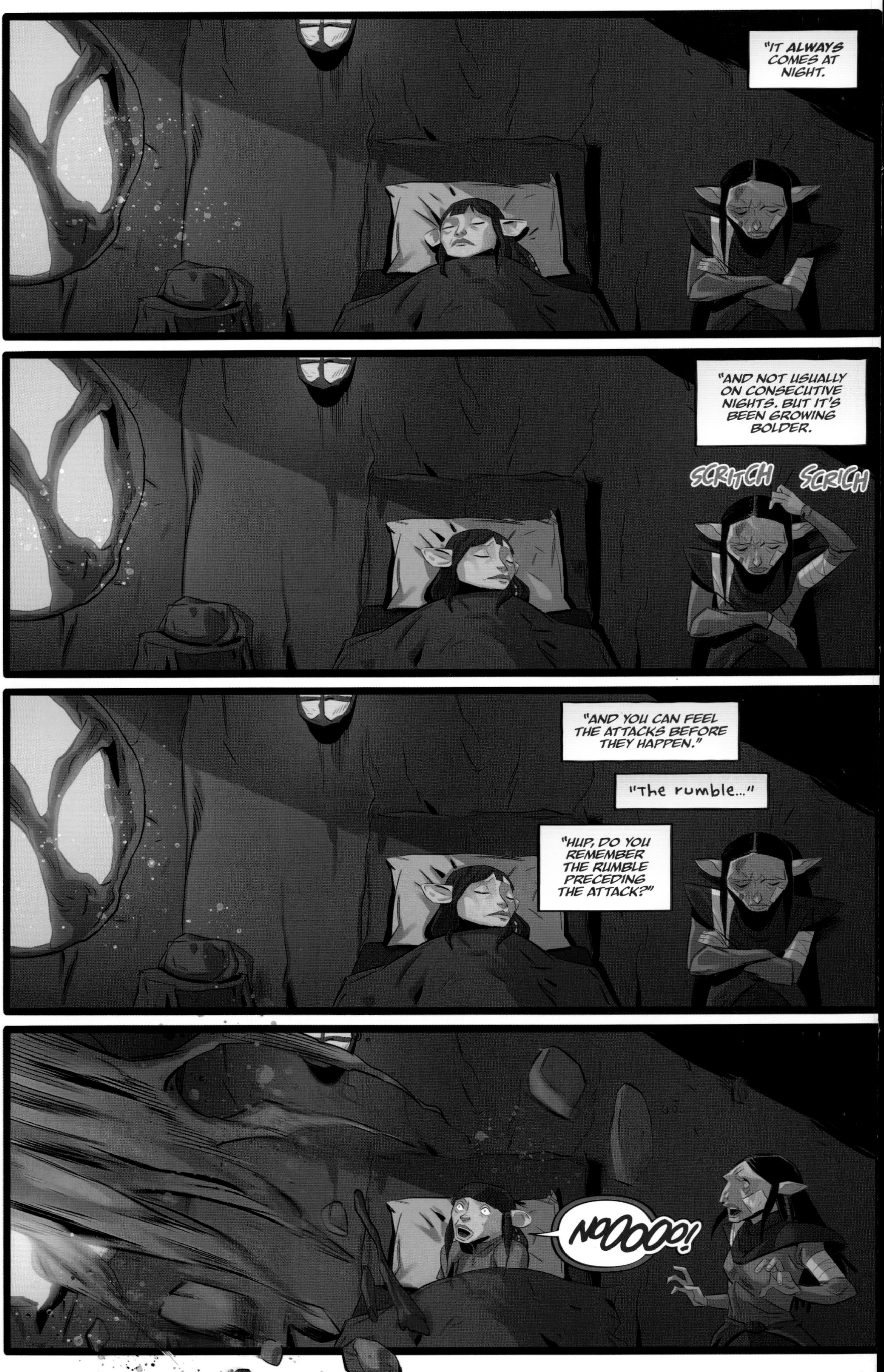
"IT ALWAYS COMES AT NIGHT.
"AND NOT USUALLY ON CONSECUTIVE NIGHTS. BUT IT'S BEEN GROWING BOLDER.
SCRITCH
SCRICH
"AND YOU CAN FEEL THE ATTACKS BEFORE THEY HAPPEN."
"The rumble..."
"HUP, DO YOU REMEMBER THE RUMBLE PRECEDING THE ATTACK?"
NOOOOO!

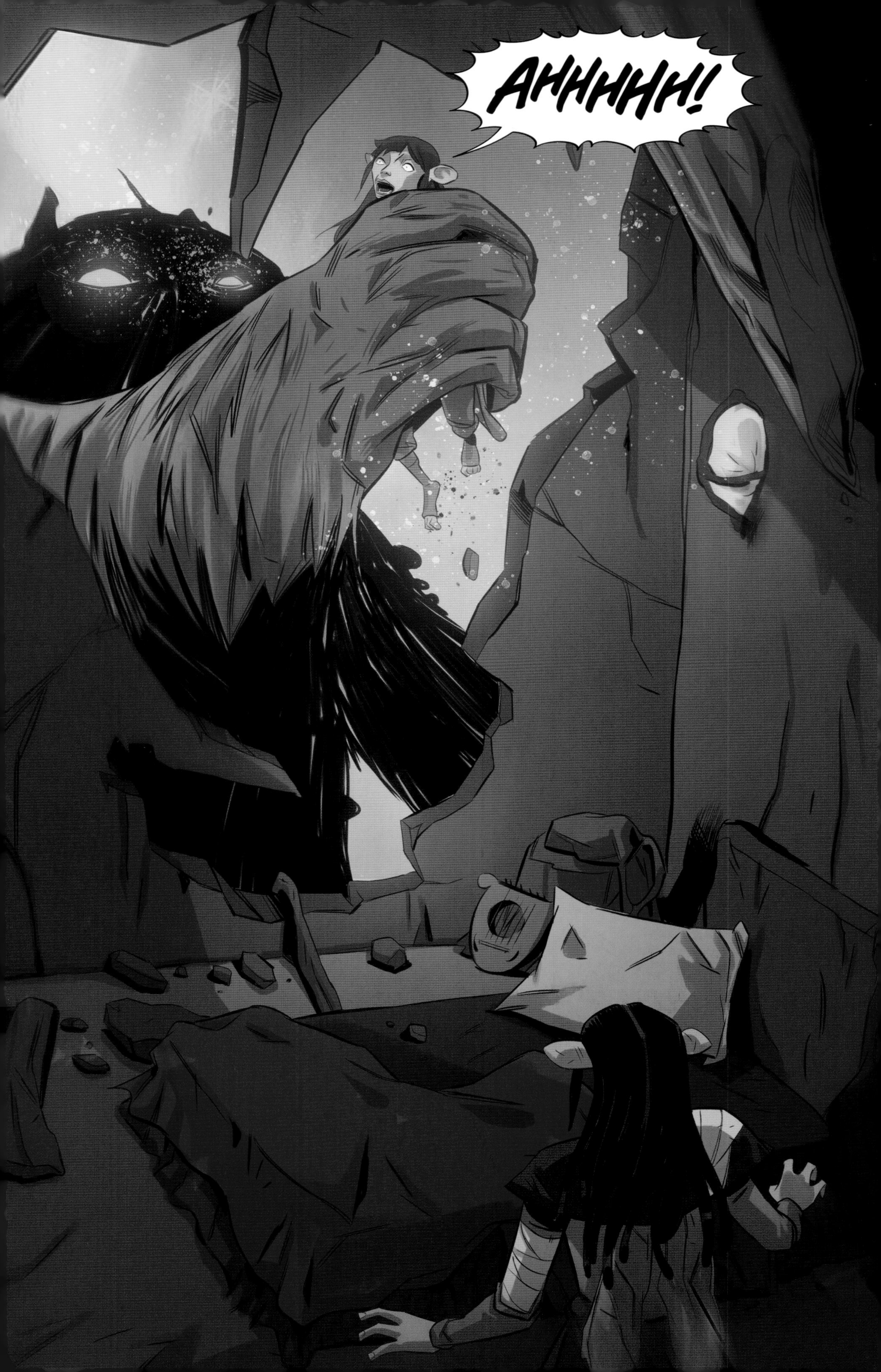
AHHHHH!

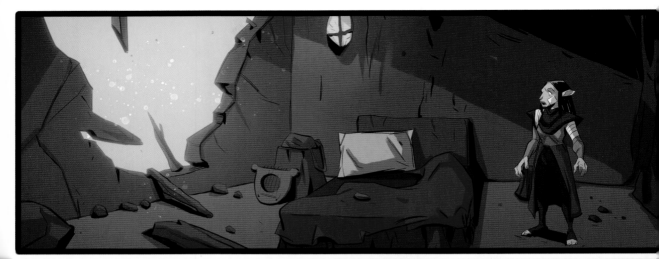

WH-WHAT HAPPENED?

THE NORTH WOODS. IT TOOK HER. BUT I COULD HEAR ITS FOOTSTEPS. BIG FEET. THE NORTH WOODS. I'M SURE OF IT.

BUT... THERE WAS NO RUMBLE!

Sir! I'll saddle Marengax. We need to save her!

Sir! Ride or run? Which will be faster?

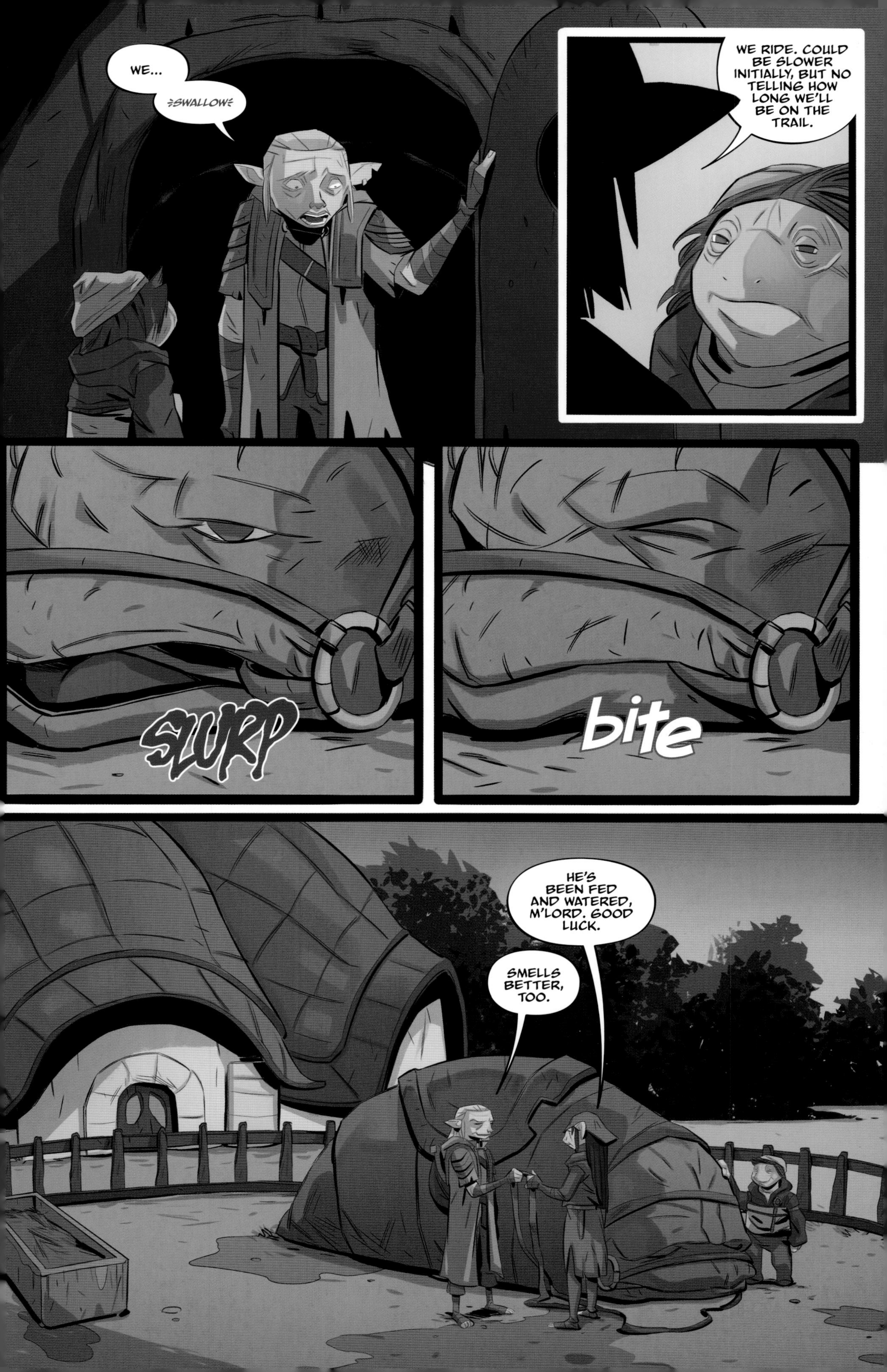
WE...
SWALLOW
WE RIDE. COULD BE SLOWER INITIALLY, BUT NO TELLING HOW LONG WE'LL BE ON THE TRAIL.
SLURP
bite
HE'S BEEN FED AND WATERED, M'LORD. GOOD LUCK.
SMELLS BETTER, TOO.

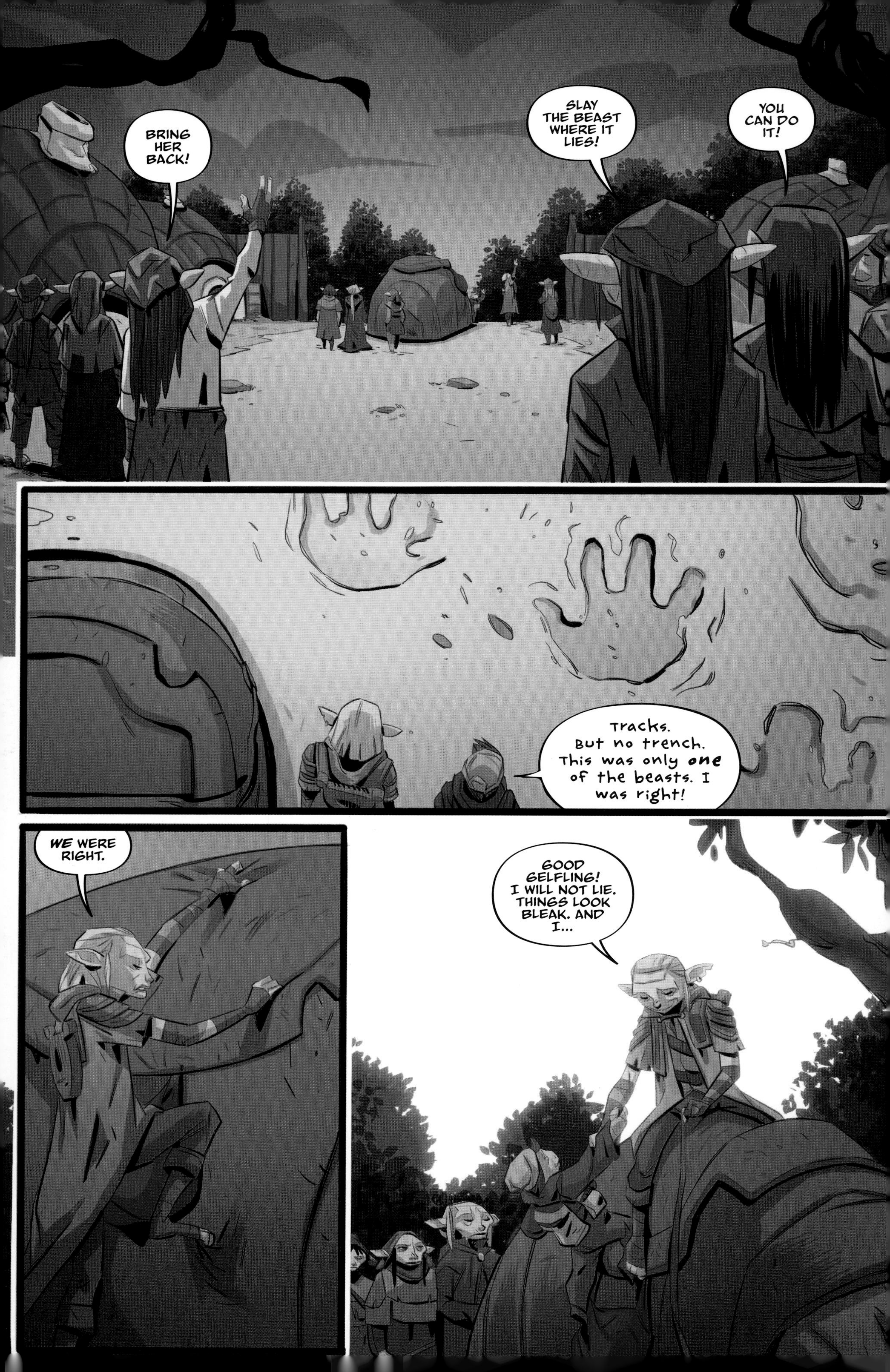
BRING HER BACK!
SLAY THE BEAST WHERE IT LIES!
YOU CAN DO IT!
Tracks. But no trench. This was only one of the beasts. I was right!
WE WERE RIGHT.
GOOD GELFLING! I WILL NOT LIE. THINGS LOOK BLEAK. AND I...

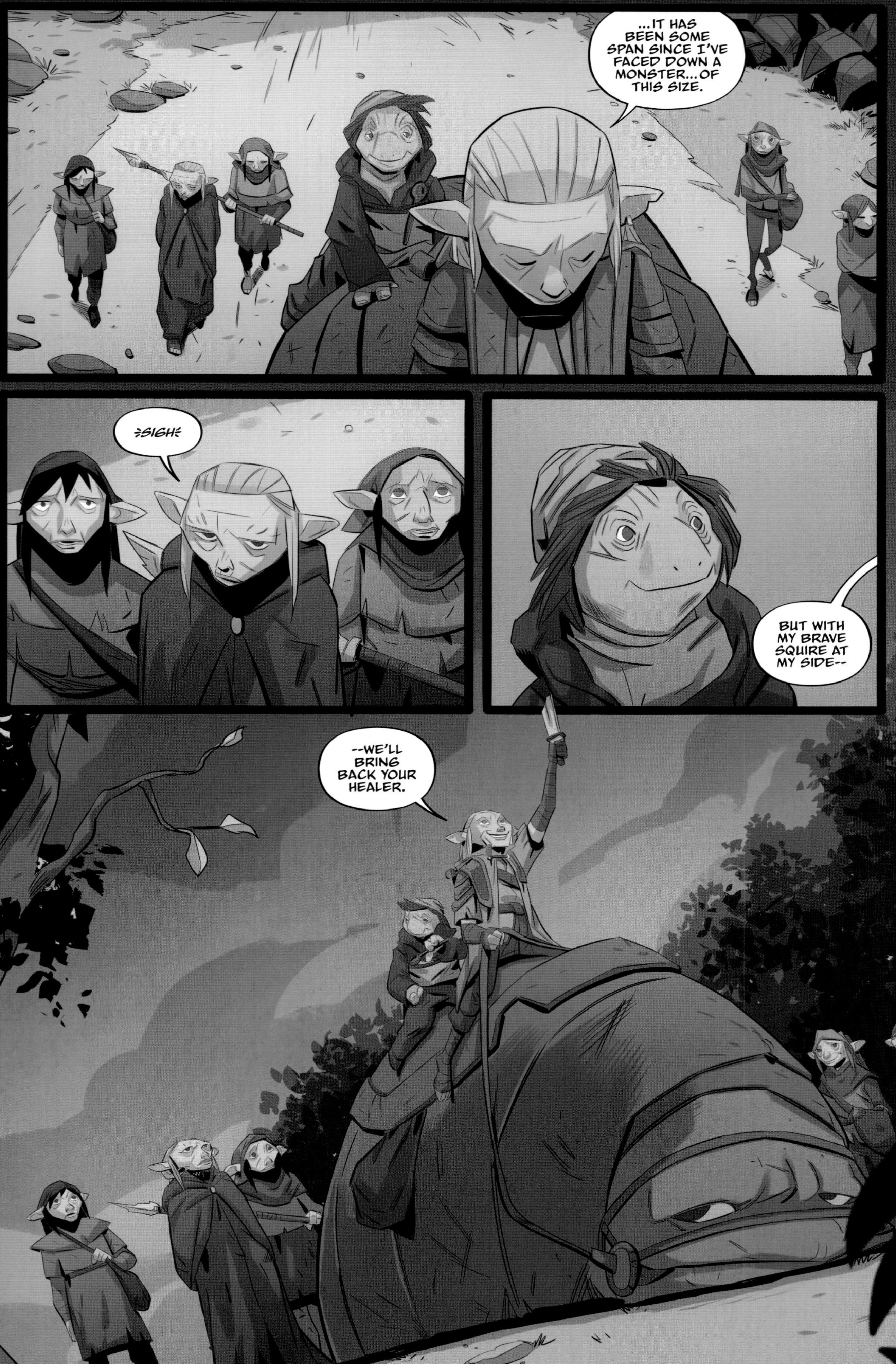
...IT HAS BEEN SOME SPAN SINCE I'VE FACED DOWN A MONSTER...OF THIS SIZE.
SIGH
BUT WITH MY BRAVE SQUIRE AT MY SIDE--
--WE'LL BRING BACK YOUR HEALER.

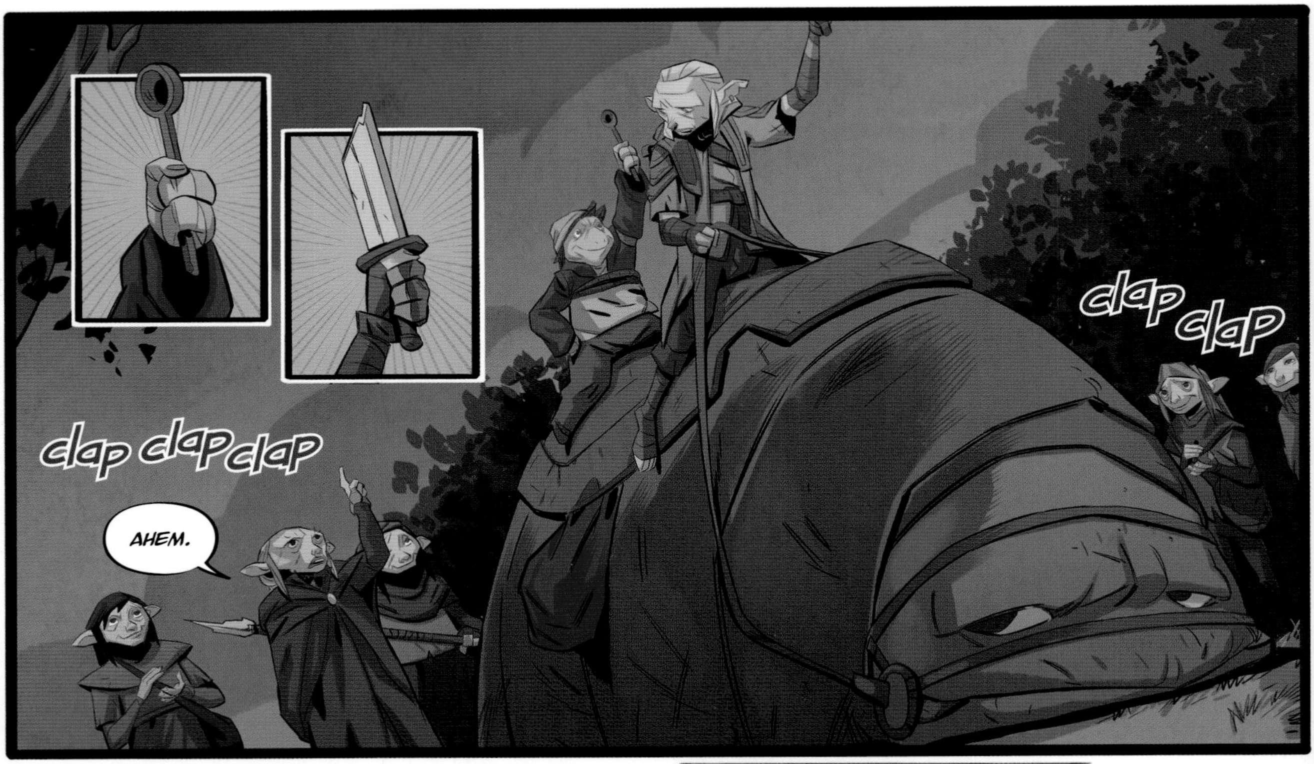
clap clap
clap clap clap
AHEM.
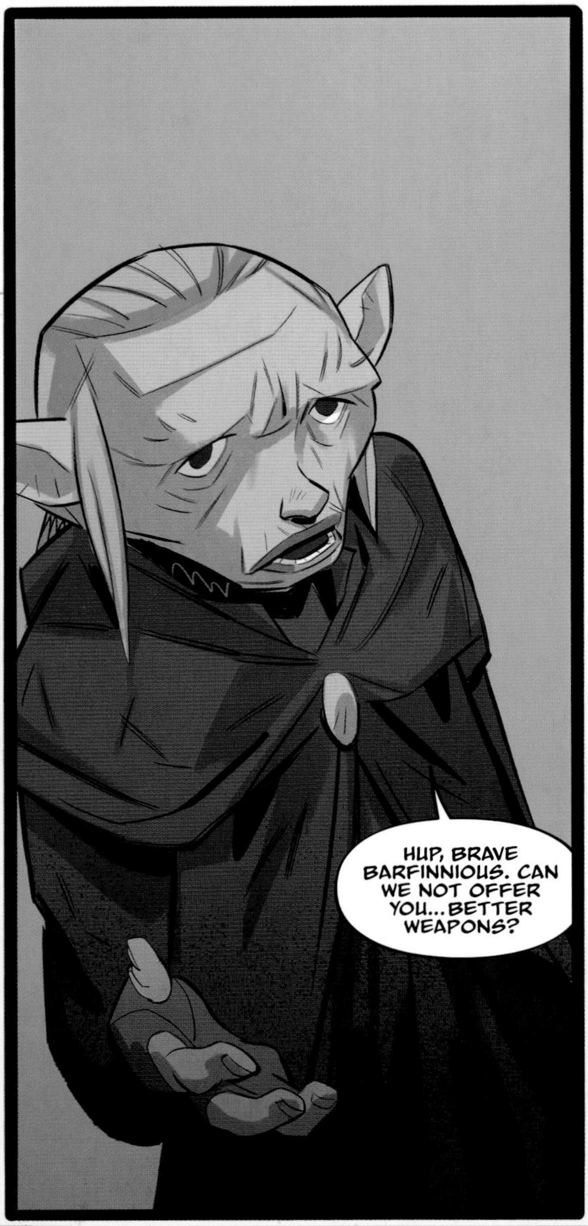
HUP, BRAVE BARFINNIOUS. CAN WE NOT OFFER YOU...BETTER WEAPONS?
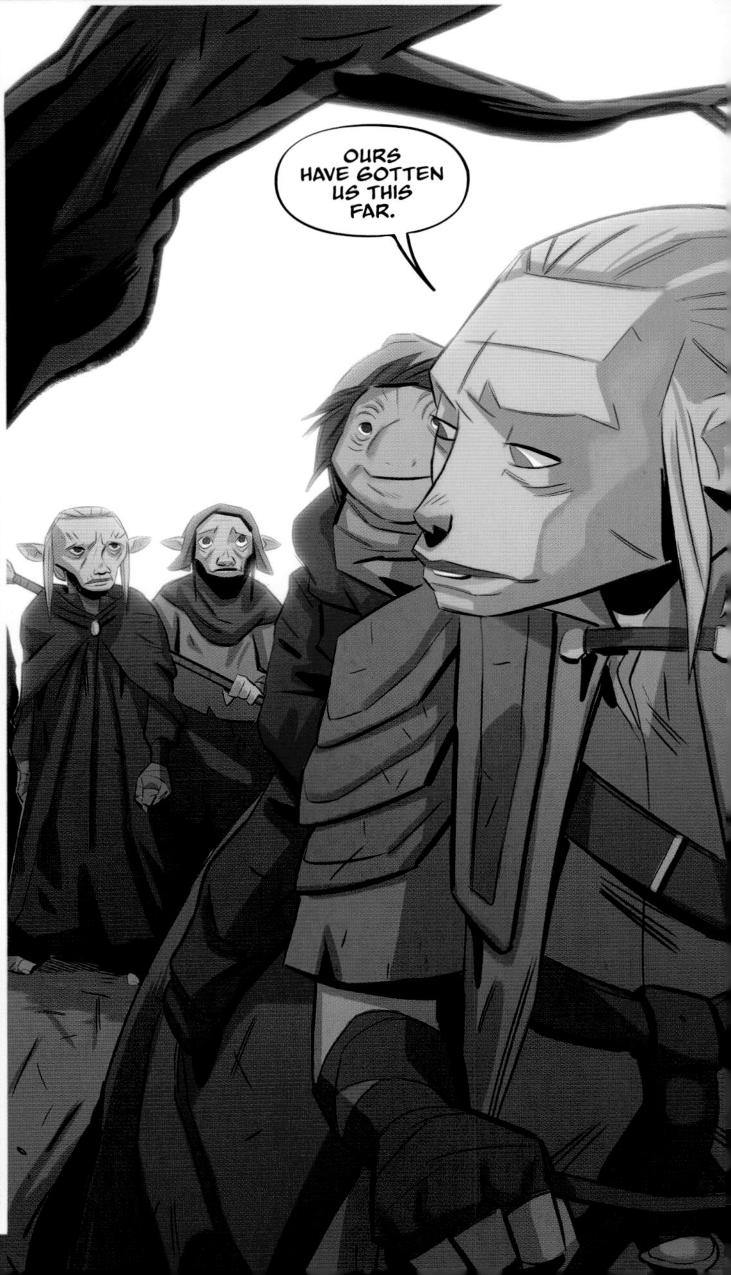
OURS HAVE GOTTEN US THIS FAR.

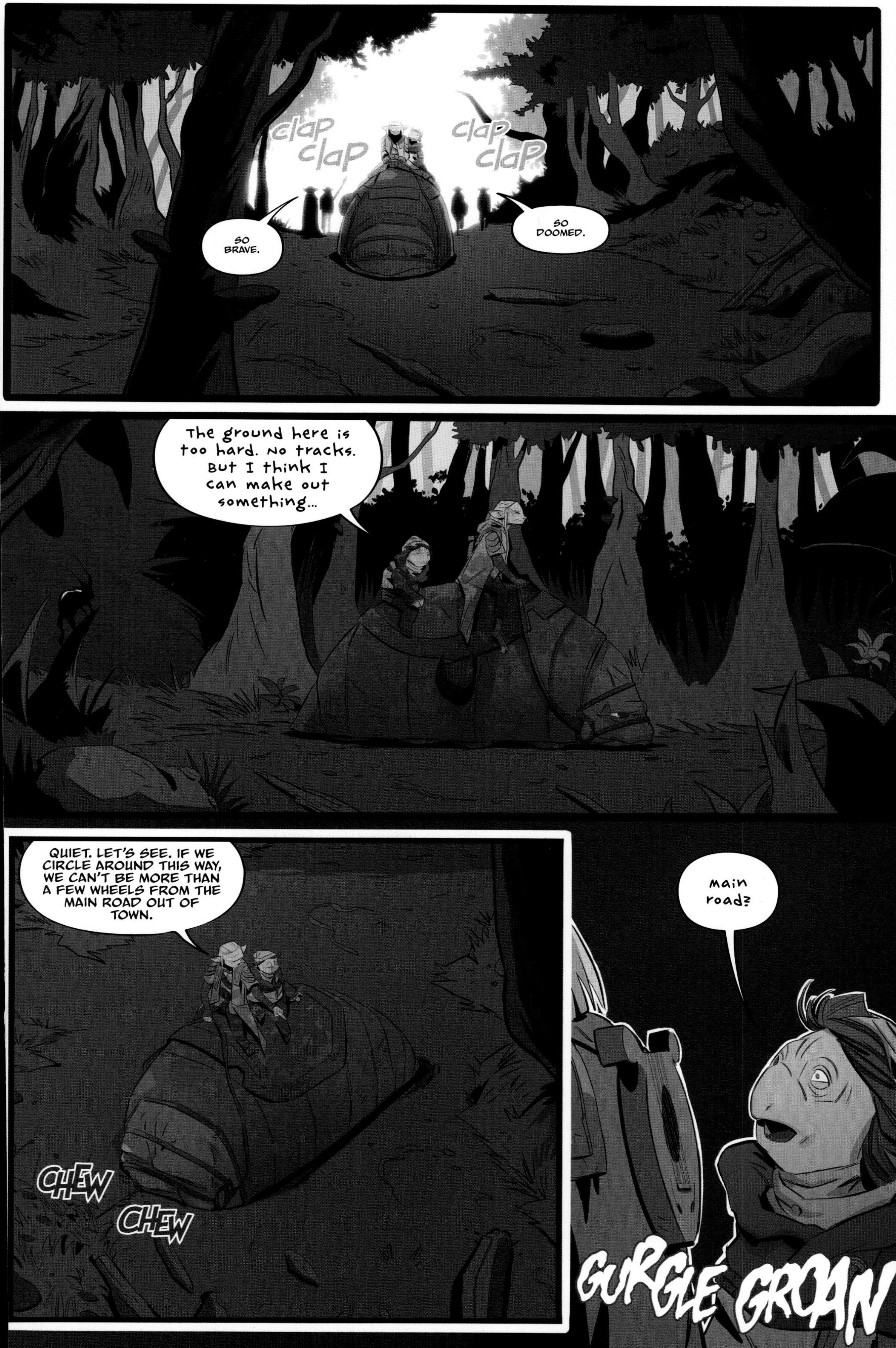
clap clap
clap clap
SO BRAVE.
SO DOOMED.
The ground here is too hard. No tracks. But I think I can make out something...
QUIET. LET'S SEE. IF WE CIRCLE AROUND THIS WAY, WE CAN'T BE MORE THAN A FEW WHEELS FROM THE MAIN ROAD OUT OF TOWN.
CHEW
CHEW
main road?
GURGLE GROAN

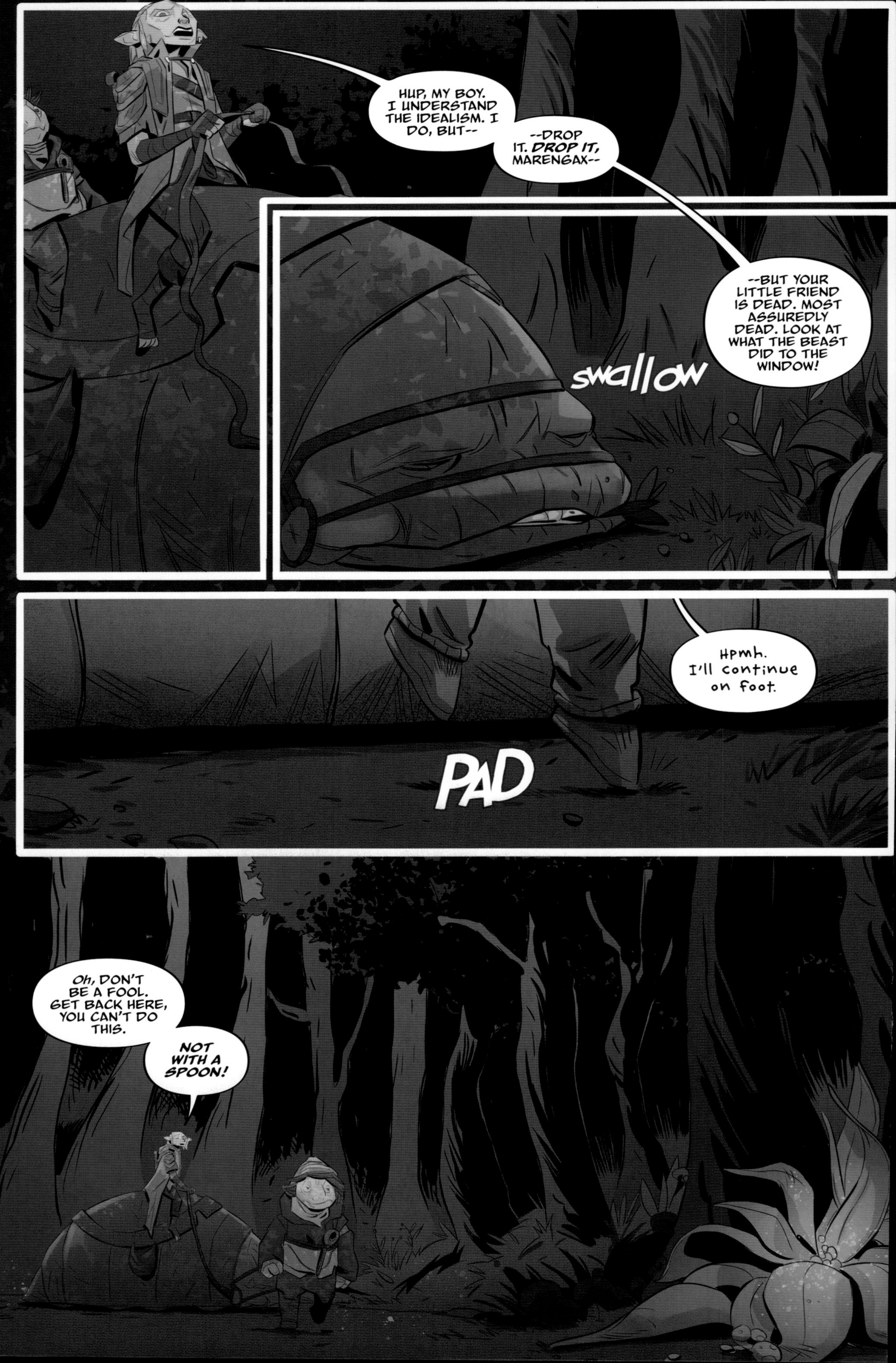
HUP, MY BOY. I UNDERSTAND THE IDEALISM. I DO, BUT--
--DROP IT. DROP IT, MARENGAX--
--BUT YOUR LITTLE FRIEND IS DEAD. MOST ASSUREDLY DEAD. LOOK AT WHAT THE BEAST DID TO THE WINDOW!
swallow
Hpmh. I'll continue on foot.
PAD
Oh, DON'T BE A FOOL. GET BACK HERE, YOU CAN'T DO THIS.
NOT WITH A SPOON!

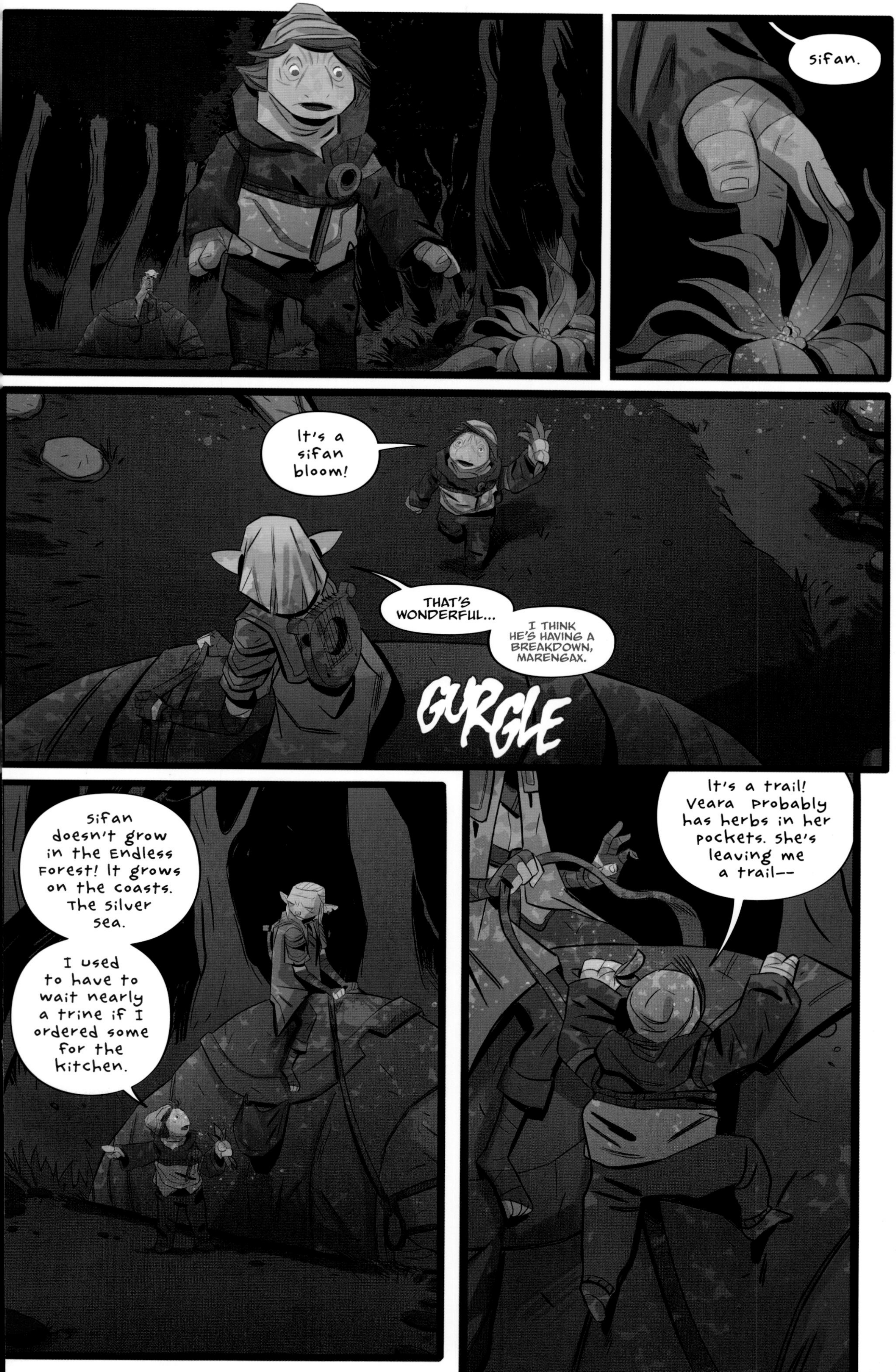
Sifan.
It's a sifan bloom!
THAT'S WONDERFUL...
I THINK HE'S HAVING A BREAKDOWN, MARENGAX.
GURGLE
Sifan doesn't grow in the Endless Forest! It grows on the coasts. The Silver Sea.
I used to have to wait nearly a trine if I ordered some for the kitchen.
It's a trail! Veara probably has herbs in her pockets. She's leaving me a trail--

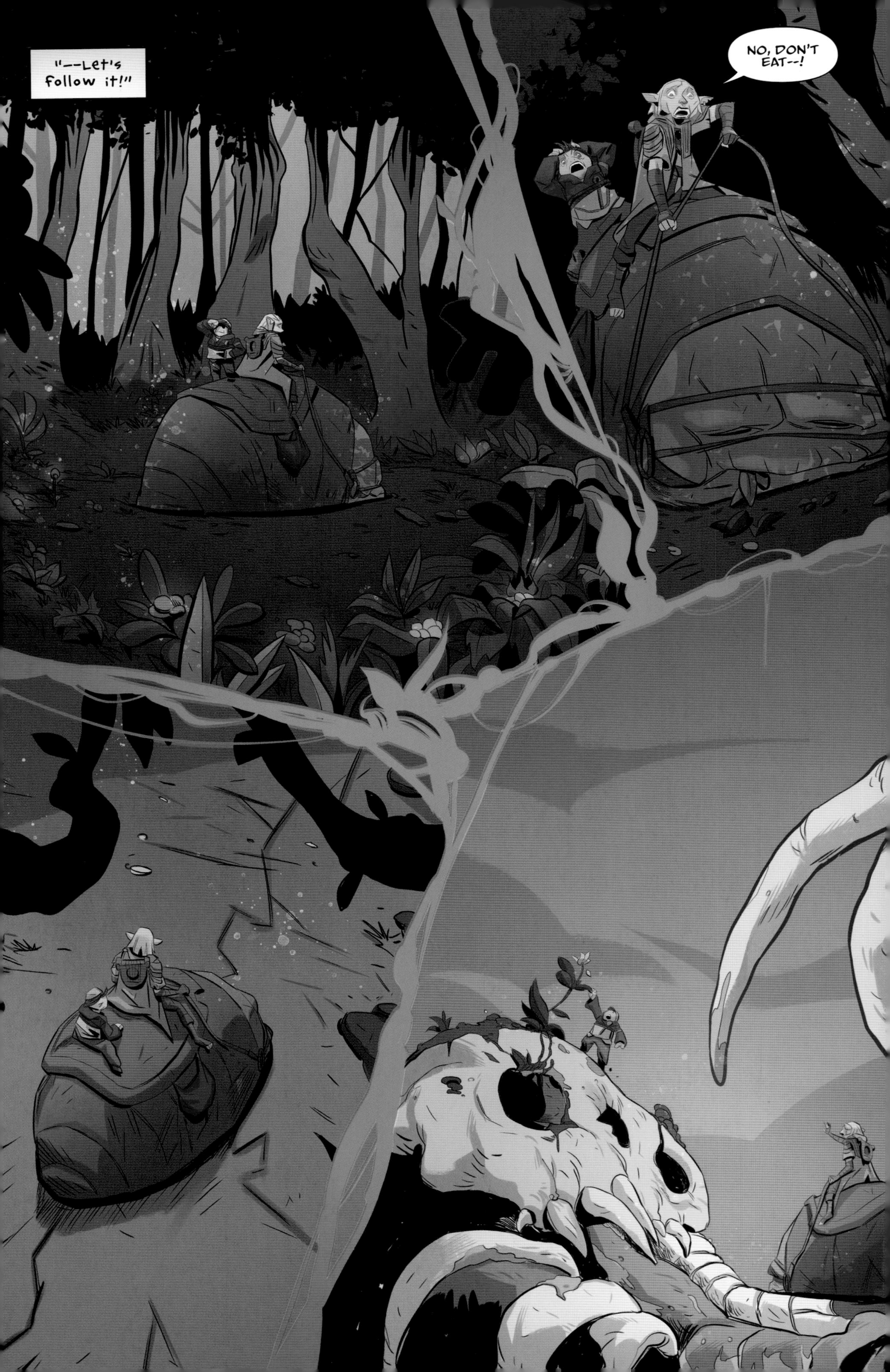
"--Let's follow it!"
NO, DON'T EAT--!

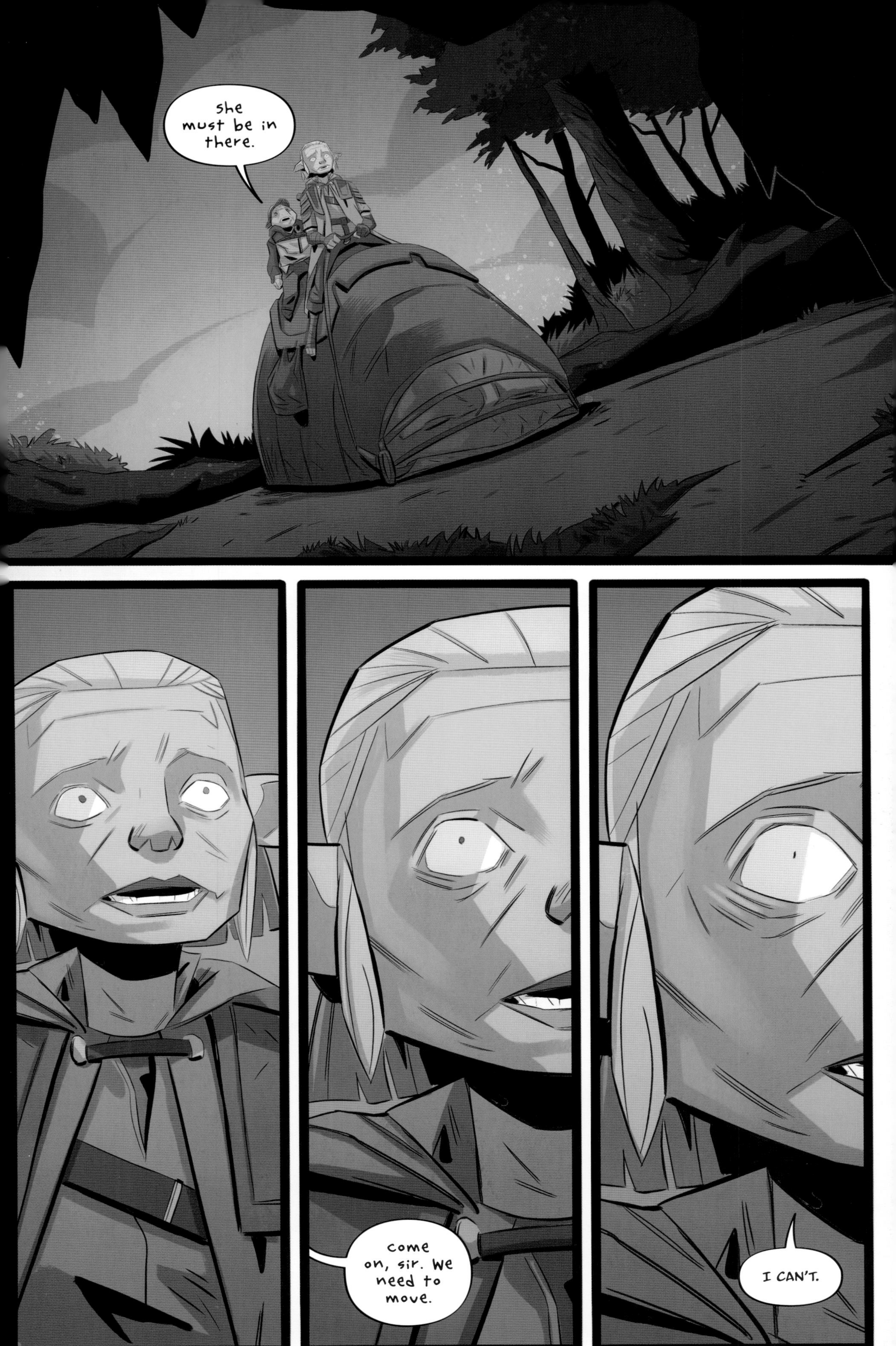
she must be in there.
come on, sir. We need to move.
I CAN'T.

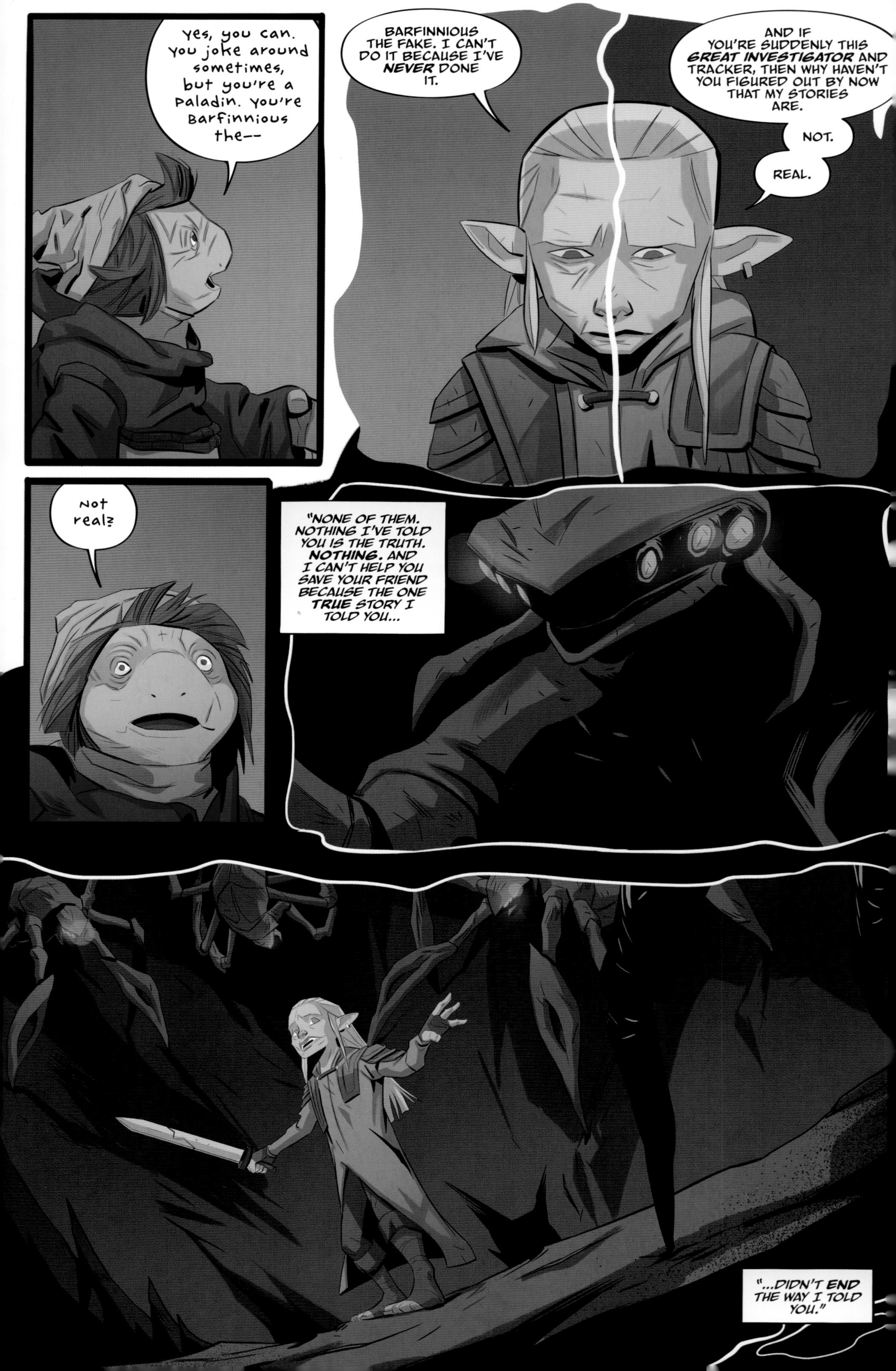
Yes, you can. You joke around sometimes, but you're a Paladin. You're Barfinnious the--
BARFINNIOUS THE FAKE. I CAN'T DO IT BECAUSE I'VE NEVER DONE IT.
AND IF YOU'RE SUDDENLY THIS GREAT INVESTIGATOR AND TRACKER, THEN WHY HAVEN'T YOU FIGURED OUT BY NOW THAT MY STORIES ARE.
NOT.
REAL.
Not real?
"NONE OF THEM. NOTHING I'VE TOLD YOU IS THE TRUTH. NOTHING. AND I CAN'T HELP YOU SAVE YOUR FRIEND BECAUSE THE ONE TRUE STORY I TOLD YOU...
"...DIDN'T END THE WAY I TOLD YOU."

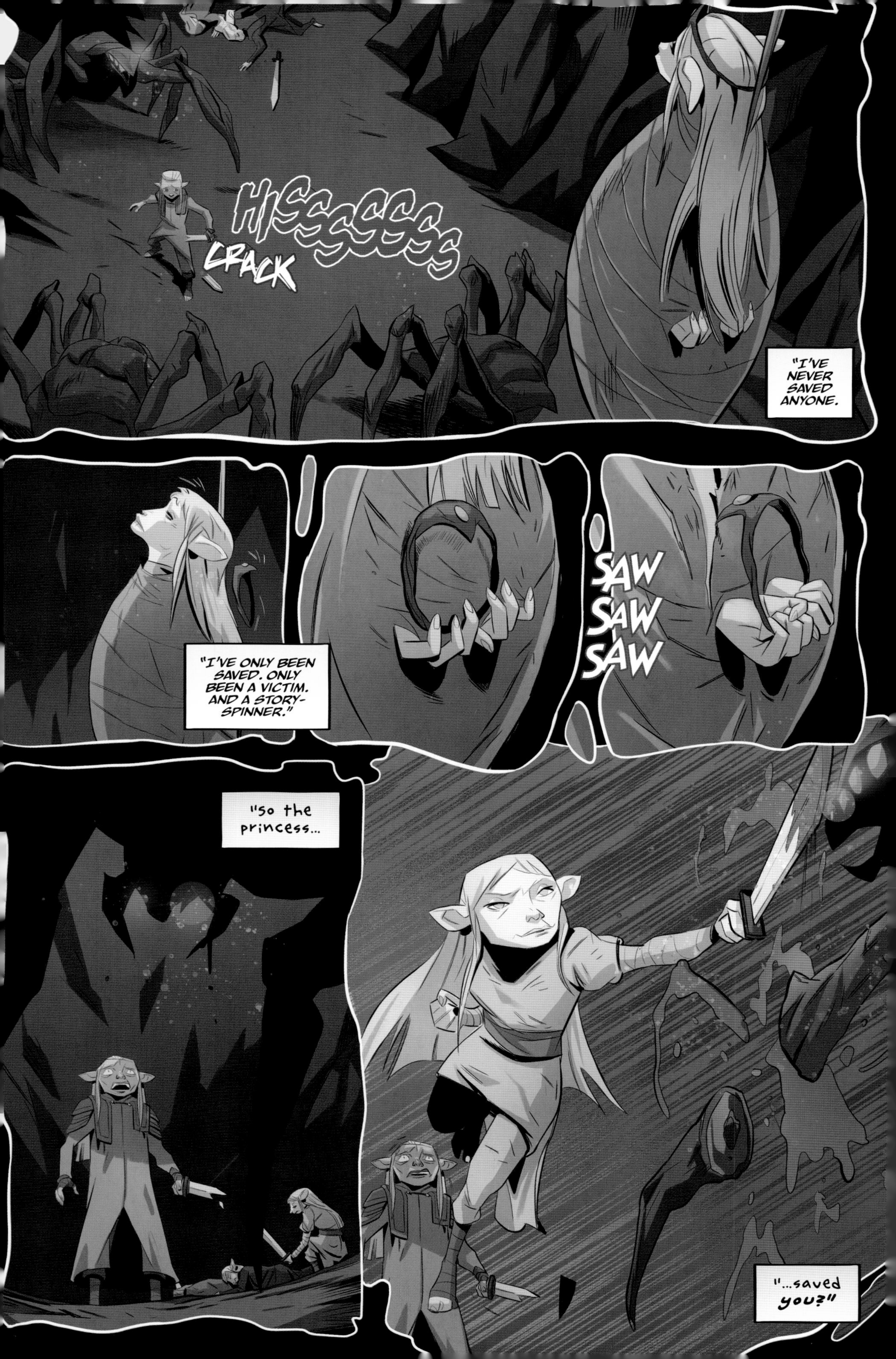
HISSSSSSS
CRACK
"I'VE NEVER SAVED ANYONE.
"I'VE ONLY BEEN SAVED. ONLY BEEN A VICTIM. AND A STORY-SPINNER."
SAW SAW SAW
"So the princess...
"...saved you?"

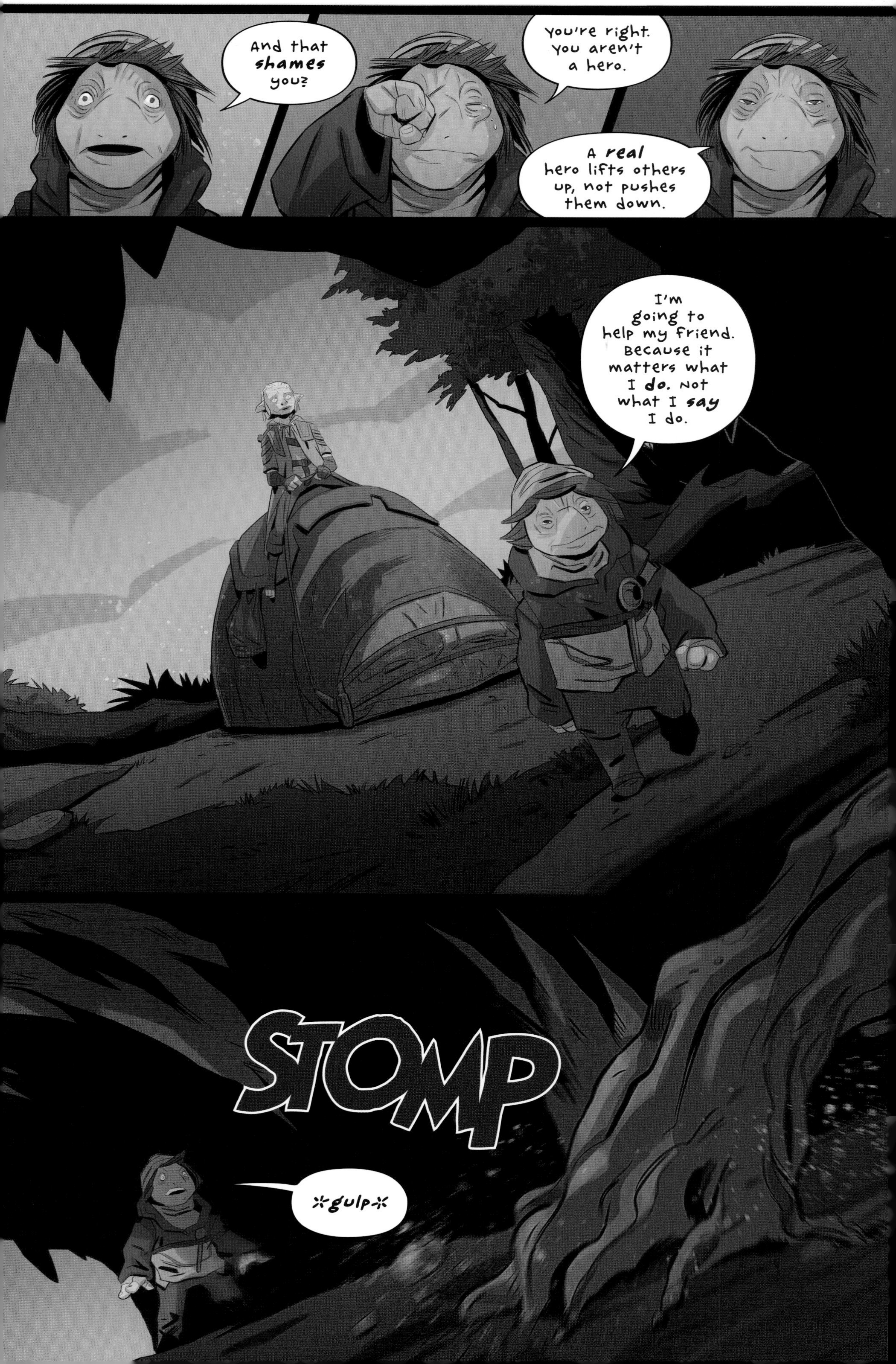
And that **shames** you?
You're right. You aren't a hero.
A **real** hero lifts others up, not pushes them down.
I'm going to help my friend. Because it matters what I **do.** Not what I **say** I do.
STOMP
gulp

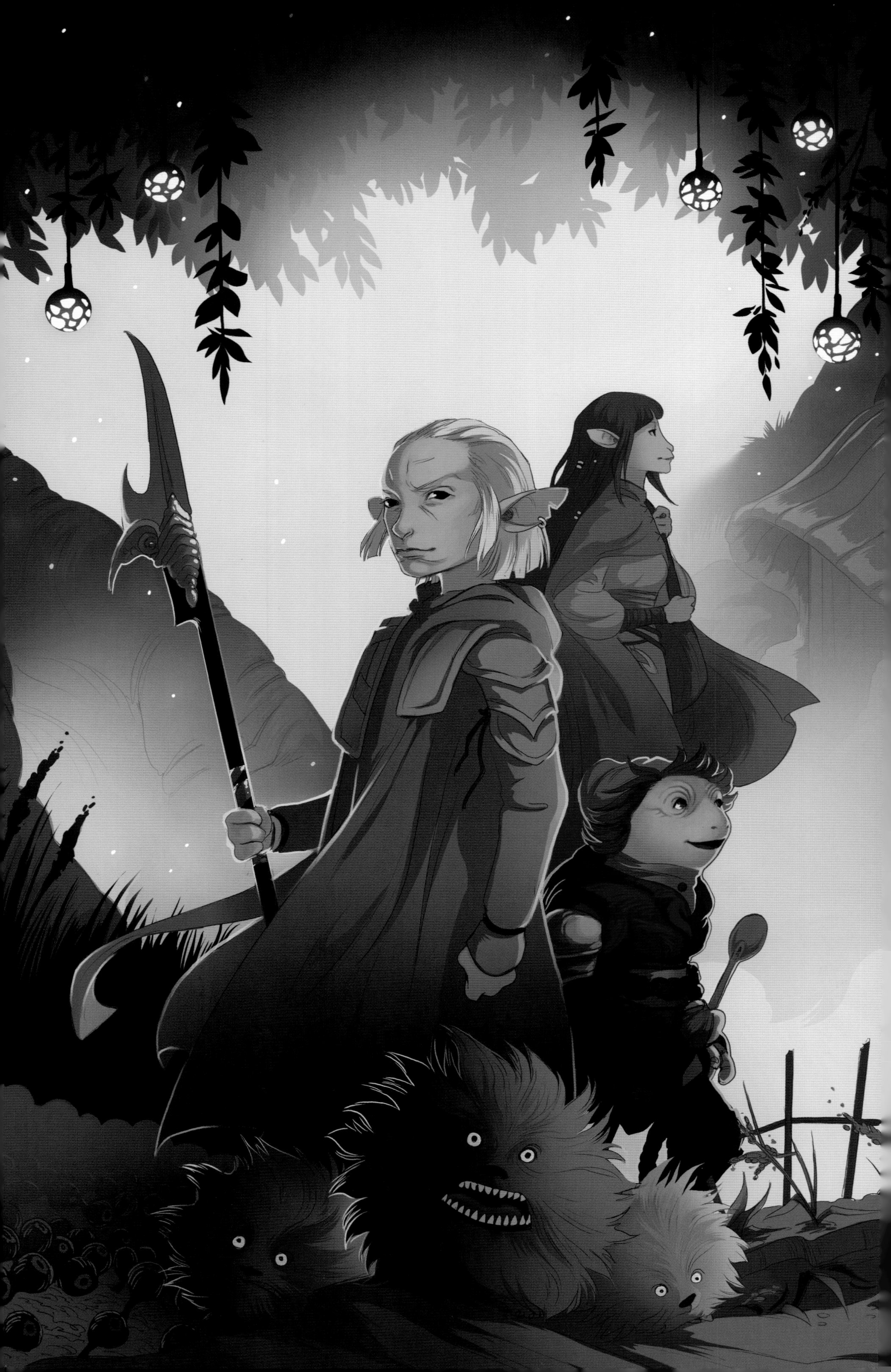

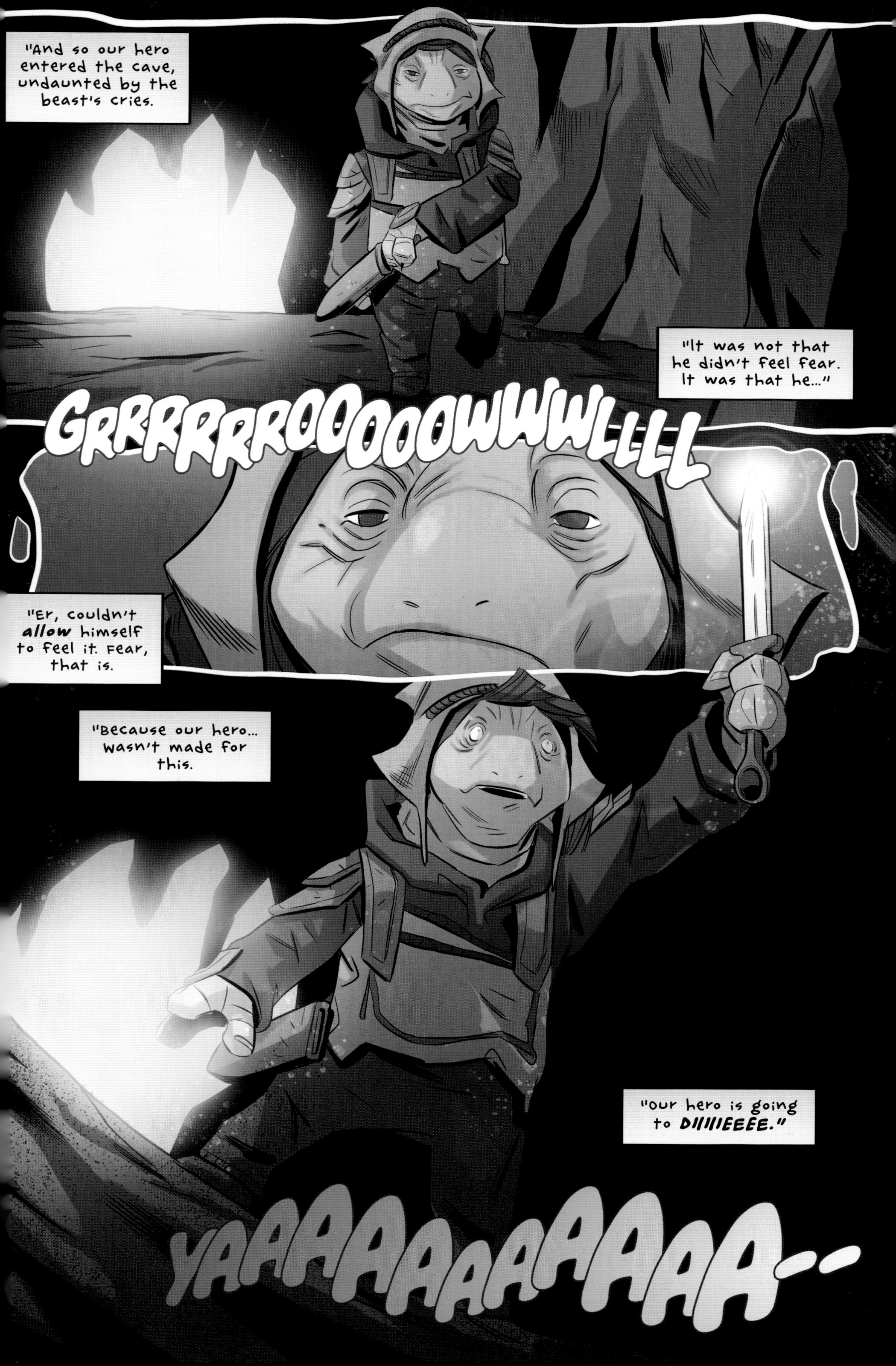

"And so our hero entered the cave, undaunted by the beast's cries.
"It was not that he didn't feel fear. It was that he..."
GRRRRRROOOOOOWWWLLLL
"Er, couldn't **allow** himself to feel it. Fear, that is.
"Because our hero... wasn't made for this.
"Our hero is going to ***DIIIIEEEE.***"
YAAAAAAAAAAAA--

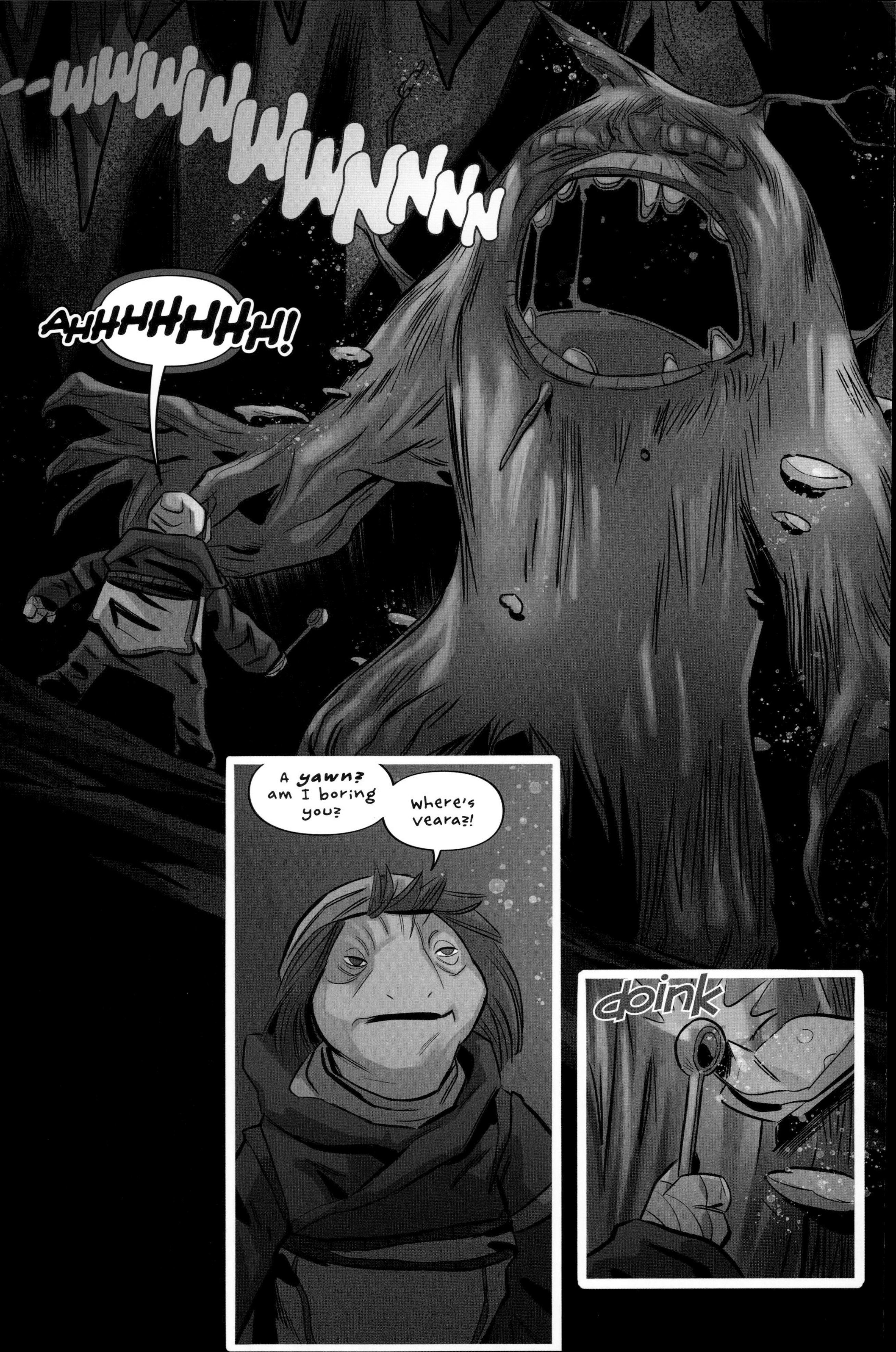
--WWWWWWWWNNNNN
AHHHHHHH!
A yawn? am I boring you?
Where's veara?!
doink

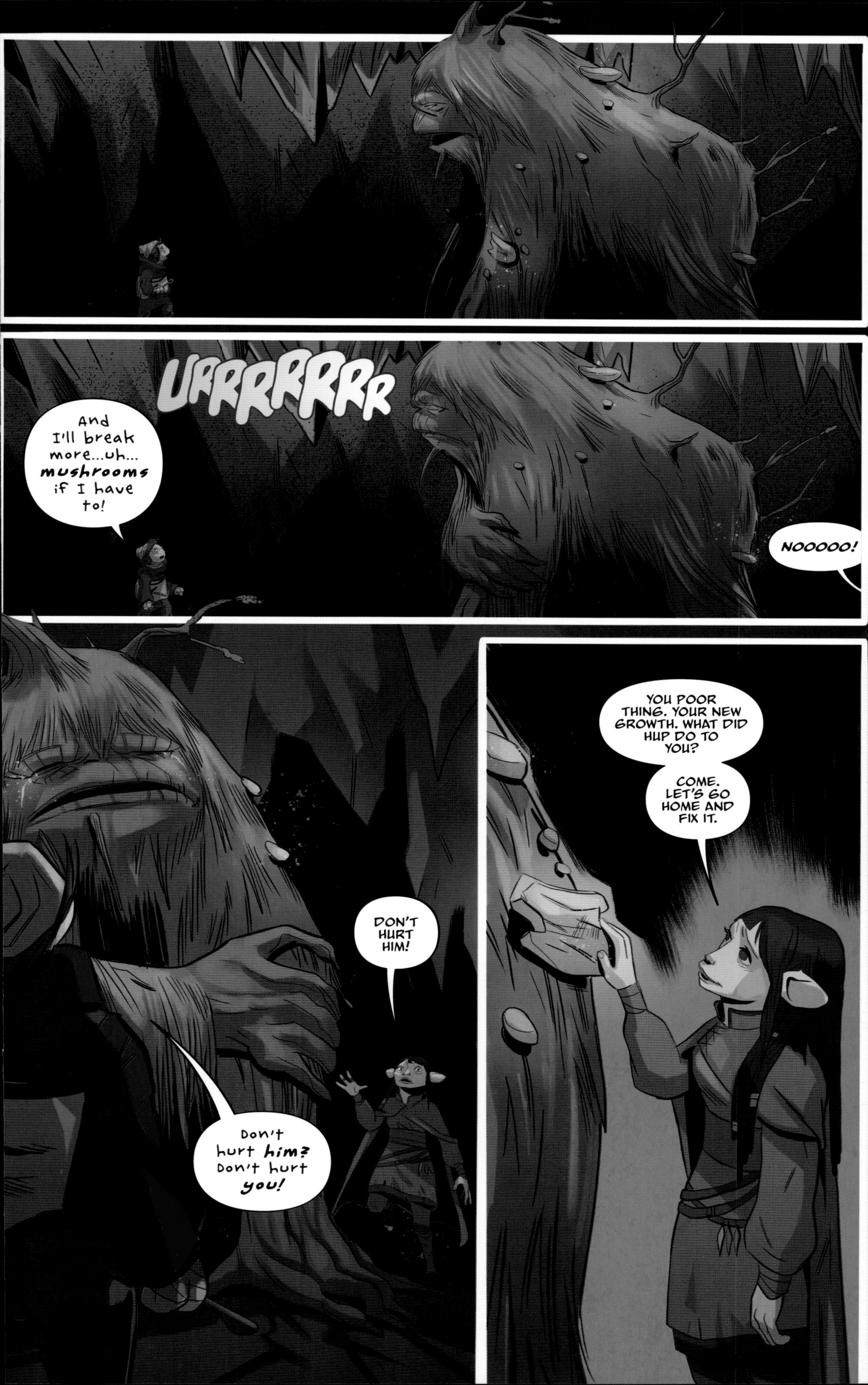
URRRRRRR
And I'll break more...uh... mushrooms if I have to!
NOOOOO!
DON'T HURT HIM!
Don't hurt him? Don't hurt you!
YOU POOR THING. YOUR NEW GROWTH. WHAT DID HUP DO TO YOU?
COME. LET'S GO HOME AND FIX IT.

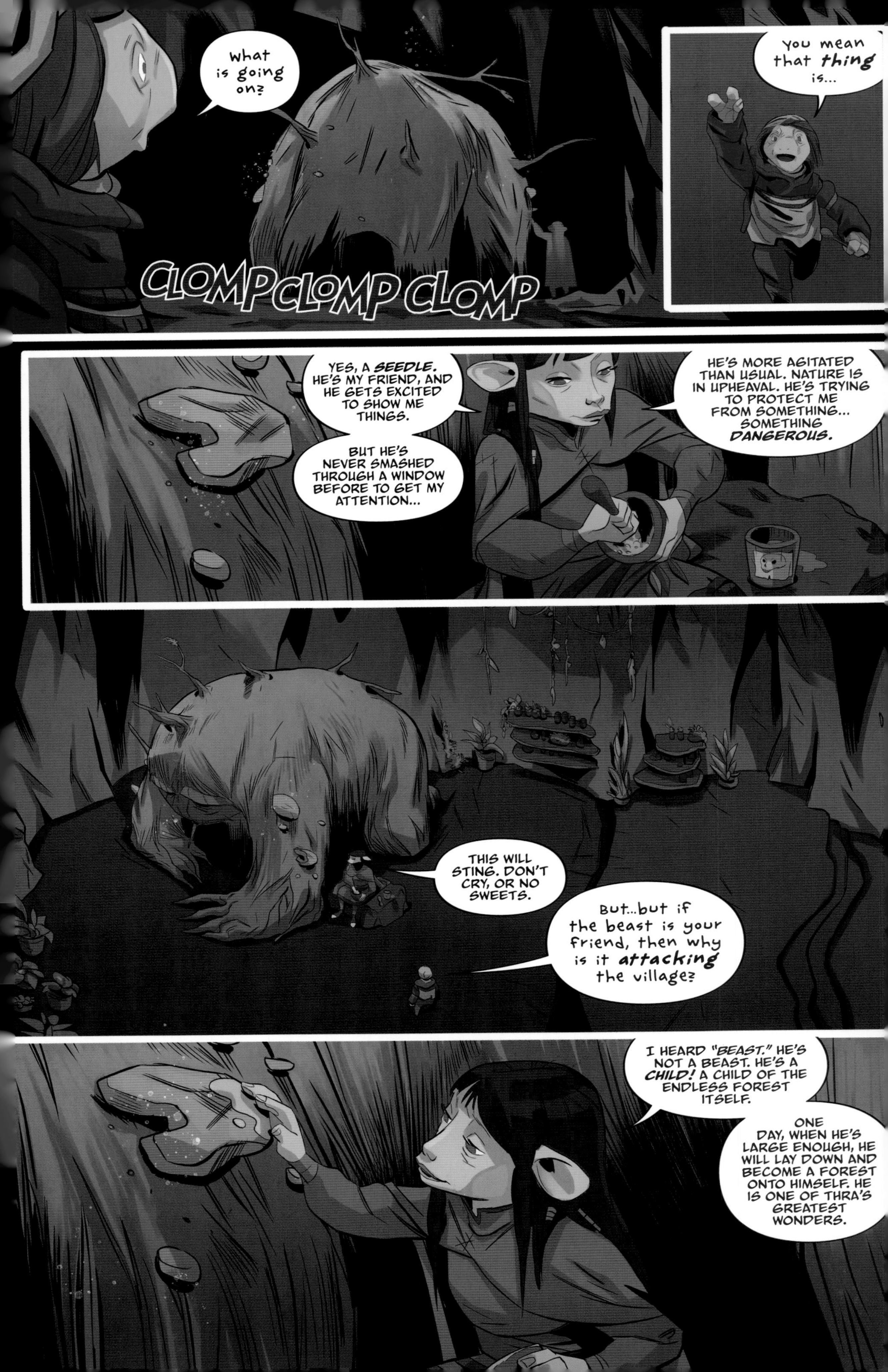
What is going on?
CLOMP CLOMP CLOMP
You mean that thing is...
YES, A SEEDLE. HE'S MY FRIEND, AND HE GETS EXCITED TO SHOW ME THINGS.
BUT HE'S NEVER SMASHED THROUGH A WINDOW BEFORE TO GET MY ATTENTION...
HE'S MORE AGITATED THAN USUAL. NATURE IS IN UPHEAVAL. HE'S TRYING TO PROTECT ME FROM SOMETHING... SOMETHING DANGEROUS.
THIS WILL STING. DON'T CRY, OR NO SWEETS.
But...but if the beast is your friend, then why is it attacking the village?
I HEARD "BEAST." HE'S NOT A BEAST. HE'S A CHILD! A CHILD OF THE ENDLESS FOREST ITSELF.
ONE DAY, WHEN HE'S LARGE ENOUGH, HE WILL LAY DOWN AND BECOME A FOREST ONTO HIMSELF. HE IS ONE OF THRA'S GREATEST WONDERS.

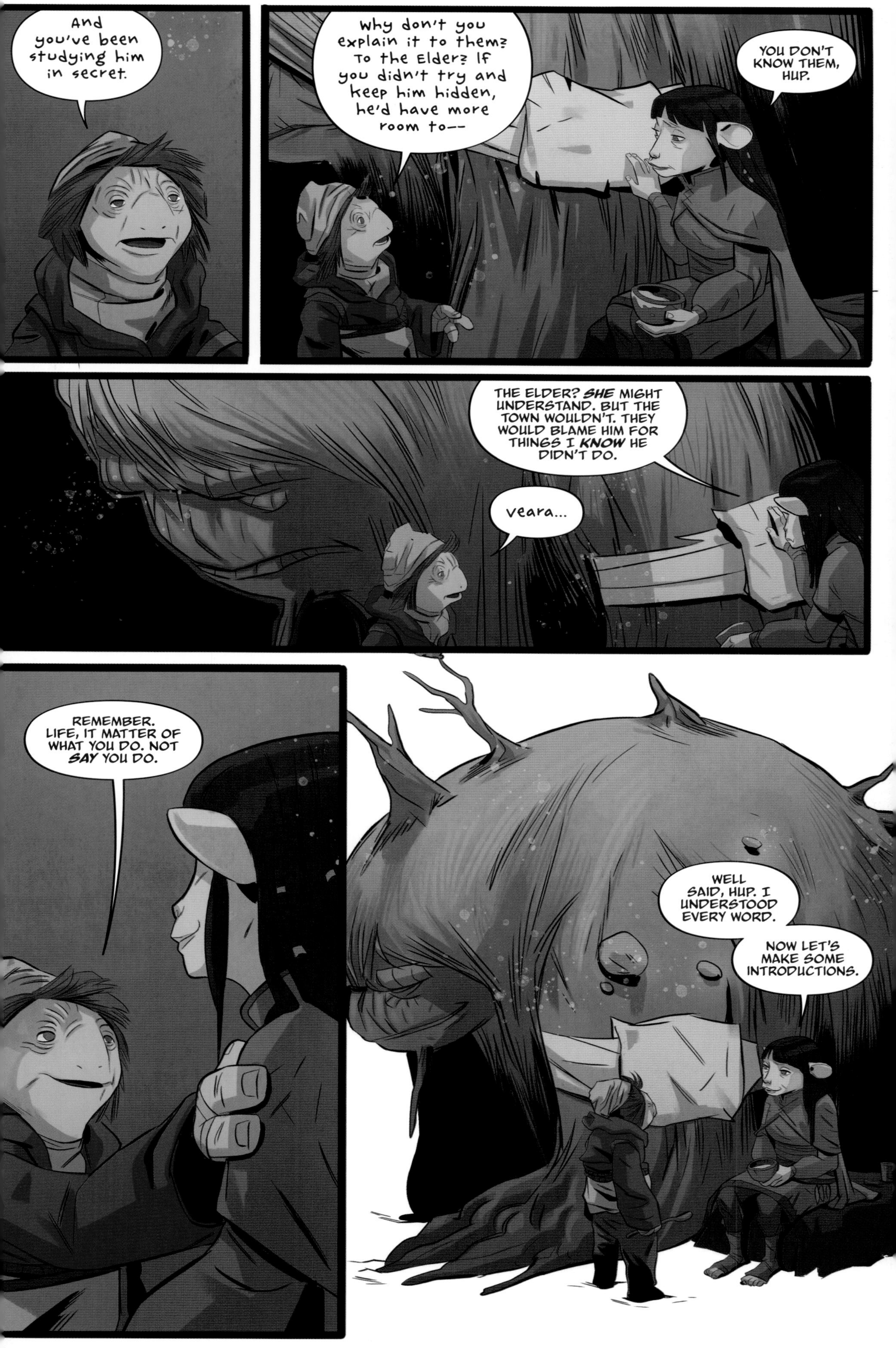
And you've been studying him in secret.
Why don't you explain it to them? To the Elder? If you didn't try and keep him hidden, he'd have more room to--
YOU DON'T KNOW THEM, HUP.
THE ELDER? SHE MIGHT UNDERSTAND. BUT THE TOWN WOULDN'T. THEY WOULD BLAME HIM FOR THINGS I KNOW HE DIDN'T DO.
Veara...
REMEMBER. LIFE, IT MATTER OF WHAT YOU DO. NOT SAY YOU DO.
WELL SAID, HUP. I UNDERSTOOD EVERY WORD.
NOW LET'S MAKE SOME INTRODUCTIONS.

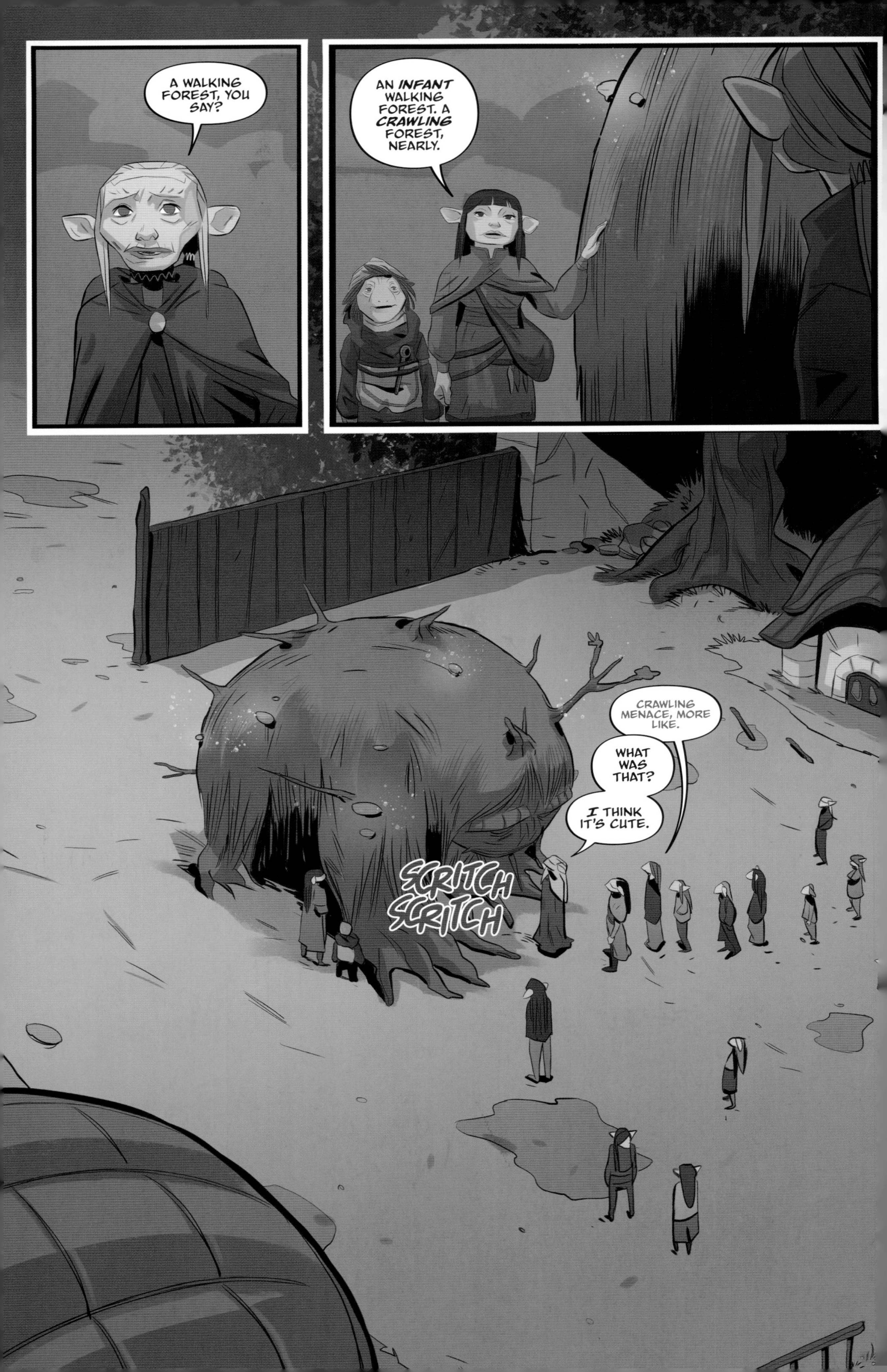
A WALKING FOREST, YOU SAY?
AN INFANT WALKING FOREST. A CRAWLING FOREST, NEARLY.
CRAWLING MENACE, MORE LIKE.
WHAT WAS THAT?
I THINK IT'S CUTE.
SCRITCH SCRITCH

FRANKLY, ELDER, *YOU* WEREN'T THE ONE CHEWED UP. *YOUR* FARM WASN'T DESTROYED.

chewed? chewed!

I CARE FOR EVERYONE IN THIS TOWN, BUT THE SEEDLE IS--

WHAT?!

veara! veara!

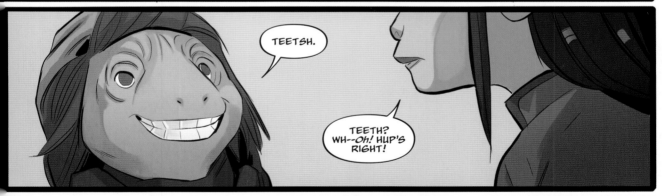

TEETSH.

TEETH? WH--*OH!* HUP'S RIGHT!

THE SEEDLE'S TEETH ARE TOO LARGE AND TOO BLUNT TO HAVE MADE THE BITEMARKS I DRESSED.

THEN--

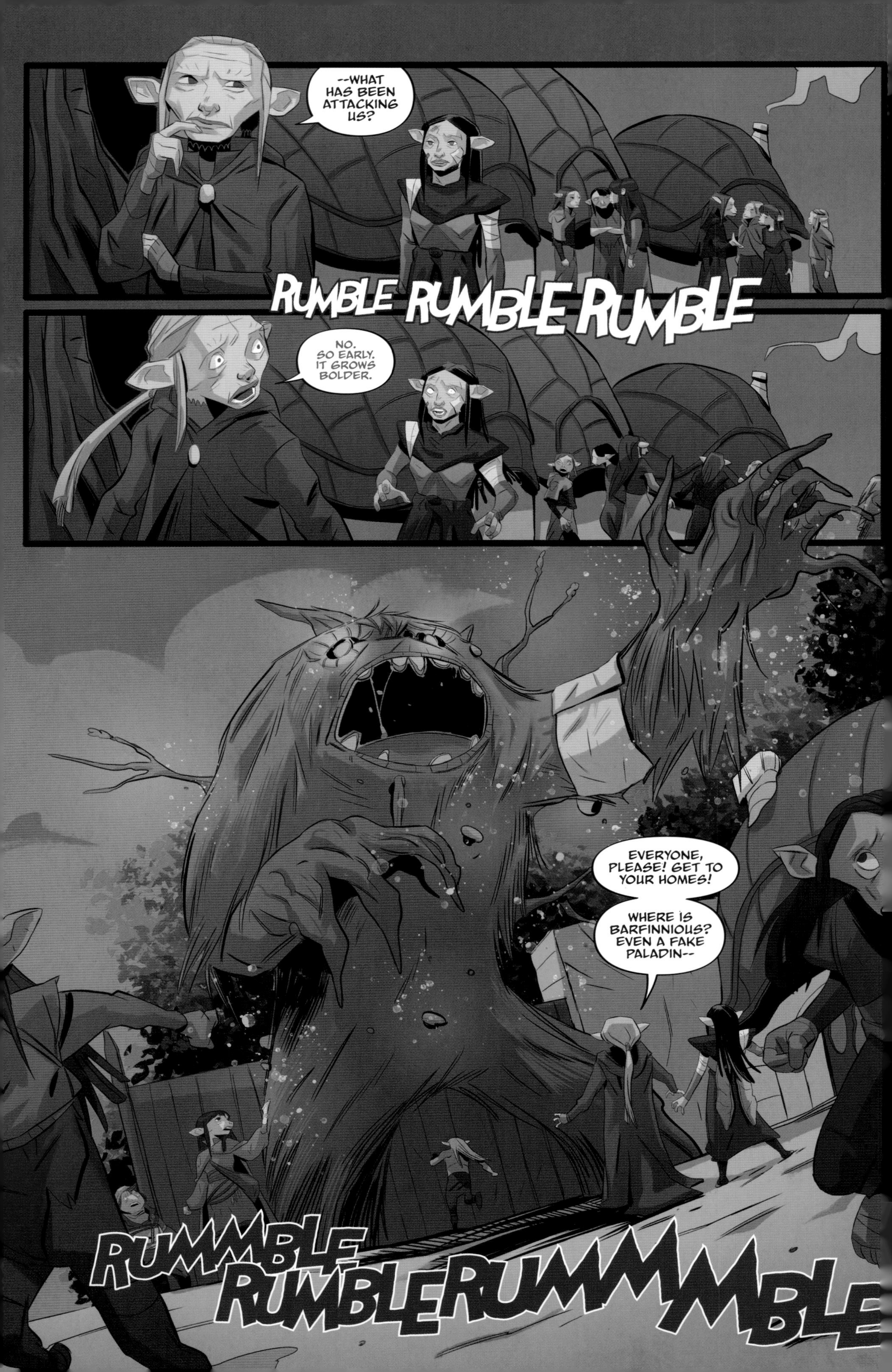
--WHAT HAS BEEN ATTACKING US?
RUMBLE RUMBLE RUMBLE
NO. SO EARLY. IT GROWS BOLDER.
EVERYONE, PLEASE! GET TO YOUR HOMES!
WHERE IS BARFINNIOUS? EVEN A FAKE PALADIN--
RUMMBLE RUMBLE RUMMMBLE

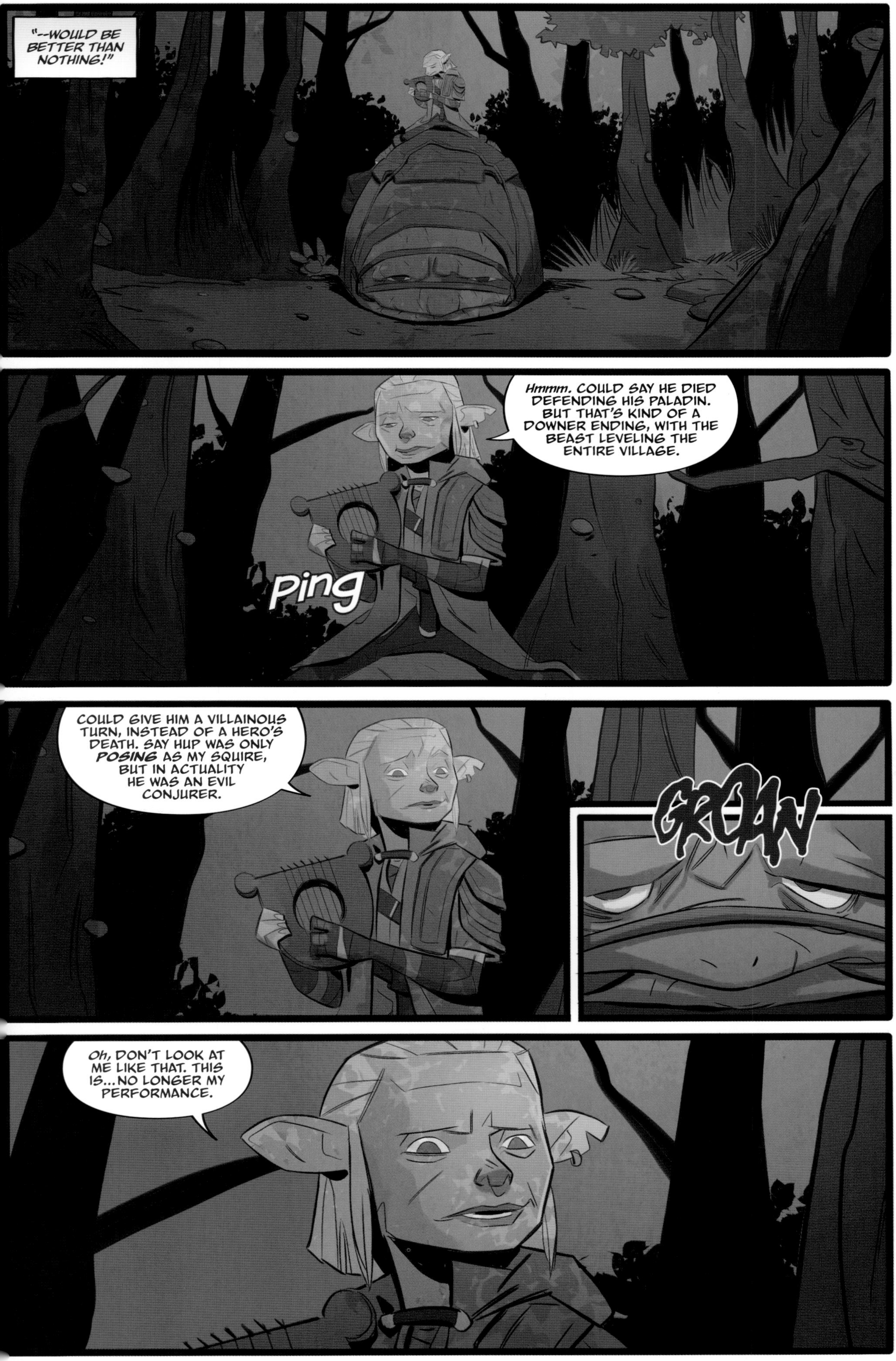
"--WOULD BE BETTER THAN NOTHING!"
Hmmm. COULD SAY HE DIED DEFENDING HIS PALADIN. BUT THAT'S KIND OF A DOWNER ENDING, WITH THE BEAST LEVELING THE ENTIRE VILLAGE.
PING
COULD GIVE HIM A VILLAINOUS TURN, INSTEAD OF A HERO'S DEATH. SAY HUP WAS ONLY POSING AS MY SQUIRE, BUT IN ACTUALITY HE WAS AN EVIL CONJURER.
GROAN
Oh, DON'T LOOK AT ME LIKE THAT. THIS IS...NO LONGER MY PERFORMANCE.

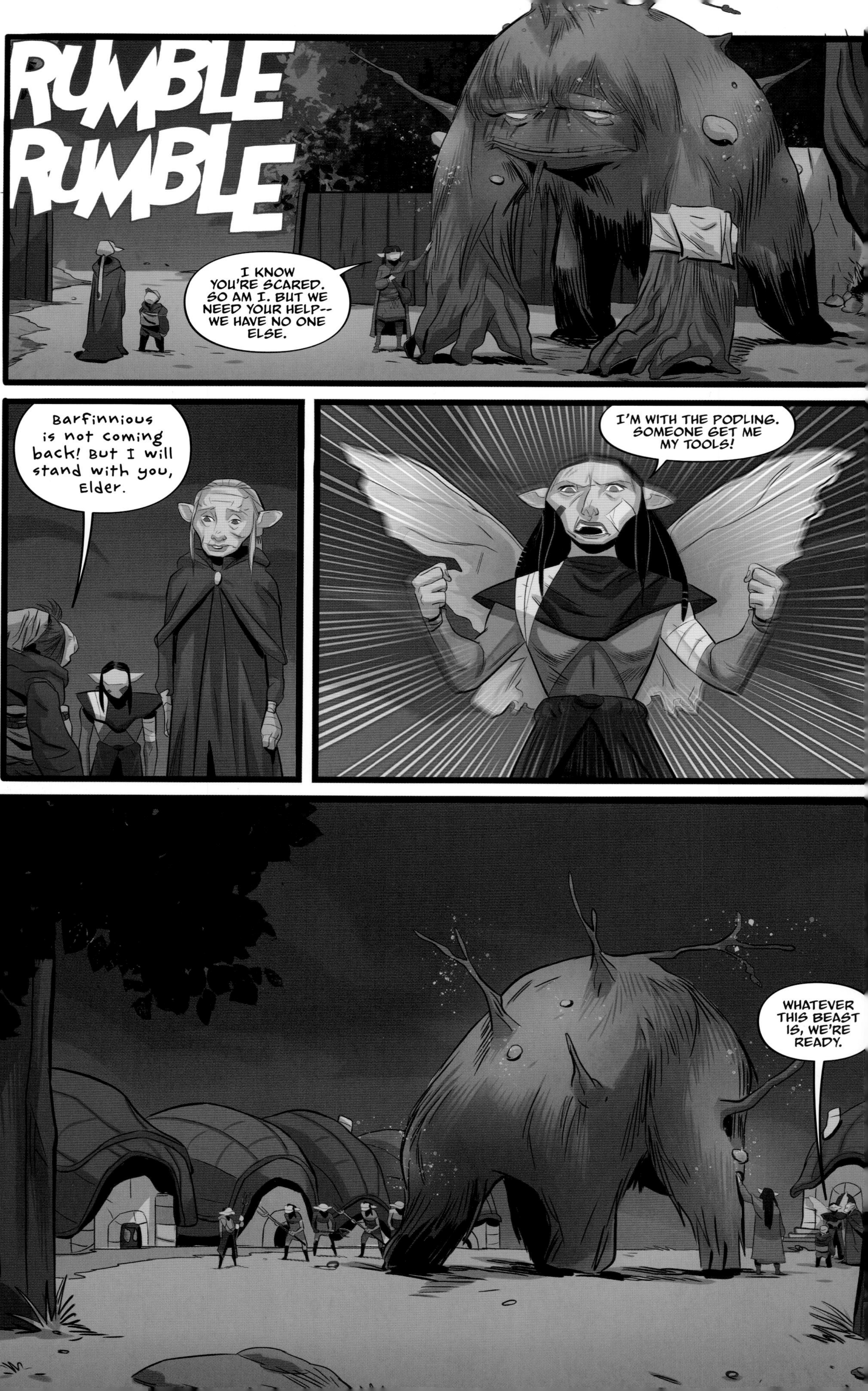
RUMBLE RUMBLE
I KNOW YOU'RE SCARED. SO AM I. BUT WE NEED YOUR HELP-- WE HAVE NO ONE ELSE.
Barfinnious is not coming back! But I will stand with you, Elder.
I'M WITH THE PODLING. SOMEONE GET ME MY TOOLS!
WHATEVER THIS BEAST IS, WE'RE READY.

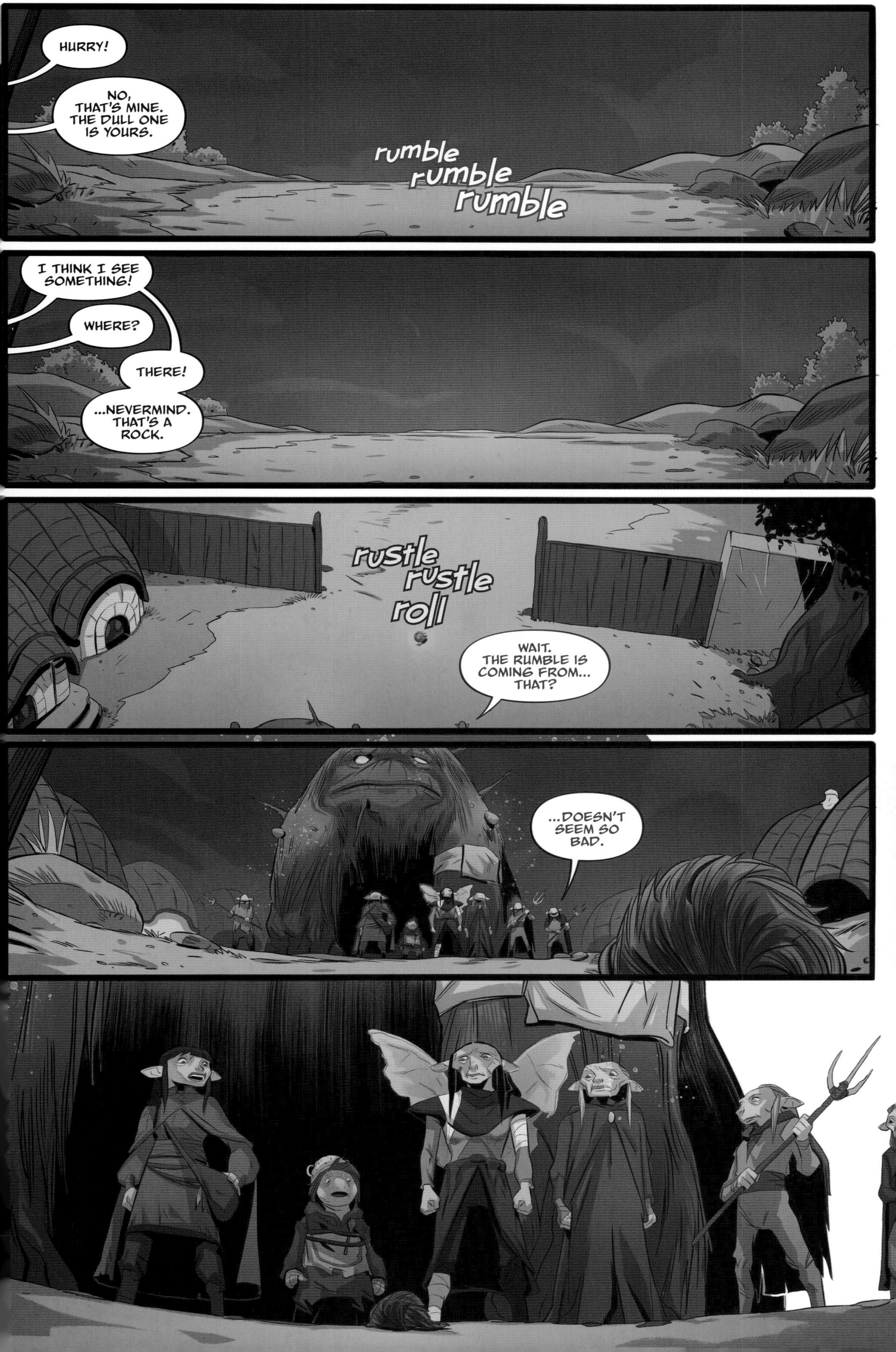
HURRY!
NO, THAT'S MINE. THE DULL ONE IS YOURS.
rumble rumble rumble
I THINK I SEE SOMETHING!
WHERE?
THERE!
...NEVERMIND. THAT'S A ROCK.
rustle rustle roll
WAIT. THE RUMBLE IS COMING FROM... THAT?
...DOESN'T SEEM SO BAD.

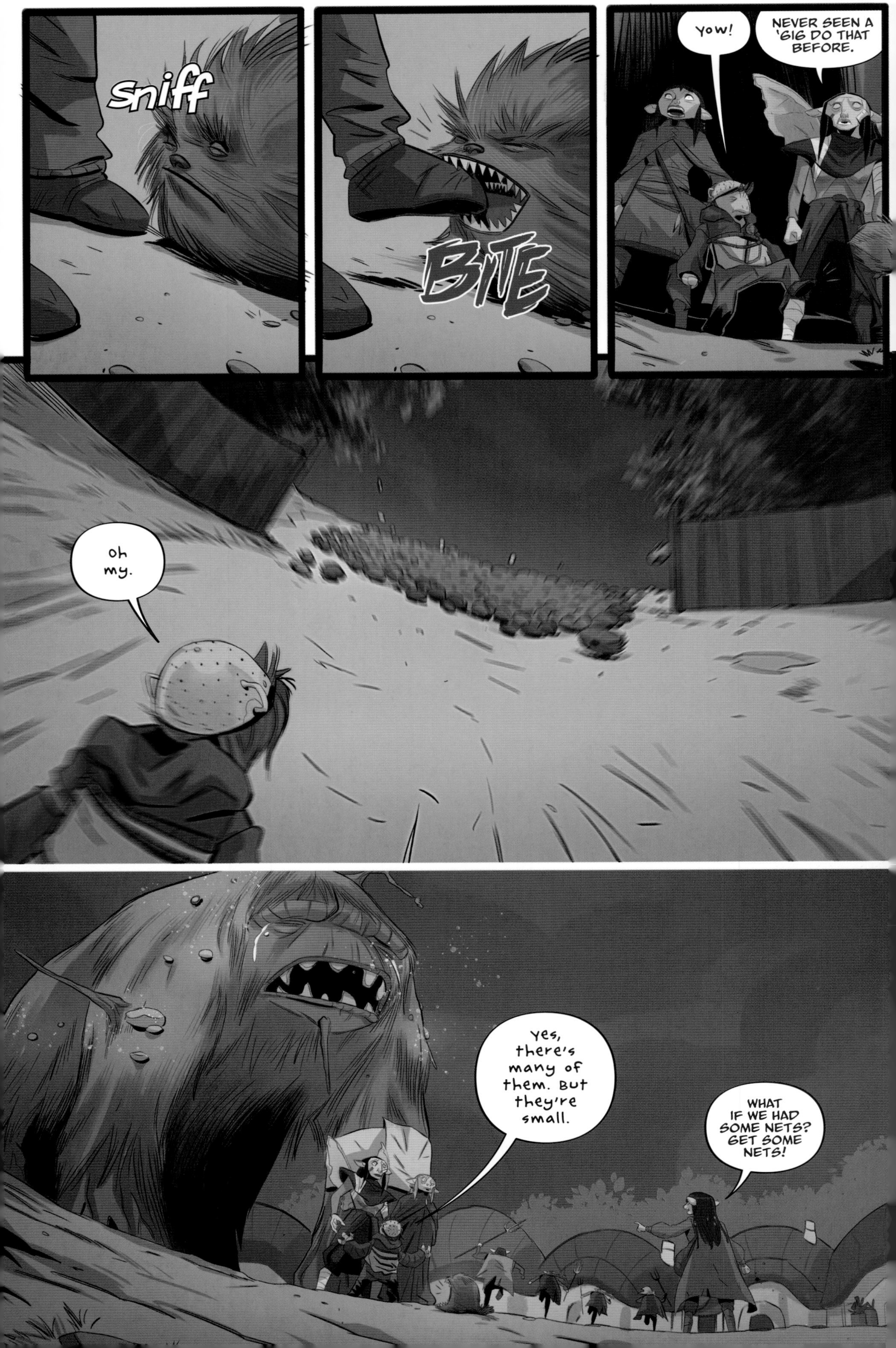

sniff
BITE
Yow!
NEVER SEEN A 'GIG DO THAT BEFORE.
oh my.
Yes, there's many of them. But they're small.
WHAT IF WE HAD SOME NETS? GET SOME NETS!

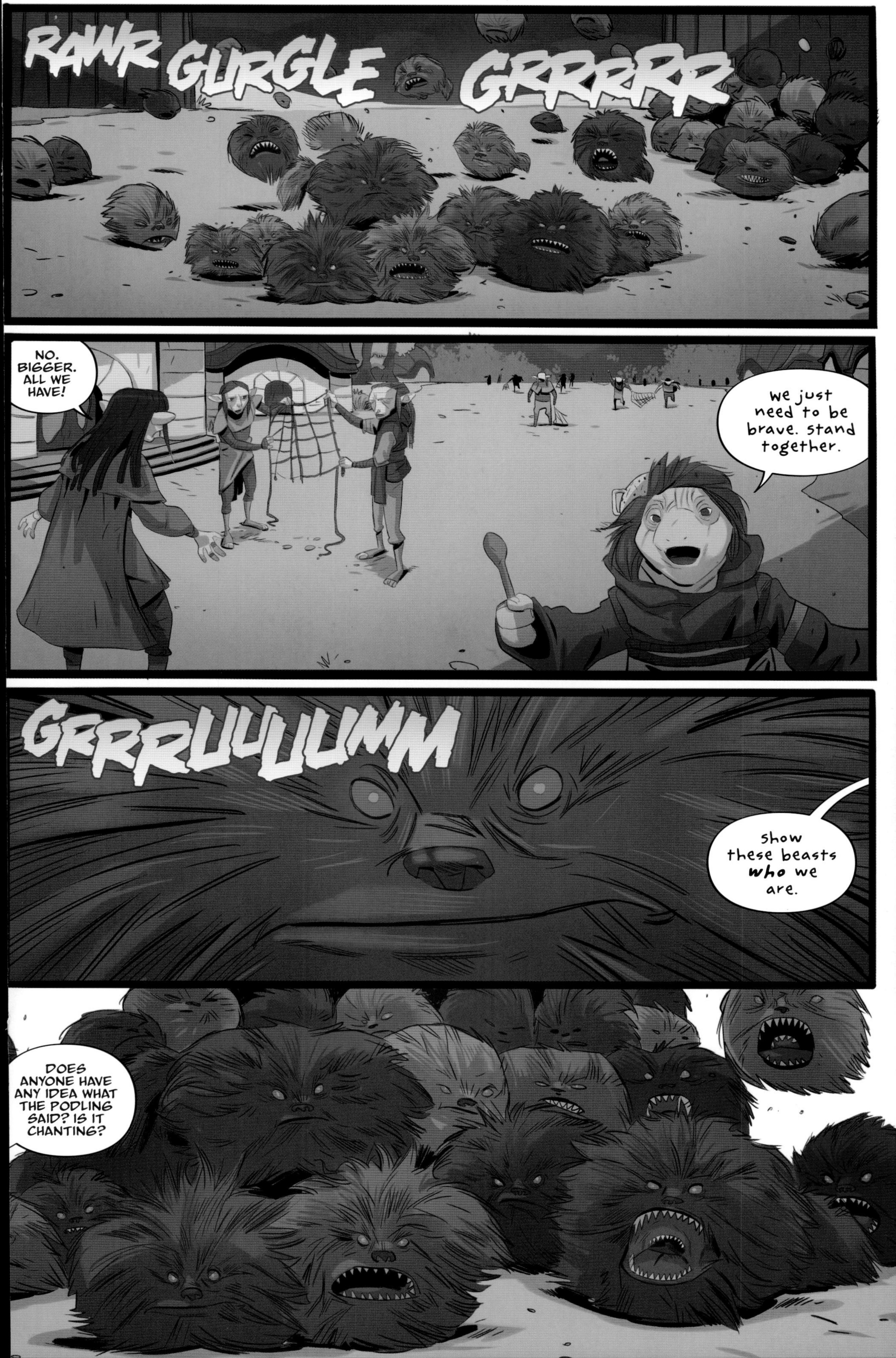
RAWR GURGLE GRRRRRR
NO. BIGGER. ALL WE HAVE!
We just need to be brave. stand together.
GRRRUUUUMM
show these beasts **who** we are.
DOES ANYONE HAVE ANY IDEA WHAT THE PODLING SAID? IS IT CHANTING?

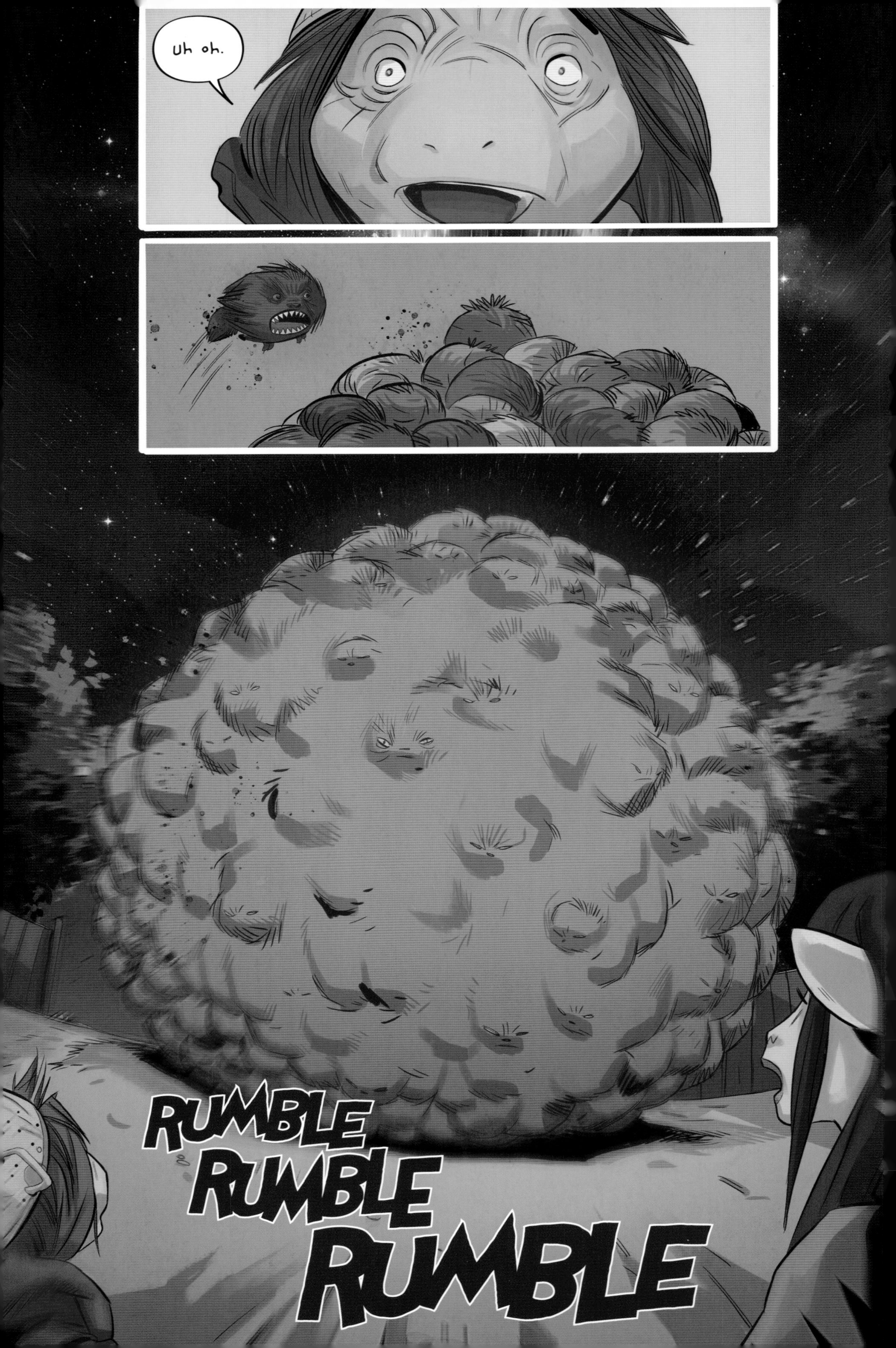
Uh oh.
RUMBLE
RUMBLE
RUMBLE

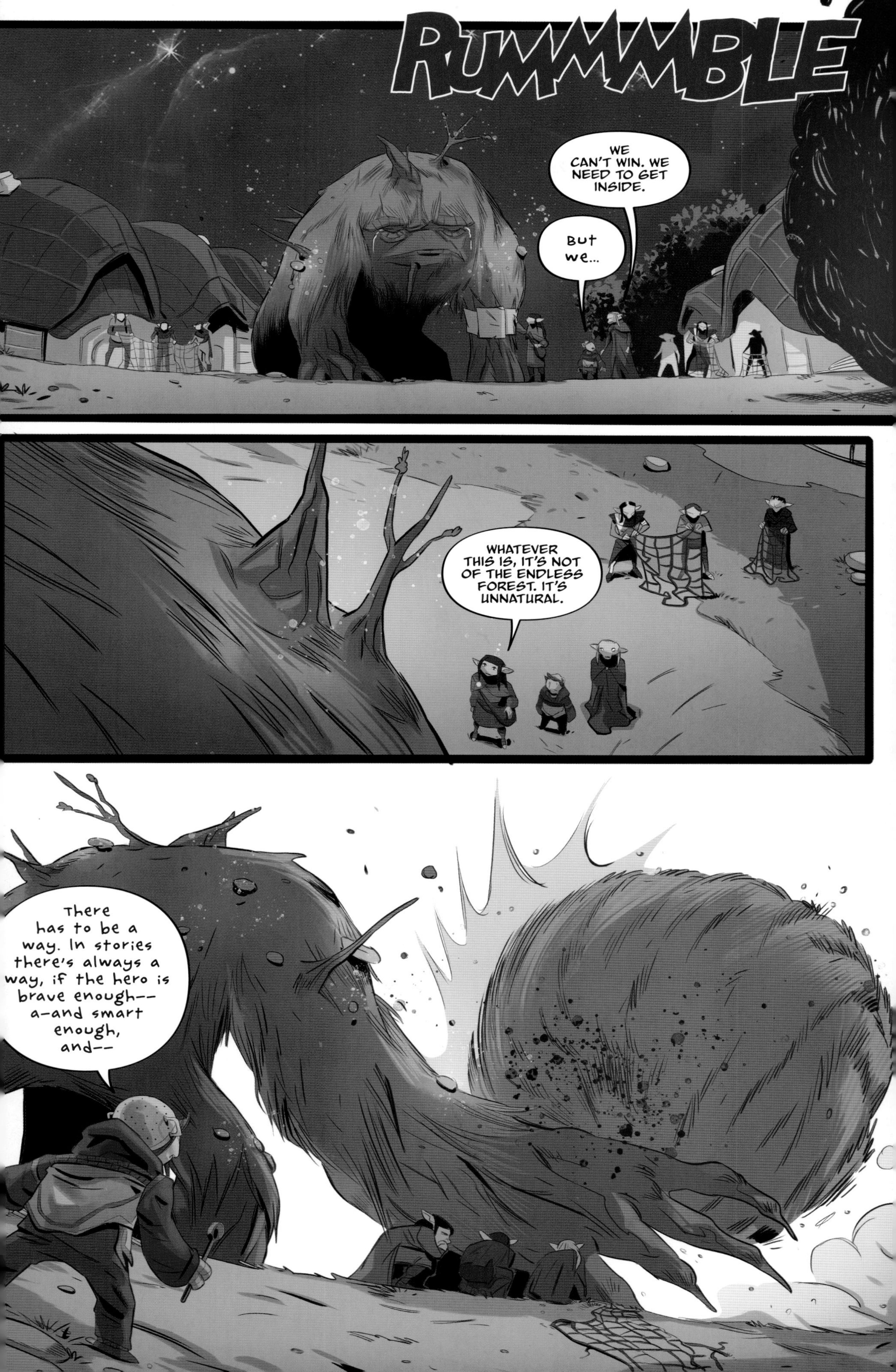
RUMMMBLE
WE CAN'T WIN. WE NEED TO GET INSIDE.
But we...
WHATEVER THIS IS, IT'S NOT OF THE ENDLESS FOREST. IT'S UNNATURAL.
There has to be a way. In stories there's always a way, if the hero is brave enough-- a-and smart enough, and--

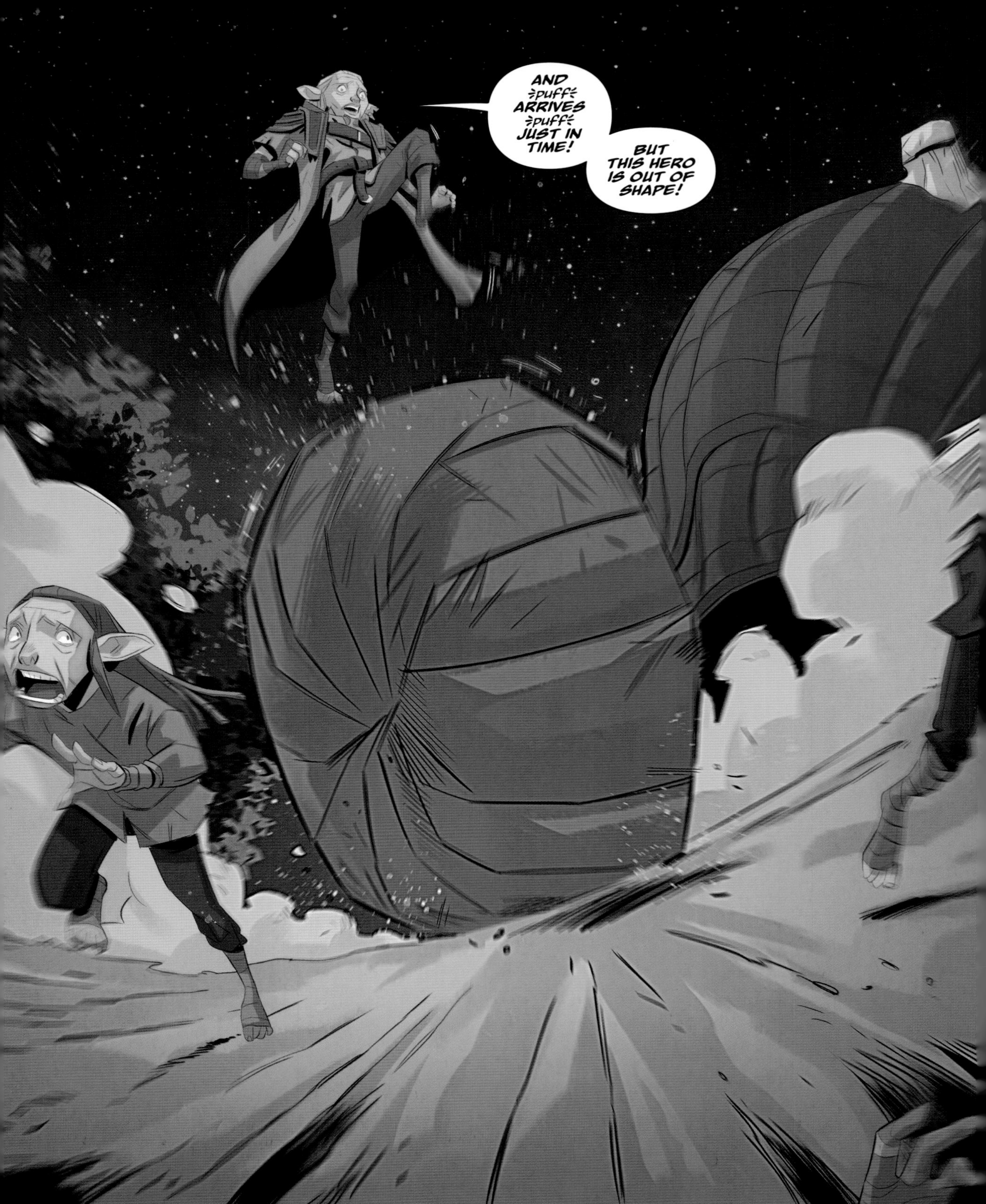
AND ≈puff≈ ARRIVES ≈puff≈ JUST IN TIME!
BUT THIS HERO IS OUT OF SHAPE!

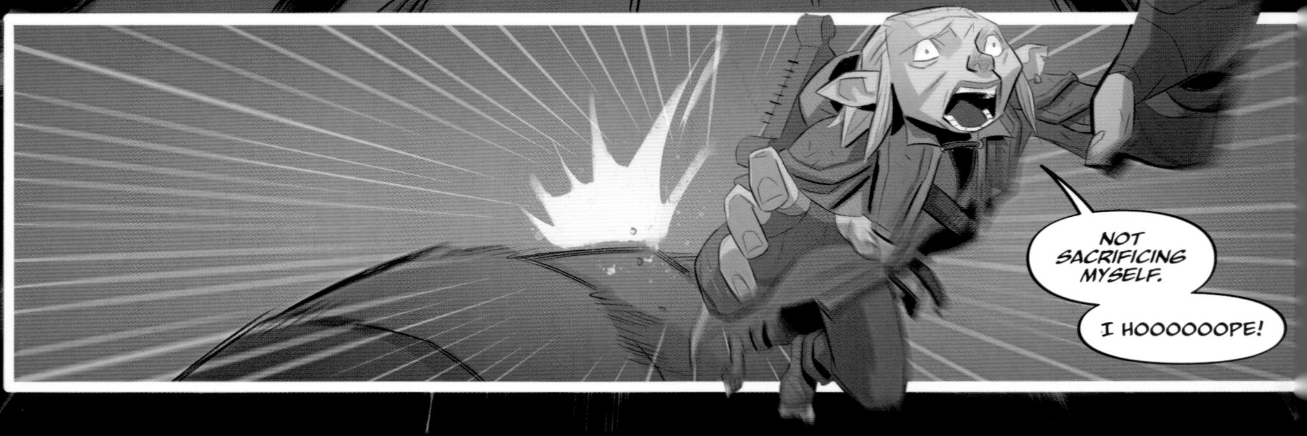
NOT SACRIFICING MYSELF.
I HOOOOOOPE!

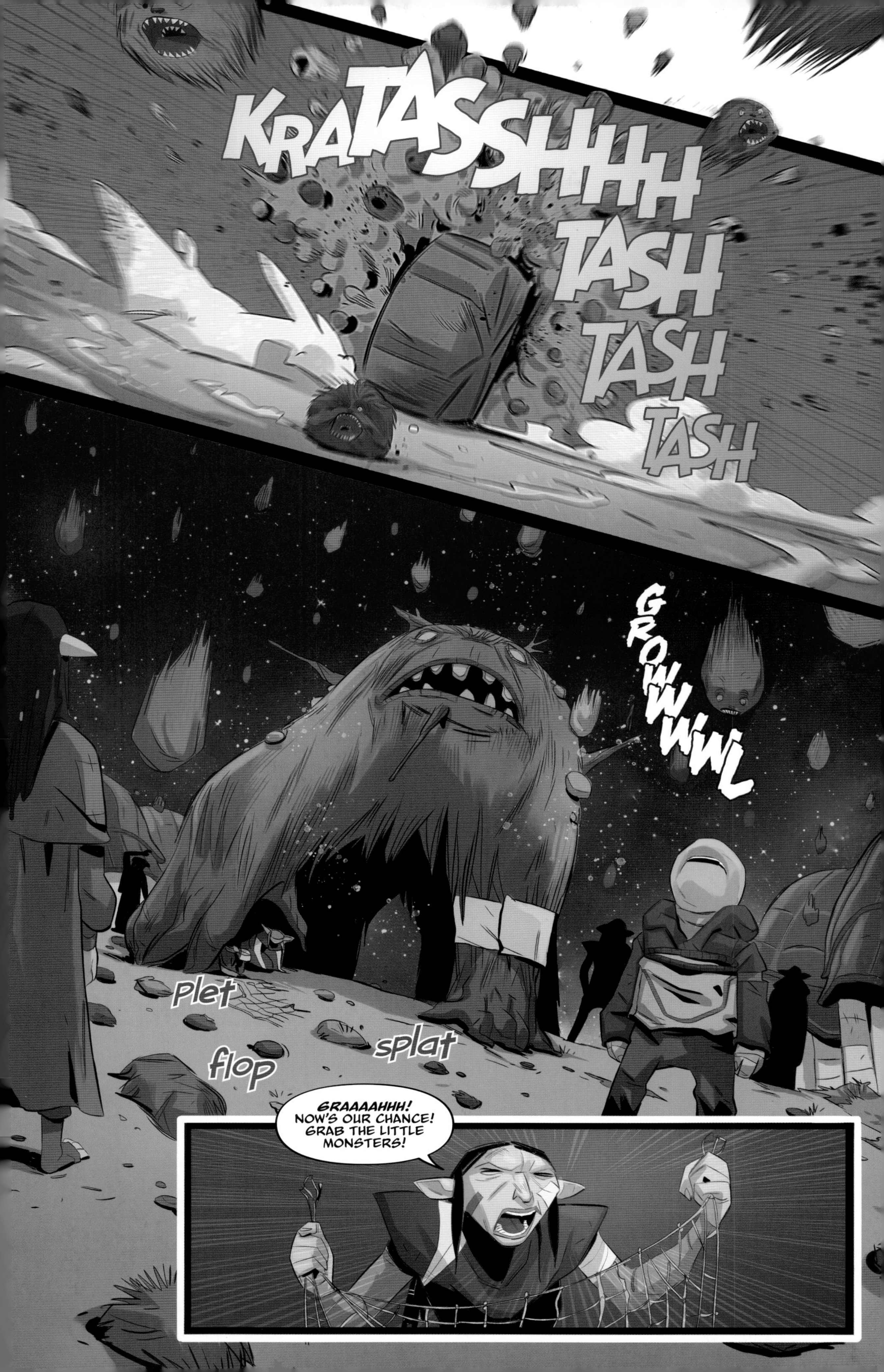
KRATASSHHHH
TASH
TASH
TASH
GROWWWL
plet
flop
splat
GRAAAAHHH! NOW'S OUR CHANCE! GRAB THE LITTLE MONSTERS!

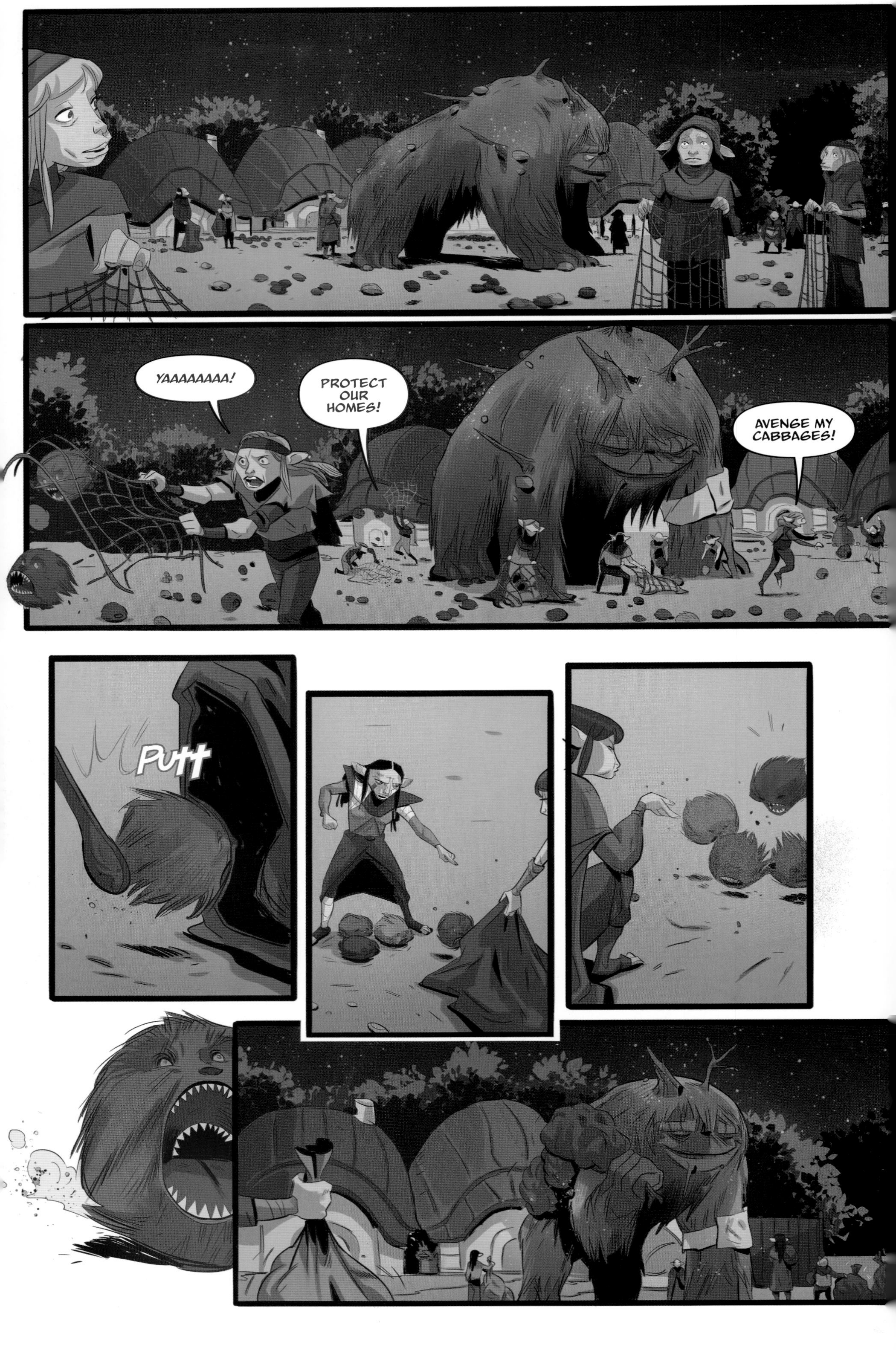
YAAAAAAAA!
PROTECT OUR HOMES!
AVENGE MY CABBAGES!
PUTT

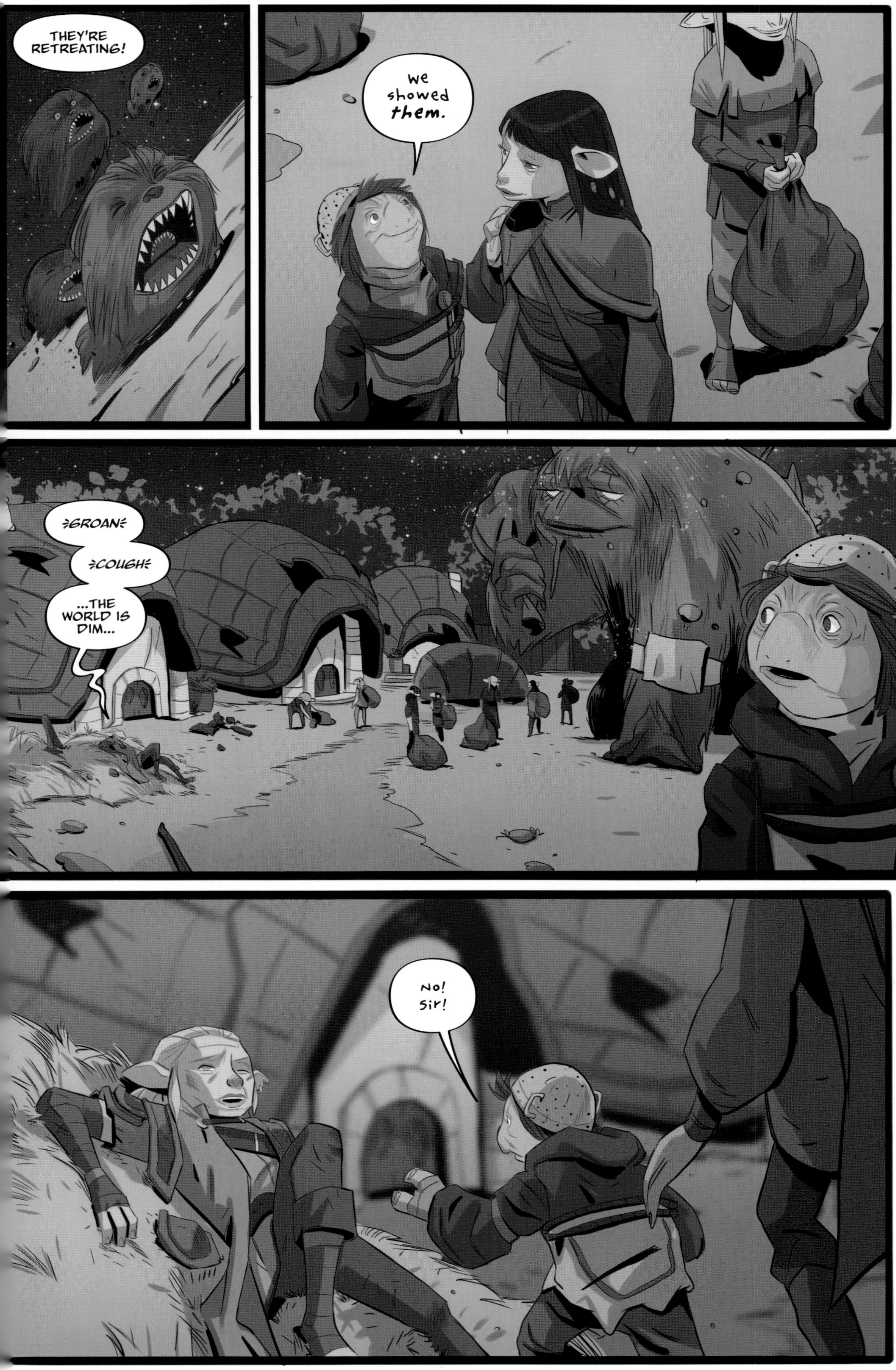
THEY'RE RETREATING!
we showed them.
GROAN
COUGH
...THE WORLD IS DIM...
No! Sir!

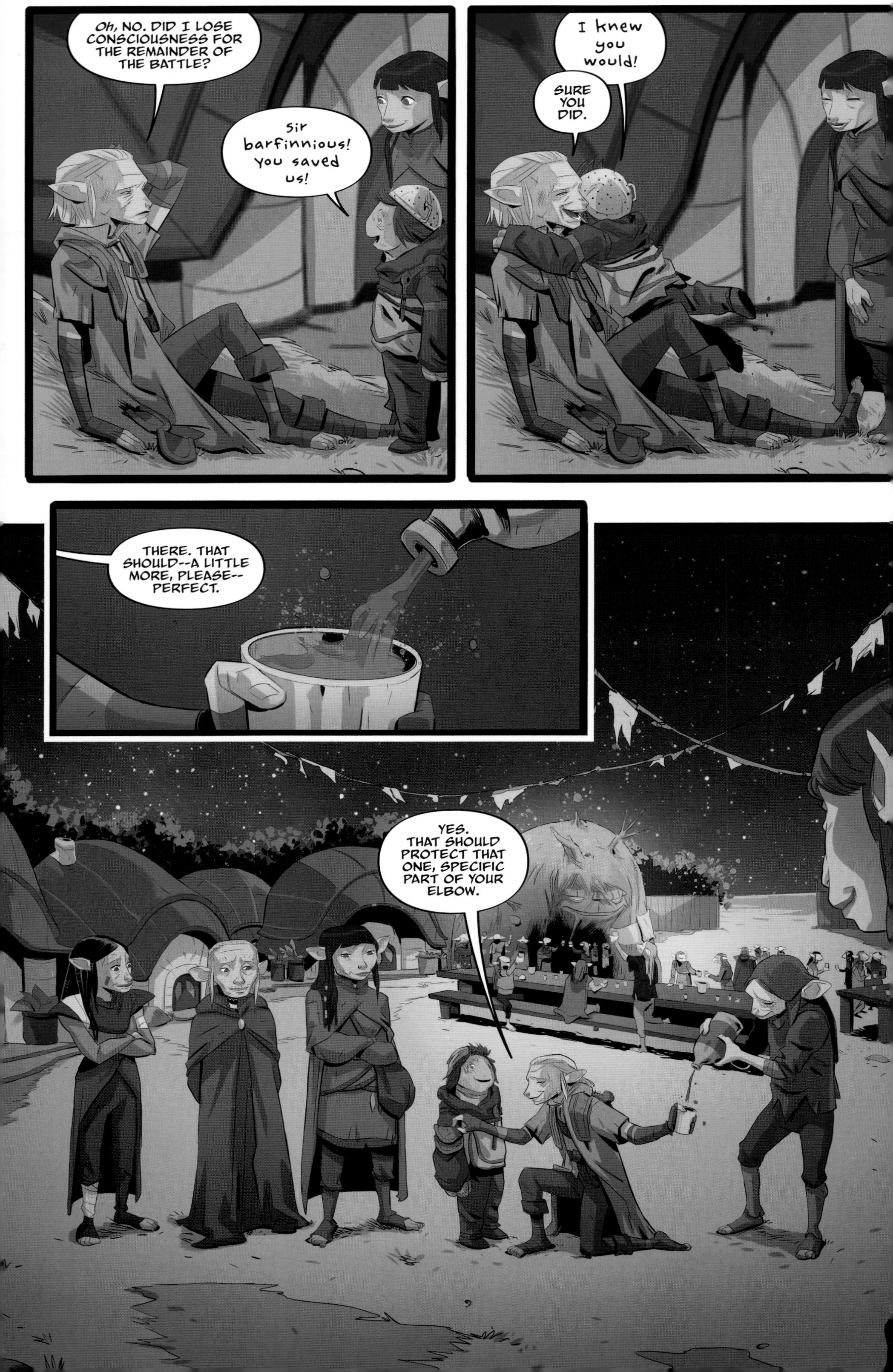
Oh, NO. DID I LOSE CONSCIOUSNESS FOR THE REMAINDER OF THE BATTLE?
sir barfinnious! you saved us!
I knew you would!
SURE YOU DID.
THERE. THAT SHOULD--A LITTLE MORE, PLEASE--PERFECT.
YES. THAT SHOULD PROTECT THAT ONE, SPECIFIC PART OF YOUR ELBOW.

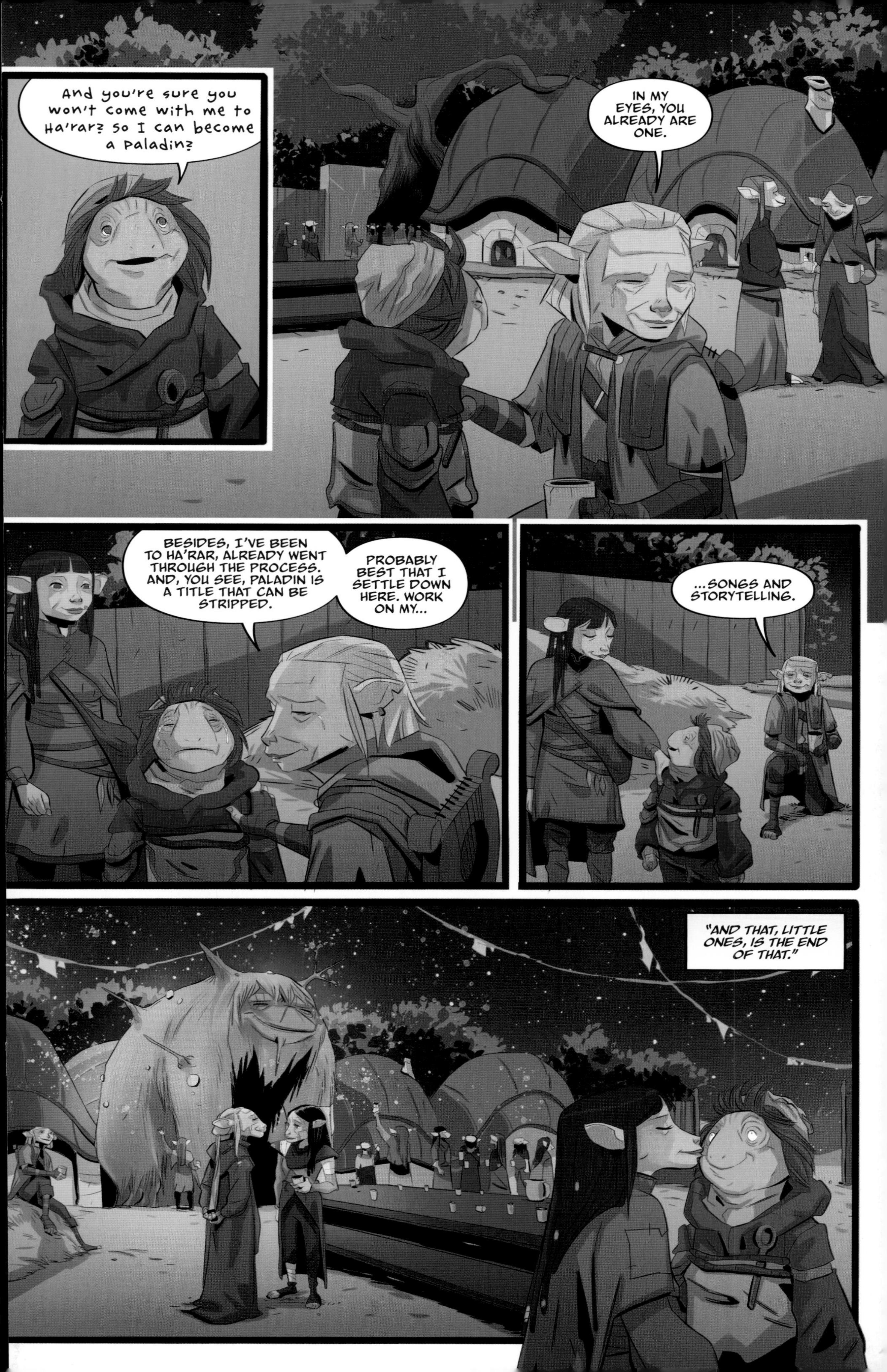
And you're sure you won't come with me to Ha'rar? So I can become a Paladin?
IN MY EYES, YOU ALREADY ARE ONE.
BESIDES, I'VE BEEN TO HA'RAR, ALREADY WENT THROUGH THE PROCESS. AND, YOU SEE, PALADIN IS A TITLE THAT CAN BE STRIPPED.
PROBABLY BEST THAT I SETTLE DOWN HERE. WORK ON MY...
...SONGS AND STORYTELLING.
"AND THAT, LITTLE ONES, IS THE END OF THAT."

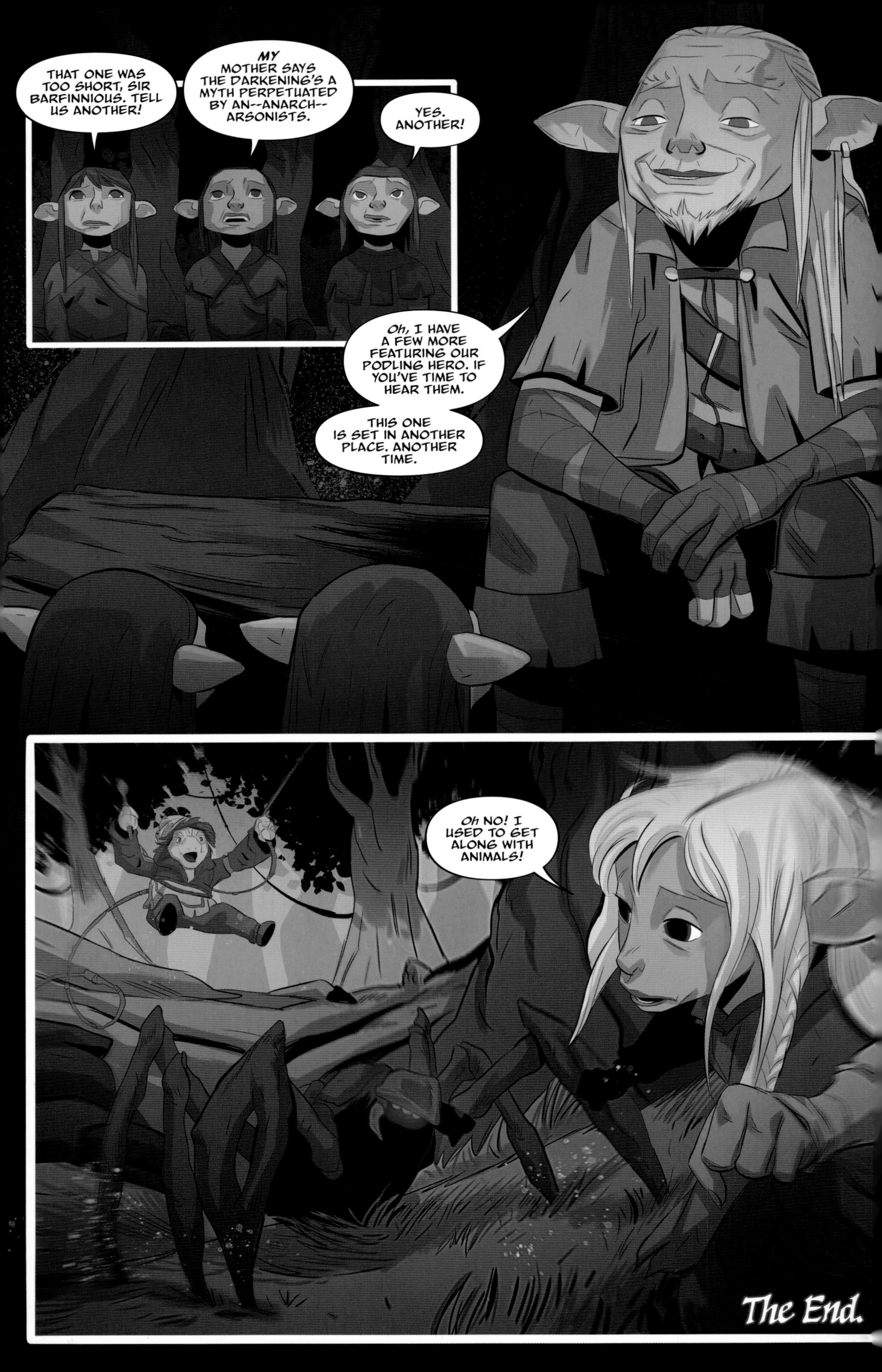
THAT ONE WAS TOO SHORT, SIR BARFINNIOUS. TELL US ANOTHER!
MY MOTHER SAYS THE DARKENING'S A MYTH PERPETUATED BY AN--ANARCH--ARSONISTS.
YES. ANOTHER!
Oh, I HAVE A FEW MORE FEATURING OUR PODLING HERO. IF YOU'VE TIME TO HEAR THEM.
THIS ONE IS SET IN ANOTHER PLACE. ANOTHER TIME.
Oh NO! I USED TO GET ALONG WITH ANIMALS!
The End.

COVER GALLERY

Issues Five-Eight Preorder Connecting Covers by
Kelly and **Nichole Matthews**

Issue Five Unlocked Retailer Variant Cover by
Christian Ward

Issue Six Unlocked Retailer Variant Cover by
David Petersen

Issue Seven Unlocked Retailer Variant Cover by
Conor Nolan

Issue Eight Unlocked Retailer Variant Cover by
Jen Bartel with **Jake Wyatt**

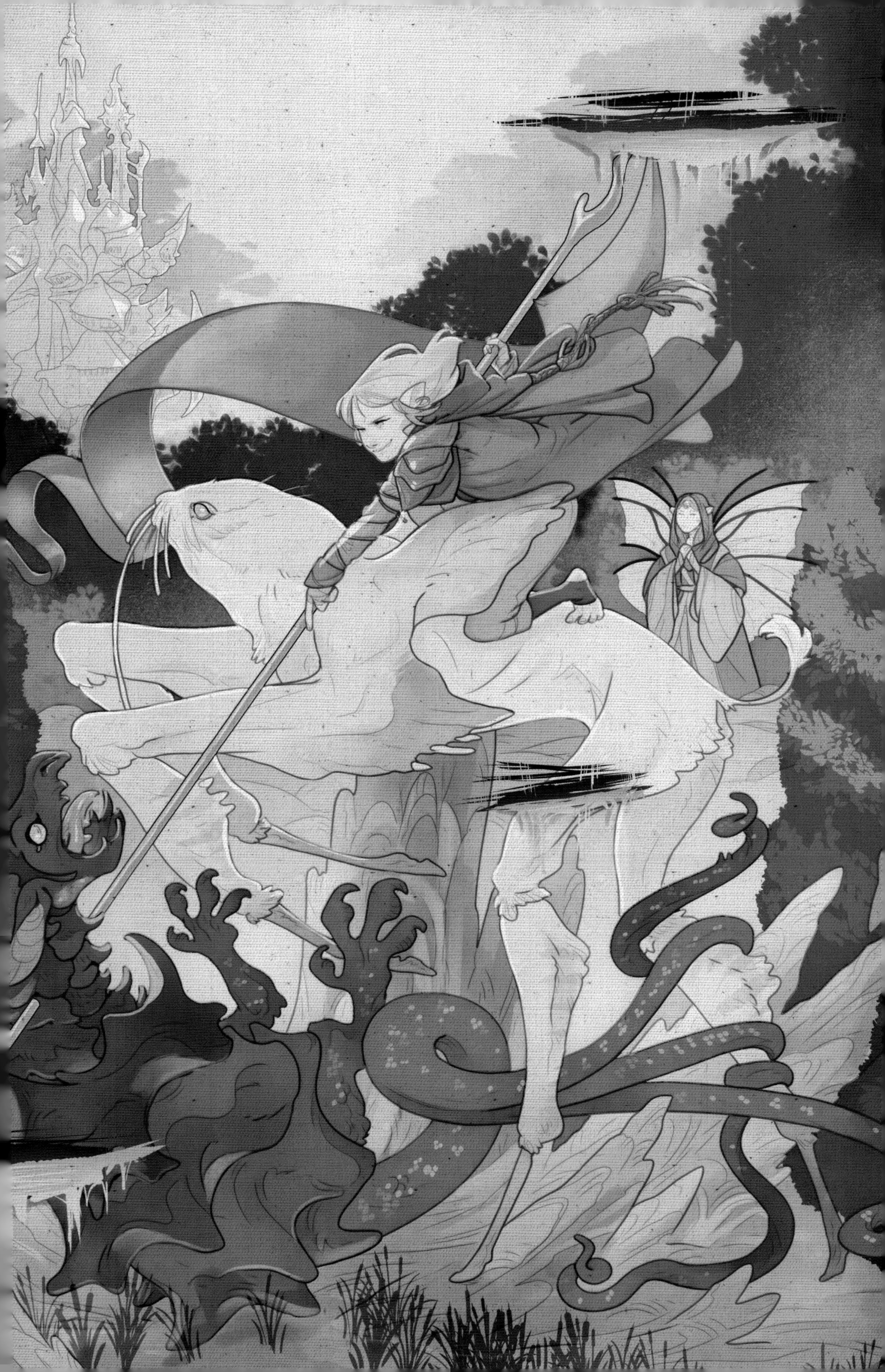

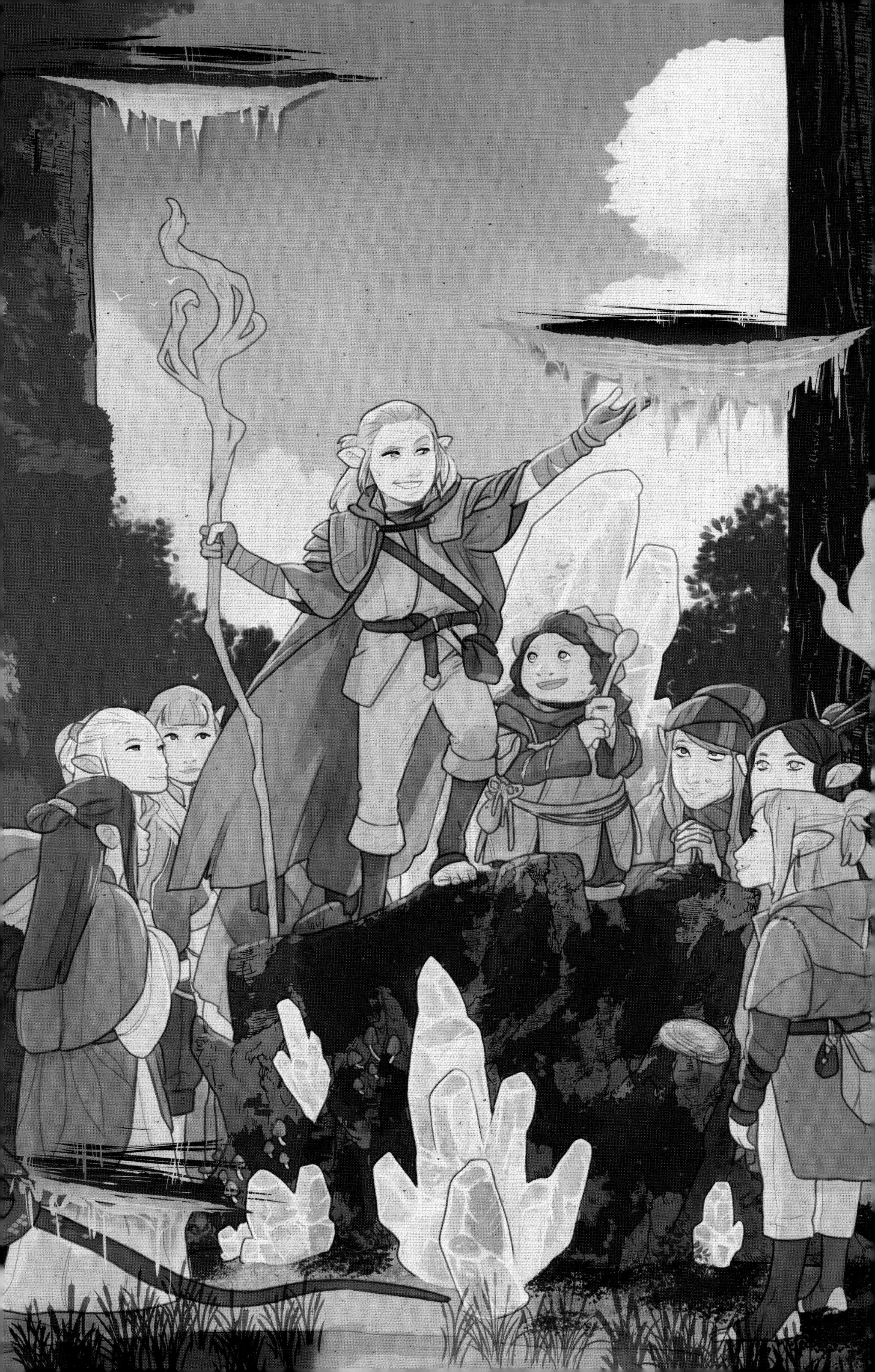

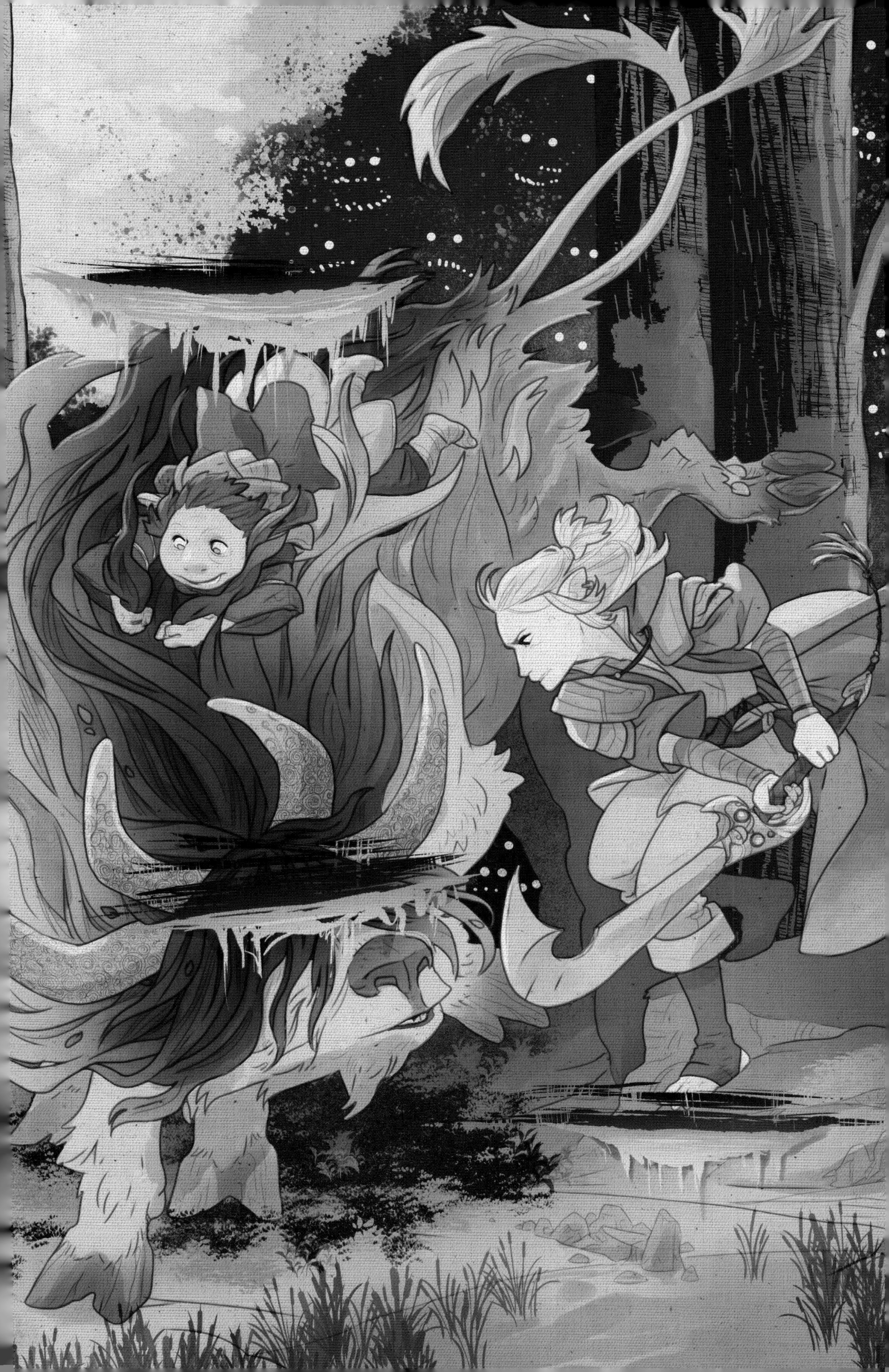

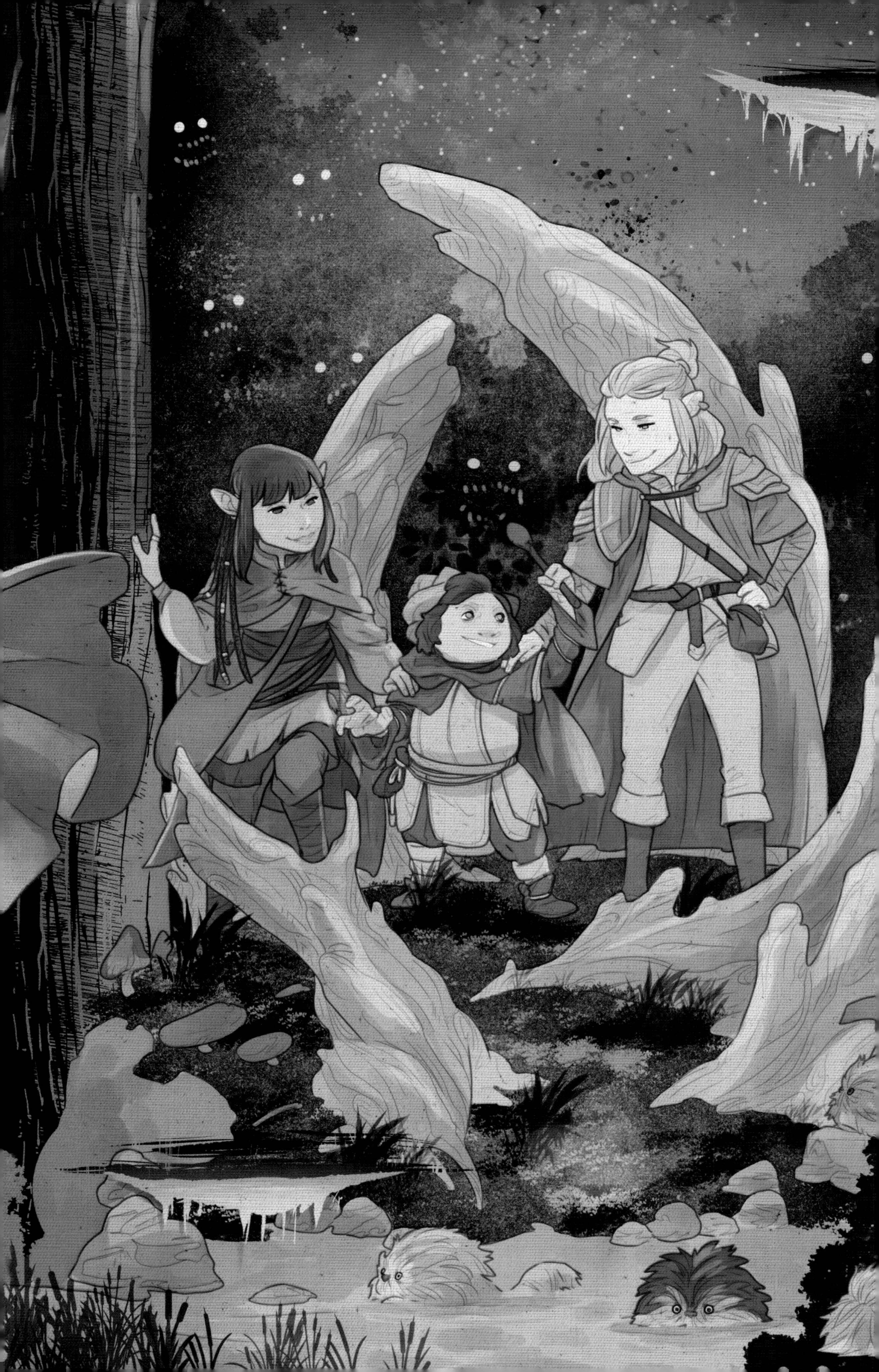

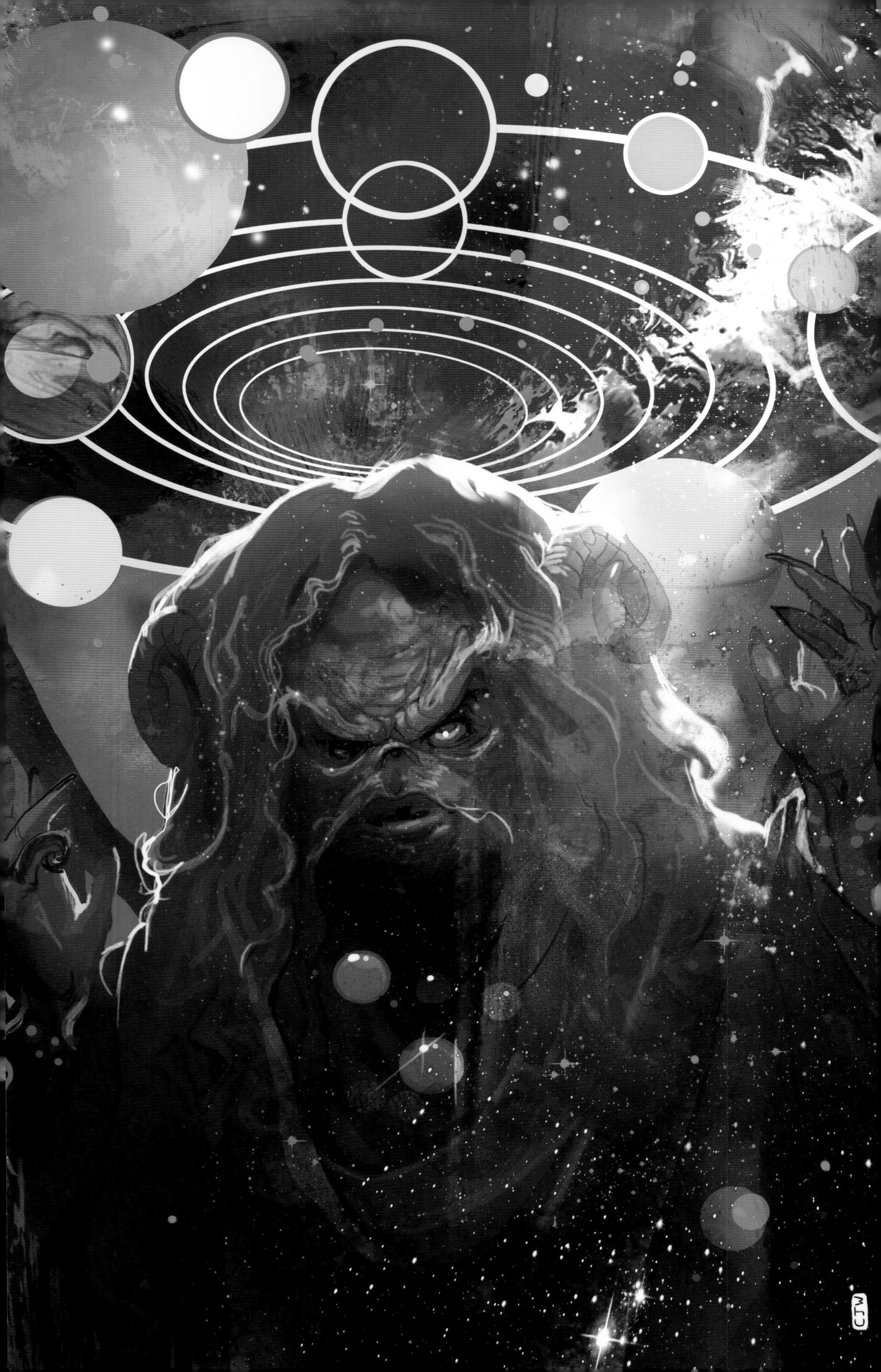

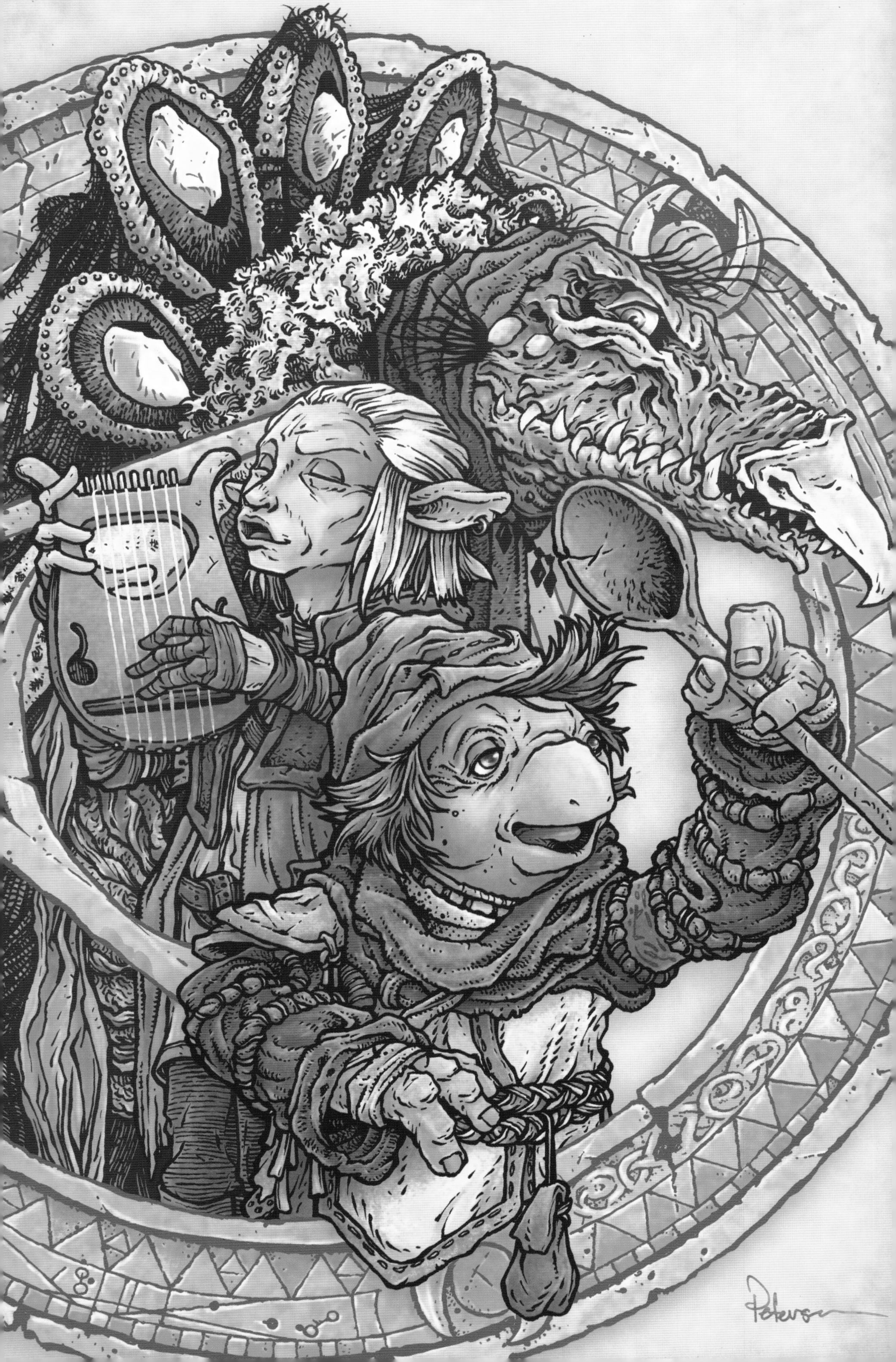

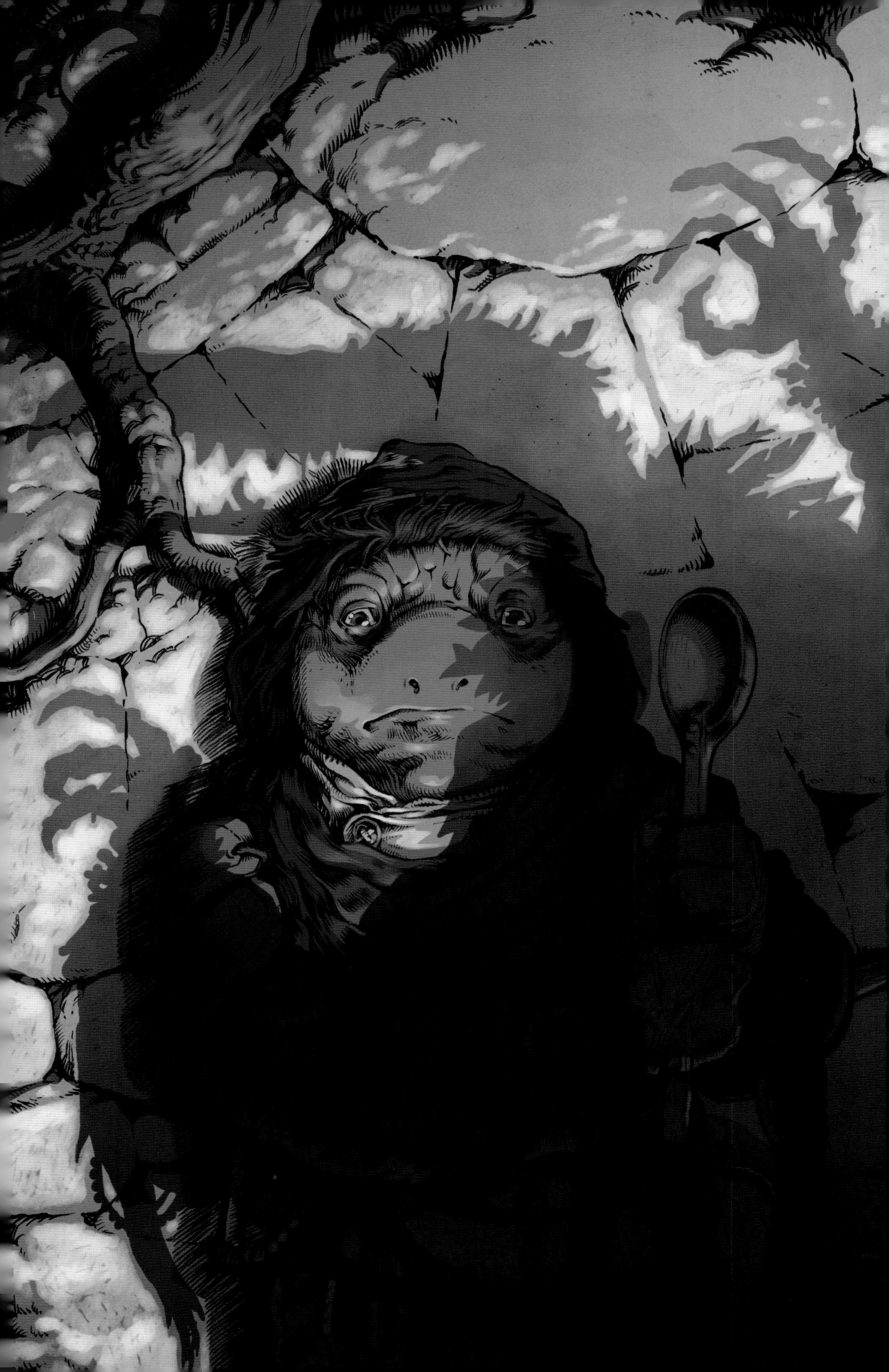

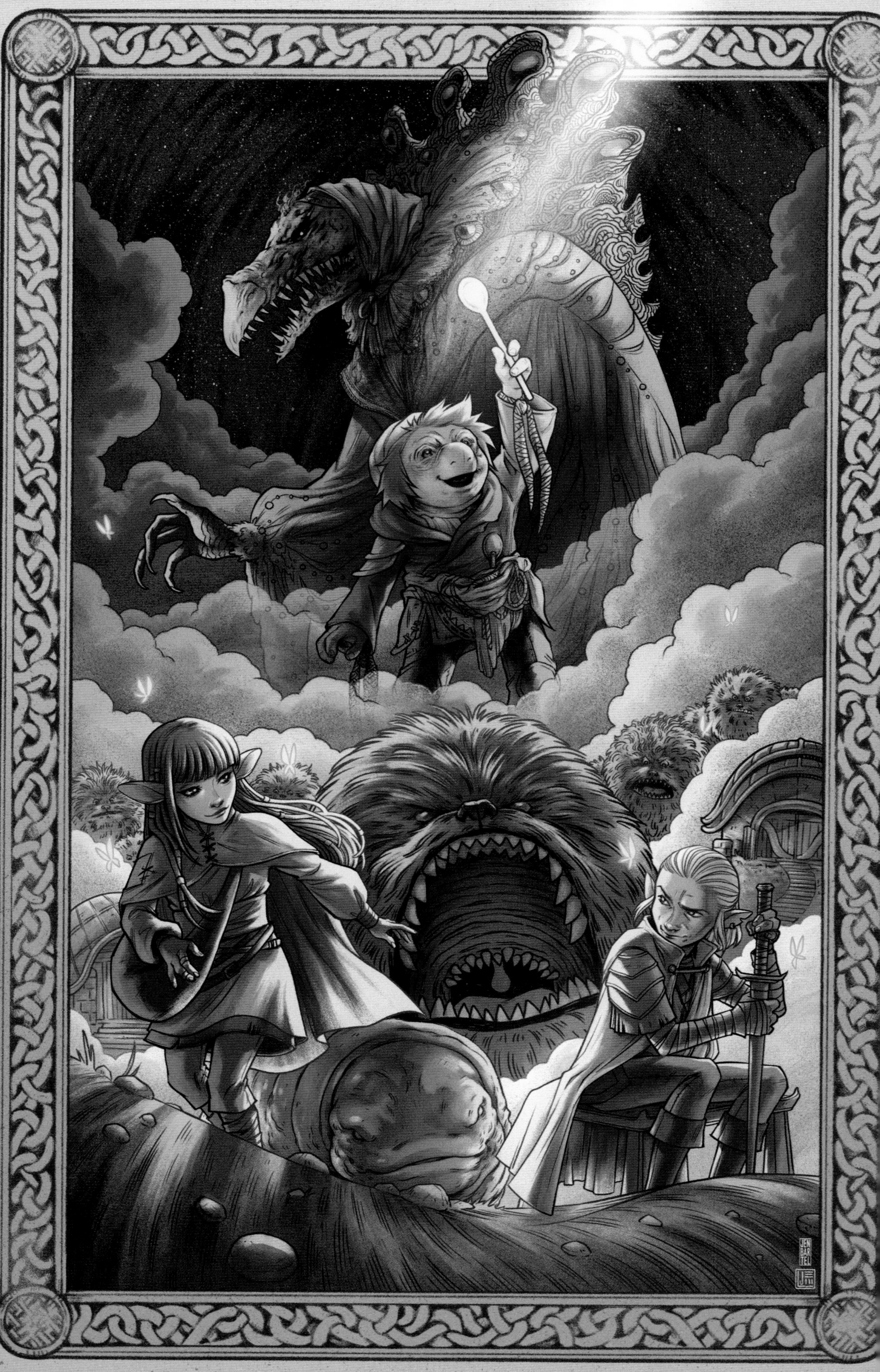

Character designs by

French Carlomagno

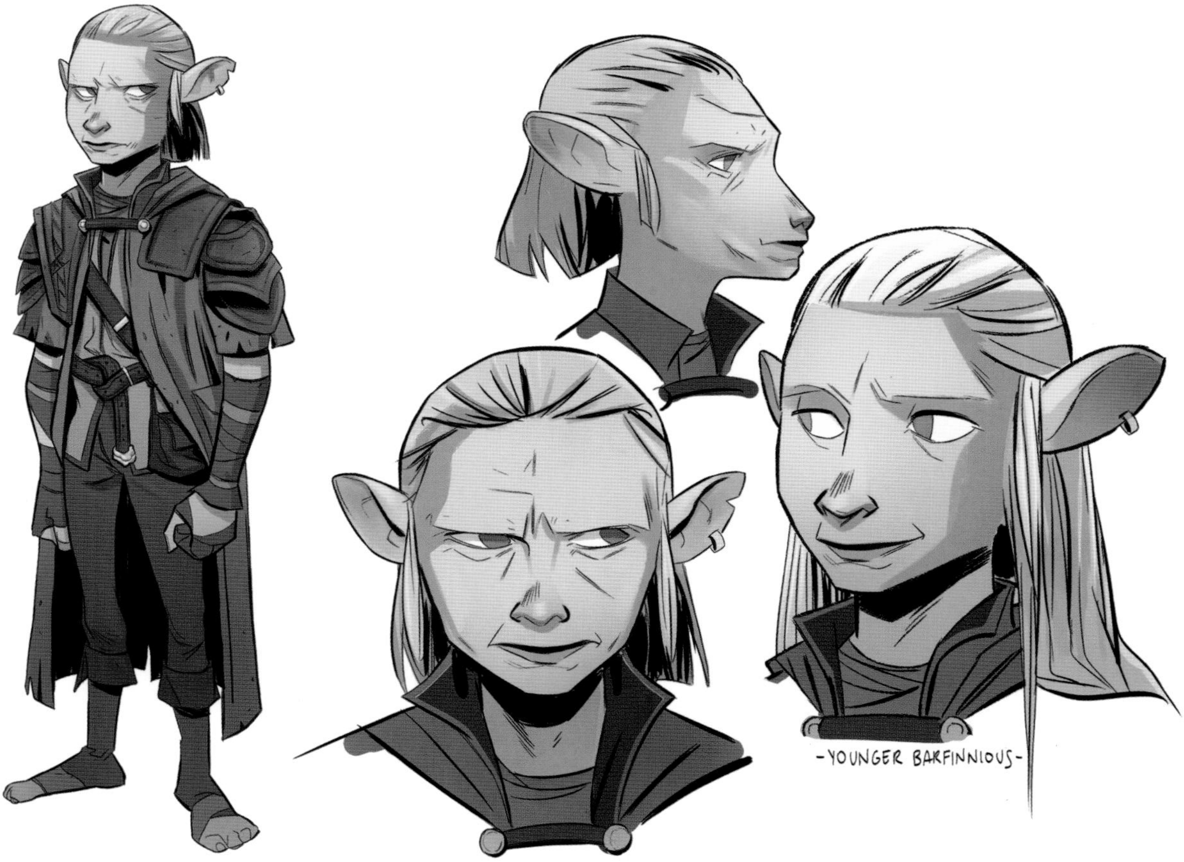
-YOUNGER BARFINNIOUS-

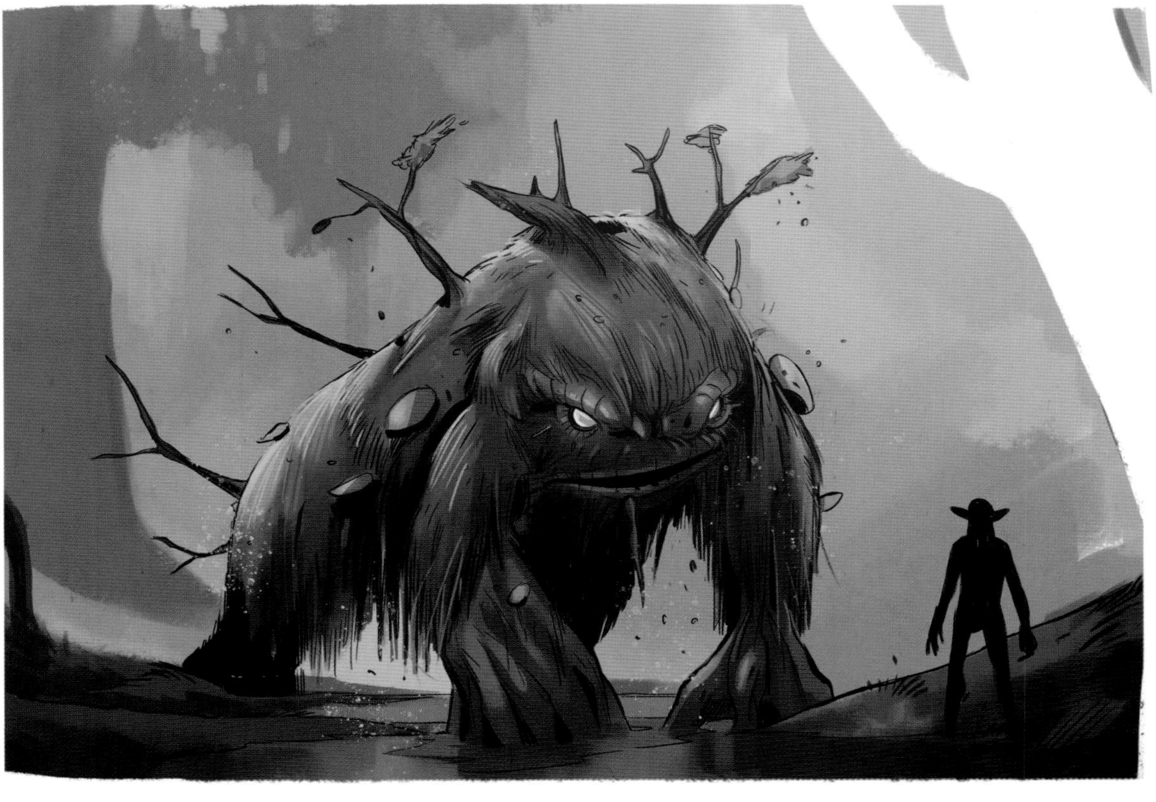

Will Matthews and Jeffrey Addiss' outline for this story arc described the Seedle (originally presumed to be the "Beast") as "a rare creature that is born as a leafy giant and grows into an entire forest."

DISCOVER
GROUNDBREAKING TITLES

ASAF HANUKA
THE REALIST

LONG WALK TO VALHALLA
ADAM SMITH MATTHEW FOX

THE MARCH OF THE CRABS
THE CRABBY CONDITION
ARTHUR DE PINS

Jane
ALINE BROSH McKENNA
RAMÓN K. PÉREZ

ROYDEN LEPP
RUST
VOLUME ONE
VISITOR IN THE FIELD

MOUSE GUARD
THE BLACK AXE
DAVID PETERSEN

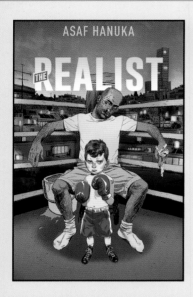

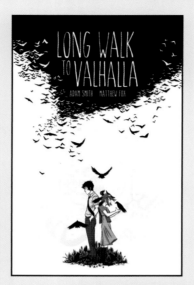

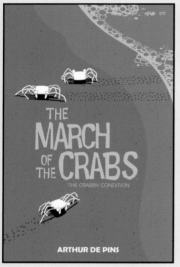

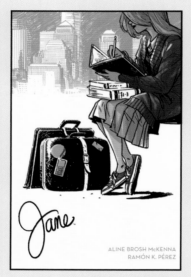

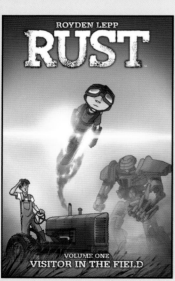

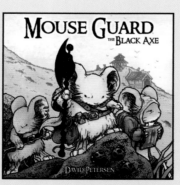

The Realist
Asaf Hanuka
ISBN: 978-1-60886-688-5 | $24.99 US

The Realist: Plug and Play
Asaf Hanuka
ISBN: 978-1-60886-953-4 | $24.99 US

Long Walk to Valhalla
Adam Smith, Matt Fox
ISBN: 978-1-60886-692-2 | $24.99 US

The March of The Crabs
Arthur De Pins
Volume 1: The Crabby Condition
ISBN: 978-1-60886-689-2 | $19.99 US
Volume 2: The Empire of the Crabs
ISBN: 978-1-68415-014-4 | $19.99 US

Jane
Aline Brosh McKenna, Ramón K. Pérez
ISBN: 978-1-60886-981-7 | $24.99 US

Rust
Royden Lepp
Volume 0: The Boy Soldier
ISBN: 978-1-60886-806-3 | $10.99 US
Volume 1: Visitor in the Field
ISBN: 978-1-60886-894-0 | $14.99 US
Volume 2: Secrets of the Cell
ISBN: 978-1-60886-895-7 | $14.99 US

Mouse Guard
David Petersen
Mouse Guard: Fall 1152
ISBN: 978-1-93238-657-8 | $24.95 US
Mouse Guard: Winter 1152
ISBN: 978-1-93238-674-5 | $24.95 US
Mouse Guard: The Black Axe
ISBN: 978-1-93639-306-0 | $24.95 US

The Cloud
K.I. Zachopoulos, Vincenzo Balzano
ISBN: 978-1-60886-725-7 | $24.99 US

Cursed Pirate Girl Coloring Book
Jeremy A. Bastian
ISBN: 978-1-60886-947-3 | $16.99 US

ARCHAIA™

AVAILABLE AT YOUR LOCAL COMICS SHOP AND BOOKSTORE
To find a comics shop in your area, visit www.comicshoplocator.com
WWW.**BOOM-STUDIOS**.COM

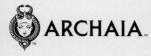